About this book

Jordan emerged from the ruins of the Ottoman Empire on a territory so marginal, barren and sparsely populated as to be initially of only glancing interest to the Turks' imperial successors, France and Britain, then busily drawing the map of the modern Middle East. Piecemeal, it expanded, absorbing first the northern part of the ill-fated Kingdom of Hejaz and then, controversially, Palestine's West Bank, a step that bestowed a Palestinian majority. Despite the pan-Arab nationalist challenge in the 1950s, the loss of the West Bank in 1967 and civil war in 1970, Jordan and its monarchy have survived and prospered, thanks to enduring alliances with the US and Britain and a strategic location at the Middle East's hub.

As well as tracing the kingdom's often turbulent history, *Jordan: Living in the Crossfire* paints a portrait of Jordan today, under its young King Abdullah II, focusing on its politics, economics and main state institutions and also on the daily lives of individual Jordanians, from the monarch to a Palestinian refugee camp dweller. More than other Arab states, Jordan has permitted the development, albeit halting, of civil society, and the regime maintains control as much through the skilful co-option of opponents as through the heavy hand of its secret police. What are the limits of personal, political, media and academic freedoms in this 'constitutional monarchy'? And in a region rocked by the invasion of Iraq and the ongoing Palestinian *intifada*, swept by Islamism and plagued by terrorism, what are the future prospects for this buffer 'state without a nation'?

Based on numerous visits to the country and interviews with a wide array of Jordanians, from King Abdullah down, this highly readable account by an experienced and well-regarded journalist offers specialists and generalists alike illuminating insights into this complex and fascinating kingdom.

About the author

After graduating from Oxford University in 1970, Alan George gained his MA on Middle Eastern geography at Durham in 1972 and his PhD on Syria, also at Durham, in 1978. Since 1984 he has worked as a freelance journalist and researcher, contributing to a wide range of UK and international publications including the *Observer*, the *Independent* and *Private Eye* in the UK; *Profil* and *Der Standard* in Austria; *Panorama* in Italy; *Berlingske Tidende* in Denmark; and the London-based pan-Arab daily papers *Ash-Sharq al-Awsat* and *Al-Quds*. He frequently commentates on Middle Eastern affairs for radio and television. He is a former Assistant Director of the Council for the Advancement of Arab-British Understanding (CAABU), of whose Executive Committee he was a member for many years, and is a Senior Associate Member of St Antony's College, Oxford University. He has visited Jordan and the wider Arab region repeatedly since 1967. His first book, *Syria: Neither Bread Nor Freedom,* was published by Zed Books in 2003.

JORDAN
Living in the Crossfire

Alan George

Zed Books
LONDON AND NEW YORK

Jordan: Living in the Crossfire was first published in 2005 by
Zed Books Ltd, 7 Cynthia Street, London N1 9JF, UK and
Room 400, 175 Fifth Avenue, New York, NY 10010, USA
www.zedbooks.co.uk

Cover designed by Andrew Corbett
Set in 10/13 pt Berkeley Book by Long House, Cumbria, UK
Printed and bound in Malta by Gutenberg Ltd

Distributed in the USA exclusively by Palgrave Macmillan, a division of
St Martin's Press, LLC,175 Fifth Avenue, New York, NY 10010

The right of Alan George to be identified as the author
of this work has been asserted by him in accordance with
the Copyright, Designs and Patents Act, 1988

A catalogue record for this book is available from the British Library

US Cataloging-in-Publication Data
is available from the Library of Congress

ISBN Hb 1 84277 470 0
ISBN Pb 1 84277 471 9
US CIP is available from the Library of Congress

Contents

Acknowledgements

Written in London, Barcelona and the delightful Languedocien village of Salasc, near Montpellier, this book is the product of two years of intermittent research that included six visits to Jordan and interviews with over sixty individuals. It would have been impossible to complete without the generous assistance of many people, most but not all in the kingdom. I owe a particular debt of gratitude to my loyal assistant and friend, Riham al-Baqa'in, for her invaluable logistical and research support. She never, ever faltered. Another huge debt is owed to my friend and mentor George Joffé, of Cambridge University's Centre of International Studies, for his steady interest, encouragement and advice. Dr Eugene Rogan, of the Middle East Centre at St Antony's College, Oxford University, was another crucial source of encouragement and guidance.

The sections dealing with King Abdullah and the royal family would have been infinitely weaker without the assistance of Dr Sima Bahous, Director of the Communications and Information Division at the Royal Court and Media Adviser to King Abdullah. I also thank two members of her staff, Dimah al-Khalili and Alia al-Kadi, for their helpful responses to my endless questions. Rula Awwad, of Queen Rania's Office, deserves praise on similar grounds.

In Amman, I stayed at the admirable Sabeel Hotel in the Jabal Amman district, where I was always treated with great warmth and kindness. I have come to regard its proprietor, Nabil Sawalha, and his staff, especially Umm Tewfiq, her son, Usama al-Bileh, and Faris al-Ya'acoub, as my 'Jordanian family'. Another member of this 'family' is the taxi driver Ali Atwan (known as Abu Muhammad), who was always reliable, considerate and of good cheer. In Aqaba, I received similar friendship and hospitality from Omar Almetwaly, proprietor of Jordan Sinai Hotels & Tours, and his wife, Jennifer. Before embarking on my research in Jordan, I wanted to learn how to ride a camel. I did so – to the best of my ability at least – in Nuweiba, on the Red Sea coast of Egypt's Sinai Peninsula, staying at the charming Habiba Holiday Village. There, too, I received nothing but kindness and hospitality, especially from its proprietor, Maged al-Said, and his associate, Angela Wierstra, and from Ibrahim Aliyan, of the Muzeina tribe, who oversaw my riding exploits with much skill, humour and patience.

I should like to thank all my interviewees: King Abdullah; Muhammad Halaiqah, Deputy Prime Minister for Economic Affairs and Minister for Administrative Development; Muhammad Idwan, Information Minister; Muhammad Daoudia, Minister for Political Development and Parliamentary Affairs; Nabil Sharif, Chief Editor of *Ad-Dustour* and subsequently Minister of Information; Samir ar-Rifa'i, Minister of the Royal Court; Taher al-Masri, former Prime Minister; Ahmad al-Obeidat, former Prime Minister, now Chairman, National Centre for Human Rights; Muhammad Hammouri, former Minister of Higher Education and of Culture and National Heritage, now of Hammouri & Partners; As'ad Abdul Rahman, a former Minister in the Palestine National Authority; Akel Biltaji, Chief Commissioner, Aqaba Special Economic Zone Authority and latterly an Adviser at the Royal Court; Barjas al-Hadid, shaikh of the Hadid tribe; Ali Abu as-Sukkar, Deputy Speaker, House of Representatives; Bassam Hadidin, MP; Ghazi Obeidat, former MP; Toujan Faisal, former MP; Laith Shubeilat, former MP; Hamzah Mansour, Secretary-General, Islamic Action Front; Abdul Majid al-Thnaibat, Superintendent-General, Muslim Brotherhood, Jordan; Bassam Saket, Chairman, Jordan Securities Commission; Mazen al-Ma'aytah, President, General Federation of Jordanian Trade Unions; Abul Feilat Abdul Razzaq, Director-General, Hejaz Jordan Railways; Charles Kapes, Deputy Director, UNRWA Operations, Jordan; Farouq al-Kilani, former Chairman, High Judicial Council; Hussain al-Mujalli, President, Lawyers' Association; Salah al-Armouti, former President, Lawyers' Association; Muhammad Tarawneh, Appeal Court Judge; Salman al-Badur, President of Aal al-Bayt University; Abdul Rahim Hamdan, President, Al-Ahliya Amman University; Mustafa Hamarneh, Director, Centre for Strategic Studies, University of Jordan; Ahmad Ziadat, Dean of Law Faculty, University of Jordan; George Joffé, of Cambridge University's Centre of International Studies; Baker al-Hiyari, Assistant Director, Royal Institute for Inter-Faith Studies; Ibrahim Izzadine, President, Higher Media Council; Jennifer Hamarneh, Chief Editor, *Jordan Times*; Nidal Mansour, Chief Editor, *Al-Hadath*; Tariq al-Mumani, Secretary-General, Jordan Press Association;

Muwafaq Muhardeen, Editor, *Al-Wahda*; Fahd al-Rimawi, Chief Editor, *Al-Majd*; Nicolas Pelham, freelance journalist; Sa'eda Kilani, Director, Arab Archives Institute; Labib Kamhawi, former President of the Arab Organisation for Human Rights in Jordan; Fawzi Samhouri, former President, Jordanian Society for Citizens' Rights; Hani Hourani, Director-General, New Jordan Research Centre; Adel Hamdan, Director of Department of Palestinian Affairs Office, Baqa'a Camp; Sir Wilfred Thesiger, explorer and writer; Nabil Sawalha, playwright; Edgar Solenthaler, Regional Manager, Mövenpick, Jordan; Peter Hoesli, Manager, Mövenpick Aqaba; Hisham Bustani, dentist; Ali Abdul Fatah Atwan, known as Abu Muhammad, taxi-driver; Abd al-Fatah al-Bustani, dentist; Awad Ash-Shubaiki, *bedu* farmer; Anisa Salim, refugee camp dweller; Rajai Khoury, CEO, Khoury Drug Store; Abeer Arafat, Senior Investment Analyst, Export & Finance Bank; Omar Almetwaly, proprietor of Jordan Sinai Hotels & Tours; Sawsan Fakhri, Director, Aqaba Office of Antiquities; Hussain and Barakah As-Swelhayin, of the Howeitat tribe, tourist guides; Atteig Audah, of the Zalabiya branch of the Annazeh tribe, tourist guide; Ismail ad-Dumour, proprietor, Al-Fida Restaurant, Karak; Abd as-Salam al-Fandi, Imam of the Ahmad bin Taimiyah Mosque, Badr al-Jadid village; Muhammad Abdullah Amira, *khatib* (preacher), Aqaba. From this list, I should like to single out for special tribute those who generously permitted themselves to be the subjects of the 'profile' chapters that form the book's central section.

I also thank Muntaha Sabah, for her help with translation from Arabic; Peter Sluglett, Professor of Middle Eastern History at the University of Utah in Salt Lake City, for recommending books that proved to be critical; T. E. Lawrence's biographer, Michael Asher, for sharing his thoughts on camel-riding and Lawrence early in the project; freelance journalist Oula Farawati, for interpreting during interviews with Barjas al-Hadid and Awad ash-Shubaiki; Nadim Shehadi, Director of the Centre for Lebanese Studies in Oxford, for helping with translation and with identifying potential interviewees; Ann Kutek, for prompting me to interview Wilfred Thesiger, and for much more besides; and Professor John Kerrigan, Head of the English Faculty at Cambridge University, for confirming that a quotation attributed to Shakespeare on the menu cards in an Amman restaurant was not in fact Shakespearian.

Throughout this often solitary marathon, I have been sustained by the encouragement, interest and support of a circle of family and close friends. In addition to George Joffé, whom I have mentioned earlier, I pay special tribute to Z, who has always been there for me, and to our superb children, Emily, Katherine and Michael; to the sculptor Timothy Holmes of Usclas du Bosc, whose spirit is generous indeed; to Nataly Firmin-Grillet, who understands the romance of the desert; and to Dorys Ardila Muñoz, whose courage was an inspiration, counsel wise and patience boundless.

Introduction

Jordan is a constitutional monarchy that practices democracy, which is governed by the rule of law and where human rights and media and academic freedoms are respected. That, at least, is the carefully cultivated official version, promoted especially in the Western capitals upon whose goodwill the kingdom so much depends. Scratch the surface, however, and the reality quickly emerges. The Constitution is revealed as a tool to perpetuate the *status quo*, affirming the king as the unchallenged master of his realm. It is summed-up in Article 30, which stipulates: 'The King is the Head of State and is immune from any liability and responsibility'. The Constitution's numerous high-sounding safeguards of personal and other liberties all take second place to 'the law'. But laws are proposed by governments appointed by the king and debated by a parliament whose upper house is royally appointed and whose lower house has a built-in majority of regime loyalists who in large measure owe their parliamentary seats to electoral engineering on a grand scale. Parliament and political parties, key attributes of any democracy, play only marginal roles in national life, not least in the crucial area of scrutinising public finances. The media is free only within the constraints of a series of overlapping and vaguely worded laws that ban all criticism of the king and forbid the publication of anything that might upset national unity or foreign relations. The nominally independent judicial system is subject to interference by the authorities, albeit occasional and usually subtle.

Jordan, however, is not Saddam Hussain's Iraq or Hafiz al-Asad's Syria. The security services are feared and effective, but do not function routinely as instruments of terror. Dissidents can be detained but are not 'disappeared' and, these days at least, torture does not generally occur. There's no blanket surveillance of the populace. Within the prescribed limits, the media is lively and diverse and, again within the limits, parliamentary debates can be vigorous. While the laws with which it deals are framed by and for the establishment, the judicial system is largely fair.

Like all national institutions, the universities must toe the official line but they and their academic staff enjoy much independence. Most Jordanians, most of the time, enjoy a freedom that sets them apart from most peoples of the region.

If Jordan is no police state it is mainly because its monarchs to date have not been demagogues. When cornered, they have shown themselves as ruthless as any other absolute rulers. In 1956–57, when his regime seemed in danger of being swept away by a rising tide of radical Arab nationalism, and again in 1970–71, when its existence was threatened by the Palestinian guerrilla movement, King Hussain did not hesitate to use the iron fist. Generally, however, Jordan's kings have preferred to rule by consent, heavily tempered by co-option. Once diehard opponents of the regime have often re-emerged as stalwart members of the establishment, sometimes after spells in prison or exile. Partly, this has reflected a personal magnanimity on the part of the monarchs. More importantly, it has reflected an intelligent appreciation of political benefit. The present king, Abdullah, records that his father, shortly before his death, reminded him 'to keep your friends close, and your enemies even closer' (see p. 165). It is inescapable, however, that constitutional and other constraints on royal power are extremely limited. To date, Jordanians have been fortunate that their kings, while sometimes ruthless, have not been vicious or cruel. Had they been, Jordan's story might have been much darker, and without profound change to the institutional framework there can be no guarantees that the kingdom will be spared despotic rule in the future.

A main purpose of this book is to explore the limits of freedom in Jordan, the precise locations of the system's 'red lines', explicit and tacit, and thus the extent of the political space where relations between rulers and ruled are mediated: the realm of civil society. This theme runs throughout the book, and separate chapters focus on the key civil society arenas: parliament, the legal system, the media and the universities. My first book, on Syria, had a similar objective and format. For both countries, it was essential to probe beyond the official veneers to the informal, primordial structures and relationships, tribal, ethnic, religious and familial, that are often far more important. But unravelling the realities of power in Syria was simpler. That country's Ba'athist regime, installed and maintained by brute force, its tentacles stretching into every nook and cranny of national life, dominates so completely that civil society barely exists. In Jordan, the regime wields its authority much more lightly. Its own survival is no less a priority than for its Syrian counterpart, but its methods of control are far more subtle and nuanced, and often far less visible.

Another main objective was simply to paint an accurate portrait of modern Jordan, its society, royal family, politics, foreign relations and economy, focusing especially on the five years since Abdullah succeeded to the throne. To set the context, initial chapters review the kingdom's creation and its two main phases, under the first King Abdullah and his grandson, the redoubtable King Hussain. Originally, I had not intended to delve much into the past. It quickly became clear, however, that, more than most states, Jordan can be understood only by reference to its origins and history. It emerged almost by chance from the ruins of the Ottoman Empire, on a marginal territory with few people, hardly any natural resources and no legacy of existence as a discrete political unit. It was a land that even the British, who held Palestine to the west and Iraq to the east, had neglected to occupy. With the Palestine war in 1947-48, it acquired both the West Bank and a majority Palestinian population, more than half of them refugees. The West Bank was lost in the 1967 Arab-Israeli war but Palestinians probably still form a majority of Jordanians, co-existing sometimes uneasily with the East Bankers who formed the core of the original state.

In the end, however, countries are the sum of their individuals, and I have sought to shed further light on the kingdom and its diversity through a series of shorter chapters focusing on the daily lives and concerns of Jordanians from each of the main sectors of society: the king; a leading tribal shaikh who is a pillar of the establishment; a wealthy businessman whose parents arrived as refugees from Palestine in 1948; an upper middle class dentist whose parents immigrated from Damascus after the First World War; a lower middle class taxi driver, originally from the West Bank; a *bedu* farmer whose tribe settled in Jordan centuries ago; and a woman from a refugee camp whose parents fled Palestine in 1948, who previously lived in Lebanon and Kuwait and who now ekes out a living making wicker-ware handicrafts.

If history has critically shaped Jordan, so too has geography. Occupying a small buffer zone between much larger and more powerful states, Jordan has always been highly vulnerable to outside influences, a feature greatly amplified by its strategic alliances with London and Washington, its heavy dependence on foreign aid and on remittances from its nationals working abroad, and its large Palestinian population with ambivalent loyalties. Often, the distinction between domestic and foreign affairs is hard to draw. In a turbulent region, Jordan occupies a crossroads, living in the crossfire. This does not mean that it is merely a helpless victim of regional and international currents. The kingdom has an authentic life of its own, and although lacking the capacity to determine developments beyond its borders, it can sometimes influence them. Iraq's future does not depend on Amman, but Jordan is playing a role, albeit limited, in shaping affairs in its eastern neighbour. Likewise, Jordan by itself cannot bring peace in Palestine, but Amman can and will do more than watch from the sidelines. The kingdom also exerts influence by example. Its political system, quasi-liberal and quasi-democratic, with the monarch at its centre as the ultimate arbiter of affairs, holds lessons for the wider region. So too does the manner in which the kingdom has contained Islamism, allowing it a political role, albeit within limits, while clamping down on its more extreme manifestations. Jordan today – along with Kuwait and Bahrain – could well be a model for the United Arab Emirates, Oman and even Saudi Arabia of tomorrow, although it is perhaps Morocco that offers a template for a subsequent phase, in which the Arab kings reign rather than rule.

Jordan has a darker side, for sure. It is not the liberal democracy of the official discourse, and poverty and unemployment are widespread, especially in the Palestinian camps, jarring with the elite's ostentatious wealth and with official claims about the benefits of economic liberalisation. But the regime is broadly popular and its legitimacy not in question, and there is little of the heavy-handed repression of other Middle Eastern states. With good reason, Jordanians are proud of what they have achieved, usually against heavy odds. I hope earnestly that I have managed to present them and their country in a way that does them justice.

Chronology

May 1920	League of Nations grants Britain a mandate over Palestine, including the territory east of the Jordan river.
November 1920	Amir Abdullah arrives in Ma'an from Mecca with armed followers as the first step towards establishing Hashemite rule in Transjordan.
March 1921	Amir Abdullah arrives in Amman. The Cairo Conference resolves that he should rule Transjordan under British tutelage.
September 1922	League of Nations exempts Transjordan from pro-Zionist clauses of the Palestine mandate.
May 1923	London formally recognises an independent government in Transjordan, under Amir Abdullah.
February 1928	Anglo-Transjordanian Agreement recognises the territory as an Amirate.
1937–38	Arab rebellion in Palestine.
March 1946	Anglo-Transjordanian Treaty grants Transjordan formal independence.
May 1946	Transjordan renamed the Hashemite Kingdom of Jordan, with Abdullah as king.
1947	The UN resolves to divide Palestine into Arab and Jewish states.
1948	Israel established. War in Palestine ends with the Israelis in control of most of the country but with Jordan holding Jerusalem and the rest of the West Bank.
April 1950	Jordan annexes West Bank.
July 1950	King Abdullah assassinated.
September 1951	Talal crowned king.
July 1952	Egyptian monarchy toppled.
August 1952	Talal abdicates.

May 1953	Hussain crowned king.
March 1956	Glubb Pasha dismissed as commander of the Arab Legion.
October 1956	Anglo-French-Israeli invasion of Egypt.
March 1957	Anglo-Jordanian Treaty abrogated.
April 1957	The Zarqa Affair, in which King Hussain intervenes to thwart an alleged army coup. Martial law declared and political parties banned.
February 1958	Egypt and Syria merge into the United Arab Republic. Jordan and Iraq form an Arab Federation.
July 1958	Iraqi monarchy toppled.
February 1963	Ba'athist coup in Iraq.
March 1963	Ba'athist coup in Syria.
June 1967	Arab-Israeli war. Israel occupies the West Bank.
September 1970	Fighting erupts between Palestinian and Jordanian forces.
July 1971	Final defeat for the Palestinians.
October 1973	Arab-Israeli war.
October 1974	Arab summit in Rabat declares the Palestine Liberation Organisation (PLO) the 'sole legitimate representative of the Palestinian people'.
November 1974	UN General Assembly affirms Palestinian right to self-determination.
1975–90	Lebanese civil war.
March 1979	Egypt and Israel sign peace treaty.
1980–88	Iran-Iraq war. Jordan sides with Iraq.
June 1982	Israel invades Lebanon.
December 1987	First Palestinian *intifada* erupts in the Israeli-occupied territories.
July 1988	Jordan severs legal and administrative ties with West Bank.
1988–89	The Jordanian dinar halves in value.
April 1989	Jordan signs five-year structural readjustment agreement with International Monetary Fund.
April 1989	Riots in Ma'an and other southern Jordanian towns.
November 1989	First general election since April 1967.
February 1989	Jordan, Iraq, Egypt and Yemen form Arab Co-operation Council.

August 1990– February 1991	Crisis in the Gulf prompted by Iraq's invasion of Kuwait.
June 1991	National Charter ratified.
July 1991	Martial law, in force since 1967, lifted.
October 1991	Arab-Israeli peace conference in Madrid.
September 1993	Israel and PLO sign Oslo Accords.
November 1993	General election.
October 1994	Israel and Jordan sign peace treaty.
August 1996	Riots in southern towns.
November 1997	General election.
February 1999	King Hussain dies and King Abdullah II succeeds to the throne.
July 2000	King Abdullah delays general election scheduled for November.
September 2000	Second Palestinian *intifada* starts in the Israeli-occupied territories.
September 2001	Usama Bin Laden's Al-Qa'ida organisation mounts attacks in New York and Washington.
June 2002	Washington unveils Road Map peace plan for Palestine.
October 2002	Jordan First campaign launched.
November 2002	Clashes in Ma'an.
March 2003	US-led invasion of Iraq.
June 2003	General election.
April 2004	Major terrorist attack in Amman foiled.
November 2004	King Abdullah relieves Prince Hamzah of title as crown prince.

Vital Statistics

Population: 5.48m. (2003)[1]
Annual population growth rate: 2.8% (2003)[1]
Urban population: 78.7% (2000)[1]
Population aged under 19: 50.1% (2001)[1]
Life expectancy: 71.5 (2000)[1]
Literacy rate: 90.3% (2003)[2]
Unemployment rate: 25% (2004 estimate)[3]
Gross domestic product (GDP): $9.93 billion (2003)[1]
Per capita GDP: $1,812 (2003)[1]
Inflation rate: 2.3% (2003)[1]
Balance of payments: +$992 million (2003)[1]
Exports: $3 billion (2003)[1]
Imports: $5.54 billion (2003)[1]
Trade balance: −$2.54 billion (2003)[1]
Net remittance income: $2.02 billion (2003)[1]
Foreign grants: $963 million (2003)[1]
Total public debt: $10 billion (2003)[1]
Land area: 88,778 square kilometres[1]
Cultivated area: 238,640 hectares (2003)[1]
Irrigated area: 71,320 hectares (2003)[1]
Annual water deficit (demand minus supply): 480 million cubic metres (2000)[2]
Per capita water deficit: 95.3 cubic metres (2000)[1&2]

1   *Hashemite Kingdom of Jordan Statistical Yearbook 2003* (Amman: Department of Statistics).
2   Ministry of Planning and International Co-operation; UNDP, *Jordan Human Development Report 2004: Building Sustainable Livelihoods* (Amman: MoPIC and UNDP, 2004).
3   'The EU's relations with Jordan', www.europa.eu.int.

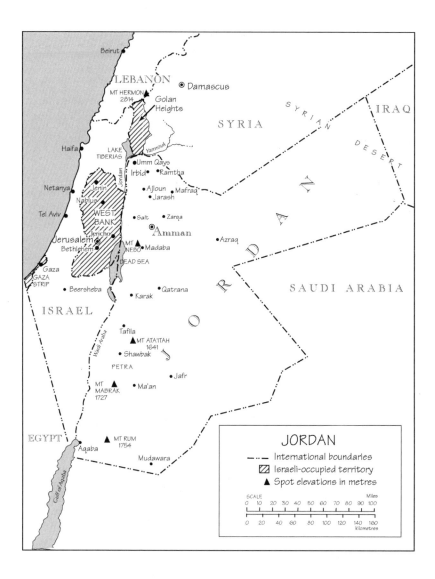

Beirut

LEBANON
MT HERMON
2814
Golan
Heights
⊙ Damascus

SYRIA

SYRIAN
DESERT

IRAQ

Haifa
LAKE
TIBERIAS
Yarmouk
Umm Qays
Irbid
Ramtha

Netanya
Jenin
Ajloun
Mafraq
Jarash

Nablus
WEST
BANK
Salt
Zarqa

Tel Aviv

Jerusalem
Jericho
⊙ Amman
Azraq

Bethlehem
MT
NEBO Madaba

Gaza
DEAD SEA

GAZA
STRIP

Beersheba
Qatrana

SAUDI ARABIA

ISRAEL
Karak

J O R D A N

Wadi Araba
Tafila
▲ MT ATA'ITAH
1641
Shawbak

PETRA
Jafr

MT
MABRAK ▲
1727
Ma'an

EGYPT
▲ MT RUM
1754
Aqaba
Mudawara

Gulf of Aqaba

JORDAN

—··— International boundaries

▨ Israeli-occupied territory

▲ Spot elevations in metres

SCALE   Miles
0   10 20 30 40 50 60 70 80 90 100

0   20   40   60   80   100   120   140   160
                                        kilometres

PART I

. . . .

Jordan

CHAPTER I

'Fulfilling our Promises':
The Creation of Jordan

'HE IS A HERO for another country, not for us', declared Bassam Saket, urbane, Oxford-educated chairman of the Jordan Securities Commission – the agency that regulates the Amman stock exchange – and a former minister of trade and industry. 'He was a British officer who helped his own country's cause' in a campaign that 'ended up in disappointment for the Arabs', he told me during our meeting at his well-appointed office. 'The freedom-fighters were stabbed in the back'.[1] Laith Shubailat, Islamist, civil engineer, ex-MP and leading democracy campaigner who in November 1992 was sentenced to death but pardoned 48 hours later, takes the same view. T. E. Lawrence – Lawrence of Arabia – was 'an instrument of the British government who felt ashamed of himself for helping his government lie to the Arabs'.[2] Even more caustic was Dr Mustafa Hamarneh, a connoisseur of Cuban cigars who directs the University of Jordan's Centre for Strategic Studies. 'Jordanians don't know him. They just know he was some white man who ran around in the desert'.[3]

It's a far cry from the Western love-affair with the Lawrence myth, a tale of courage and derring-do set against the vastness and purity of the desert. 'I was fascinated by Lawrence', said Wilfred Thesiger, the greatest of modern desert travellers, whose crossing of Arabia's Empty Quarter is chronicled in his classic *Arabian Sands*.[4] 'How others have tried to diminish him! Rubbish! I stand no talk against Lawrence!'[5] I met Thesiger, a figure in his way as enigmatic as Lawrence, at his nursing home in Coulsdon on the Surrey Downs, shortly before his death. At age 94 his eyes still shone with the vigour that once propelled him across the arid sand seas.

Sharif Hussain ibn Ali was not only the ruler of Islam's holiest city of Mecca and a Hashemite – a member of the Prophet Muhammad's branch of the Quraish tribe; he was also a direct descendant of the Prophet. These attributes underpinned his claim to leadership of the nationalist movement that was stirring in the Ottoman Empire's Arab territories early last century. In June 1916, when Sharif Hussain launched the Arab Revolt against the Turks, setting in train events that shape the Middle East to this day, Lawrence was a young Arabist officer based at British headquarters in Cairo. Posted as liaison officer to the rebels, Lawrence fought with them throughout their campaign. *Bedu* tribesmen formed the core of the rag-tag Sharifian army although its ranks also included numbers of Arab officers and men from the towns and settled agricultural areas of Iraq and Syria who had defected from the Ottoman forces. The army was commanded by Hussain's third son, the Amir (Prince) Faisal.

Having taken control of the Hejaz – the mountainous western region of the Arabian Peninsula lapped by the Red Sea – the rebels moved into Greater Syria – the territory today fractured into Israel, Palestine, Jordan, Syria and Lebanon. North of the Hejaz, they operated in tandem with a British army, commanded initially by Sir Archibald Murray and then, more successfully, by General Edmund Allenby, that had invaded Palestine along the coast from Egypt. For both the British and the Arabs, the prize was Damascus, that greatest of all Arab cities. While the British advanced via a series of set-piece battles, Faisal's highly mobile, camel-mounted irregulars harassed the Turks and disrupted their communications along the desert fringe to the east. A key target for the guerrillas was the Hejaz Railway, a 1,320 kilometre narrow gauge line linking Damascus and Medina built by the Ottomans with German technical assistance in 1900–08. Ostensibly, Sultan Abdul Hamid had launched the project to facilitate the annual *hajj* pilgrimage to Mecca. Its rolling stock included a novel mosque carriage with a large open floor area for prayers and a two-metre minaret that could be retracted to permit passage through tunnels. But the railway also had a critical strategic role as an imperial artery, supplying Turkish garrisons and outposts in a part of the Empire where the Ottomans' grip was tenuous. The fast-moving, colourful and decisive Middle Eastern war was a welcome diversion for a British public horrified by the slaughter in Flanders, where bloody advances and retreats were measured in metres. Faisal took Aqaba, at the head of the Red Sea, in July 1917 and Amman – today Jordan's capital but then little more than a large village – in September. Jerusalem fell to the British three months later. The first British unit – actually the Third Australian Division – entered Damascus on 1 October 1918, to be followed the next day by Amir Nasir, the brother of the Amir of Medina (Islam's second holiest city) and one of the key Sharifian leaders, Lawrence and the *bedu*, and on 3 October by Amir Faisal, who arrived on a Hejaz Railway train.

The Arab Revolt had been launched only after discreet negotiations with the British. In 1915–16 Sharif Hussain and Sir Henry McMahon, the British High Commissioner in Egypt, exchanged a series of letters known as the McMahon Correspondence. These outlined a *quid pro quo* under which Britain agreed to reward an Arab rebellion against its Turkish foe by recognising the independence of the Arab territories of the Ottoman Empire, within certain limits. Britain excluded from the region where independence would apply the areas west of Mersin and Alexandretta, at the junction of Anatolia and Syria; the coastal regions to the west of a line linking the Syrian cities of Aleppo and Damascus; and the Ottoman *vilayets*, or provinces, of Baghdad and Basra. It also stipulated that Arab independence would apply only where that did not conflict with the interests of its wartime ally, France. Hussain did not accept the British territorial exemptions. In the interests of securing a workable alliance, however, the two sides agreed to leave these outstanding issues for future discussion.

Perfidy

Perfidious Albion did not gain its appellation for nothing. At the same time as it was urging Sharif Hussain to rebel with promises of Arab independence, London was quietly negotiating a separate deal with France and Russia on the shape of a post-Ottoman Middle East. Concluded in May 1916, the secret Sykes-Picot Agreement, named after its negotiators, Sir Mark Sykes, under-secretary to the War Cabinet, and François Georges-Picot, former French consul general in Beirut, divided the Arab Middle East north of the Arabian Peninsula into French and British spheres of influence. The French were allocated a zone corresponding roughly to modern Lebanon, Syria and northern Iraq while the British were allocated an area corresponding to modern Israel, Palestine, Jordan and southern Iraq. At Russian insistence, Jerusalem and a part of Palestine were designated for some form of international administration in recognition of their religious significance. The Sykes-Picot Agreement – made public by the Russians after the 1917 Revolution – plainly conflicted with the British assurances in the Hussain-McMahon Correspondence. As if this was not enough, on 2 November 1917 the British issued the Balfour Declaration, named after the Foreign Secretary, Arthur James Balfour. Concluded after negotiations with the Zionist movement, the Declaration affirmed that 'His Majesty's Government view with favour the establishment in Palestine of a National Home for the Jewish people, and will use their best endeavours to facilitate the achievement of this object'. In a qualification that with hindsight looks at best naïve and at worst cruelly cynical, the Declaration insisted that 'nothing shall be done which may prejudice the civil and religious rights of existing non-Jewish communities in Palestine'.

The capture of Damascus sealed the fate of Ottoman rule over the Arabs. But the latters' euphoria was short-lived. On 30 September 1918 supporters of the Arab Revolt in Damascus had proclaimed an Arab government loyal to Sharif Hussain, who in October 1916 had been proclaimed 'King of the Arabs' by religious and other notables in Mecca although Britain recognised him only as King of the Hejaz. His son Faisal took charge of the Damascus government, albeit that Britain remained the real power in Syria. Faisal, with Lawrence as his adviser, attended the Paris Peace Conference in 1919, where they pressed in vain for the promises to the Arabs to be fulfilled. The treaties agreed in Paris provided for the former possessions of the defeated Germans and Ottomans to be administered as mandates, under the supervision of a new international body, the League of Nations. Officially, the mandates were intended to prepare the former colonies for independence. In reality, they represented a means by which France and the United Kingdom could maintain their interests under a slightly more benevolent guise than crude imperialism. It was agreed that France should have a mandate for Syria (including the area now comprising Lebanon) while Britain should have Palestine (including the area now comprising Jordan) and Iraq.

Shortly after Faisal's administration was established in Damascus the French had landed troops in Beirut, and in November 1919 Britain withdrew its forces from Syria to make way for the French. To pre-empt French designs, a General Syrian Congress of nationalist figures convened in Damascus in March 1920 and elected Faisal king of a united Syria – i.e. of the territory today encompassing Syria, Lebanon, Israel, Palestine and

Jordan. Twenty-nine Iraqis present proclaimed Faisal's elder brother, Abdullah, king of an independent Iraq. They were vain gestures. To formalise what had already been agreed in Paris, Britain and France hastily convened a meeting at San Remo of the Supreme Council of the League of Nations. On 5 May 1920 this granted France mandates over Syria and Lebanon and gave Britain mandates over Palestine and Iraq. Transjordan – the territory east of the Jordan river – was not explicitly mentioned, but as it formed part of the Sykes-Picot Agreement's zone of British influence it was understood to form part of the Palestine mandate. French troops moved inland into Syria and, after defeating a hopelessly outnumbered and out-gunned Syrian irregular force at the Pass of Maisaloun, occupied Damascus on 25 July 1920. Faisal was forced into exile, although by way of compensation the British installed him as king of Iraq the following year.

Despite the November 1918 signing of the armistice that formally ended the war in Europe, Fakhri Pasha, the commander of the Turkish garrison of Medina in the Hejaz, remained defiant until January 1919, when his own men forced him to capitulate. When Faisal had led his army north into Syria, Abdullah had stayed behind to act as his father's foreign minister and military chief in the Hejaz. The Medina garrison's surrender freed him to counter a new challenge to his family's ambitions, this time coming not from the imperial powers but from the central Arabian Peninsula. There, Abdul Aziz ibn Saud, a tribal shaikh inspired by Wahhabism, a form of Islamic fundamentalism, was rapidly extending his rule, his formidable *Ikhwan* ('Brotherhood') fighters winning a string of victories against neighbouring rivals. By spring 1919 Ibn Saud was threatening the oases of Khurma and Turaba on the eastern borders of the Hejaz. On 21 May Abdullah captured Turaba. Within days the *Ikhwan* responded, to devastating effect. Abdullah's army was cut to shreds and he barely escaped with his life. 'The battle of Turaba was a turning point in Abdullah's life and in the history of Arabia', wrote the American historian Mary Wilson in her fascinating account of Jordan's creation and early history. 'From that time on, Husayn and his sons were on the defensive while Ibn Saud grew inexorably more powerful'.[6]

By late summer 1920 Sharif Hussain's grandiose scheme for Arab independence under his family's rule was in tatters. His Hejaz kingdom was under pressure from Ibn Saud and Greater Syria and Iraq were under French and British control. Abdullah, no less than his father, felt cheated.

His bitterness was fuelled by jealousy of his younger brother, Faisal, whom the British apparently intended to install on the Iraqi throne even though Abdullah felt that his claim to Iraq was stronger than Faisal's. Boxed in, Abdullah suddenly changed tack.

North to Ma'an

During the brief Syrian monarchy, Transjordan had been administered – nominally at least – from Damascus. With Paris and San Remo, it fell nominally within the Palestine mandate, constituting a land bridge between British-ruled Palestine and Iraq. The precise borders of 'Palestine' had yet to be defined formally, however, and the Jordan river was the effective eastern limit of direct British control. Transjordan was thus a sparsely populated political and military no man's land located between Palestine proper, to the west, Syria to the north, the Hejaz and Najd to the south and south-east and Iraq to the east. Without pre-emptive action, London feared that the vacuum might be filled either by the French from the north or by Ibn Saud and the Wahhabis from the south-east. But Britain, exhausted after the Great War, was disinclined to commit the necessary funds and manpower to assert direct control. As a stopgap, it opted for local autonomy under British influence. In August 1920 Sir Herbert Samuel, the High Commissioner in Palestine, travelled to Salt to outline Britain's prescription to a gathering of 600 Transjordanian dignitaries. The outcome was a series of three British-advised mini-states. In the north was the Government of Ajloun, based in Irbid. To its south was the Government of Salt, based in the eponymous town; and in the south was the grandly named Government of Moab, centred on Karak. Underlining Transjordan's lack of political cohesion, even these statelets quickly fractured. Ajloun split into four: Irbid, Ajloun, Mazar and Jerash. In the south, the small towns of Tafila and Wadi Musa sought autonomy from Karak. 'With the powerful tribal confederations of the hinterland beginning to reassert themselves, the reach of the Karak government was by mid-November limited to the town itself', records Oxford University's Philip Robins.[7]

After the French occupation of Syria, nationalists had fled south to Amman, whence they had been calling on Abdullah to lead a campaign to recover Syria. In autumn 1920 he responded dramatically. Having agreed a truce with Ibn Saud, Abdullah gathered a force of tribesmen variously estimated at between 300 and 2,000 strong, went by camel caravan from Mecca to Medina and thence travelled by train to the small oasis town of Ma'an, today in southern Jordan but then in the kingdom of Hejaz. He arrived on 21 November 1920, basing himself at the railway station, a substantial but graceful structure of golden local limestone with a gabled roof which today houses a museum celebrating the exploits of Abdullah and his heirs. The following day Abdullah addressed a message to 'our Syrian brethren', urging them to join him in a march on Damascus to liberate Syria from the French usurpers and avenge his brother's exile. The threat was 'probably spurious and certainly unrealistic, since Abdullah was no military genius'.[8] More likely it was 'a desperate attempt to bring himself forcefully to Britain's attention' as a first step in salvaging at least something of his family's dreams.[9]Abdullah remained in Ma'an for three months awaiting the British reaction and putting in place the foundations of a power base, receiving delegations of local *bedu* chiefs and other notables, and of nationalist ex-colleagues of Faisal. Initially, Abdullah's audacious move threw the British off-balance but it forced them to focus their minds. A key concern was that he might complicate Britain's relations with France, and Abdullah plainly understood that this was his strongest card. Although his army was small it was sufficient to worry the French who were already facing armed resistance from nationalists in Syria. Paris pressed London to neutralise the threat by ejecting Abdullah from Transjordan. By early 1921 London had decided that Transjordan should be included formally in its Palestine mandate; that as a gesture to the wartime promises to the Arabs, the territory should be exempted from the mandate's provisions concerning a Jewish National Home; and that Abdullah should shelve his declared designs on Syria and instead head a British-sponsored Transjordanian administration.

Learning that the tide in London was running in his favour, Abdullah moved north, again by means of the Hejaz Railway, arriving in Amman on 2 March 1921. His timing was perfect. Ten days later a conference of British officials involved in the Middle East – including Lawrence – convened in Cairo to review Britain's policies in the region. Chaired by the newly-appointed Colonial Secretary Winston Churchill, the meeting resolved that Abdullah should govern Transjordan under the British High Commissioner in Palestine. In late March, Churchill, accompanied by Lawrence, travelled to Jerusalem, where he forged a deal with Abdullah during three days of talks. Initially Abdullah suggested that he should rule a unified Palestine and Transjordan or a merged Transjordan and Iraq. He settled for much less: Transjordan alone, for a trial period of six months and under British tutelage, together with an annual stipend of £5,000. In return, Abdullah promised to quash anti-French and anti-Zionist activity in the territory. To encourage the amir's agreement, Churchill – who would later boast that he had created Transjordan by a stroke of his pen on a Sunday afternoon – appealed to Abdullah's undimmed territorial dreams. He hinted that a successful curbing of anti-French activities in Transjordan might result in improved relations with the French and, ultimately, to his being installed in Damascus as amir.

'Despite the short term nature of the arrangement', wrote Wilson, 'Transjordan proved to be a lasting creation. For Abdullah himself, his six months stretched to a lifetime'.[10] In September 1922 the League of Nations formally exempted Transjordan from the pro-Zionist clauses of the Palestine mandate and on 23 May 1923 London formally recognised an 'independent Government in Trans-Jordan under the rule of His Highness the Amir Abdullah ibn Husain'. Lawrence, who during the Arab Revolt had professed to feel shame at Britain's duplicity towards the Arabs, was well-satisfied. '[Churchill] made straight all the tangle', he wrote, 'finding solutions fulfilling (I think) our promises in letter and spirit (where humanly possible) without sacrificing any interest of our Empire or any interest of the people concerned. So we were quit of our war-time Eastern adventure, with clean hands, but three years too late to earn the gratitude which peoples, if not states, can pay'.[11] It was an astonishing interpretation of what has elsewhere been described more realistically as 'a cheap sop to Arab nationalist ambition'.[12]

Wadi Rum

In Wadi Rum, an hour's drive east of Jordan's Red Sea port of Aqaba, echoes of the Arab Revolt linger still. It is surely one of the most spectacular sights in all Arabia: a sandy and flat-floored wadi three kilometres wide defined by 1,000 metre-high sheer walls of red sandstone. Here in 1917 the *bedu* army of Amir Faisal encamped prior to bursting from the desert to seize Aqaba. 'The Arab armies would have been lost in the length and breadth of it, and within the walls a squadron of aeroplanes could have wheeled in formation', wrote Lawrence in his celebrated history of the Revolt, *Seven Pillars of Wisdom*.[13]

The best way to appreciate Wadi Rum is by the same means of transport used by Faisal and Lawrence: the camel. Mine, Alyan, was a seven-year old male that behaved well during my two-day trek – if one discounts his outlandish gurgles and toothy coughs of complaint when being loaded. My guides, alternately Hussain as-Swelhayin and his half-brother, Barakah, were from the Howeitat tribe, whose traditional territory this is and who played an important role in the Arab Revolt. Today, many of the tribe live in Wadi Rum village, a dusty cluster of squat, breeze-block houses that has sprung up in the past 40 years around a much older police post. When Faisal and Lawrence passed this way, not even the police post existed.

We started in the late morning at Wadi Rum's northern entrance, striding out to the east, skirting Jabal Umm Ishrin ('Mother of Twenty') on our right and, to our left, the towering, yellow, brown and red Mazfar mountain – dubbed the Seven Pillars of Wisdom after its seven massive tubular abutments. Around us, the flat wadi floor was dotted with spidery *ratam* bushes and occasional thorny *siyala* trees. Clouds flitted across a rich blue sky and to the north, perhaps two kilometres distant, a sandstorm played over the shimmering plain. Stretching before us to the south was Wadi Umm Ishrin, which runs parallel to Rum, to which it is physically similar though less imposing. After perhaps five kilometres of steady plodding across the sand and gravel, we stopped for lunch with an elderly lady relative of Barakah whose traditional goat-hair tent stood in a side-valley, in the lee of spectacular rocky outcrops. Rested and fed, we pressed on for three kilometres before stopping to inspect ancient Nabatean rock drawings of camels and other animals at the base of the cliff forming the east side of Wadi Umm Ishrin – one of several such inscriptions in this district.

With the shadows lengthening and the air growing chilly, we turned right past a mountainous dune of crimson sand hosting some twenty *ghatha* plants – considered a delicacy by camels – and followed a narrow tributary wadi, Barakah breaking the profound silence with rhythmic singing as the slowly setting sun dramatically exaggerated the purples and reds of the surrounding sands and sandstone crags. Just before nightfall we reached our camp site at Umm al-Gathir, a small tributary wadi 250 metres deep and 70 metres wide cut into Jabal an-Nafishiya. On one side, a 25-metre stretch of the precipitous sandstone wall had been gouged out at its base by the wind to leave a semi-cave where mats and mattresses were laid out beside a goat-hair tent and wind-breaks. A fire was lit and thick, sugary *bedu* tea brewed, to be followed by a meal of chicken and roast potatoes. 'Went to bed (sleeping bag and blankets) at 10.00 p.m.', I recorded in my notebook. 'A warm night with no wind. The stars swim in a black lake, its shores the surrounding rocky peaks'.

Tribal memories of Lawrence are hazy. 'We don't forget him', said Atteig Audah, a member of the Zalabiya branch of the Annazeh, who lives in Wadi Rum and works as a tourist guide. More than Lawrence, the local *bedu* remember Amir Faisal and the exploits of their then chief, Audah Abu Tayyi. 'They promised to make [Abu Tayyi] great if they helped Lawrence and the Amir', said Audah. He was notably more charitable towards Lawrence than others in Jordan. 'I don't think Lawrence was so bad. I don't think the English were so bad. They helped the *bedu*', he said, adding that after the Ottoman defeat, 'we felt there was freedom'. Audah, who spent the night with us at Umm al-Gathir, had read Lawrence's famous book and once lived briefly in the west London district of Acton. Only a handful of people who witnessed the Revolt are still alive. Audah identified one as Hajj Awad Zalabiya, a resident of Wadi Rum village who was now 'around 90 years old or something like that'.[14]

After an early breakfast we plodded across the sand to Wadi Rum's southern entrance, there turning north towards the village. We called at Hajj Awad's house but he was unwell and couldn't be disturbed. Above the settlement, high up the rock wall, the springs that provided water to Faisal's army still flow. The natural rock basin beneath a waterfall known as Ash-Shallala, where Lawrence bathed, is still there, although the water is now just a trickle. So too are the ancient tribal rock engravings mentioned by Lawrence, although the rocks are now disfigured by more modern graffiti and the site is marred by discarded bottles, tins and plastic bags. From the village, we returned to the wadi's southern entrance where we lunched with Hussain's father in his family's black tent, pitched near Ain Abu Ain – popularly known as 'Lawrence's Spring'. Although not old enough to remember the Arab Revolt, he had the clearest memories of the army of actors and support staff that camped here 40 years ago to make the film *Lawrence of Arabia*, starring Omar Sharif as Faisal and Peter O'Toole as Lawrence. Elsewhere in Jordan too, the Lawrence film resonates more than the man himself. 'We don't discuss [Lawrence] or think of him much', said Nabil Sawalha, one of the kingdom's leading actors and playwrights. 'To us, he's a film really'.[15] This view was echoed by the then information minister, Muhammad Afash Idwan. 'You rarely read anything about Lawrence – but we enjoyed the movie as much as you did!' he laughed.[16] In fact, the film caused considerable consternation in Jordan. The late King Hussain had extended all facilities to the film-makers but there was disquiet at what was considered the negative portrayal of the Arabs. It must have rankled the king that his great-uncle, Amir Faisal, is described in the film as as 'a Hashemite bedouin'. Hashemite he may have been, and a leader of *bedu*. But Sharif Hussain and his sons were cultivated men who had spent their lives not in the desert but in Mecca and Constantinople, the Ottoman Empire's most cosmopolitan urban centres. Faisal's brother Abdullah would scornfully deride his Wahhabi rival, Ibn Saud, as 'that worthless man' and 'a mere *bedu*'.[17] For four years *Lawrence of Arabia* was banned in Jordan.

During the hot, clear afternoon, we trekked southwards from Wadi Rum across a broad, flat expanse of sand dotted with *rimth, ajram* and *ratam* bushes, each trailing its own mini sand-dune. I was reminded of Lawrence: 'The essence of the desert was the lonely moving individual, the son of the road, apart from the world as in a grave'.[18] We skirted the jagged, precipitous walls of Jabal Khazali and reached Hussain's delightful Sunset Camp – just as the sun was setting, plunging this surreal landscape into a multitude of reds and browns. As we warmed ourselves around the fire, sipping tea and smoking a hubble-bubble, Hussain produced a *rababa* – a single-stringed instrument with a goatskin soundbox played by means of a horsehair bow. Accompanying himself he sang plaintive, hypnotic *bedu* songs as the sky darkened and the shoals of stars emerged. In the morning, we set off early, the air crisp and clear, heading back towards Wadi Rum across a landscape that could have been plucked from a Salvador Dali painting. Ahead, thrown into sharp relief by the early morning sun, stretched the yawning avenue of the wadi. By noon, and after stopping for tea with Hussain's family at his home in the village, we reached the northern entrance to what Lawrence called 'this irresistible place: this processional way greater than imagination'.[19]

Abdullah's domain

Prince Abdullah had won a domain but his victory seemed pyrrhic when set against the old Hashemite dream of an independent Arab kingdom stretching from Turkey to Arabia and from Iran to the Mediterranean. In

1921 Transjordan 'had a population of only some 230,000, no real city, no natural resources, and no importance to trade except as a desert thoroughfare', notes Wilson. 'In short, it had no reason to be a state on its own rather than a part of Syria, or of Palestine, or of Saudi Arabia, or of Iraq, except that it better served Britain's interests to be so'.[20] Transjordan was 'a country – if it was a country at all…which was conceded to Abdullah because nobody else really cared to have it', wrote Lebanese historian Kamal Salibi.[21] A harsher assessment yet comes from Israeli scholar Avi Shlaim: 'The borders of the new principality did not correspond to any particular historic, cultural or geographical unit. Bounded by the valley of the Yarmouk on the north, by the Arabian Desert on the east, by the River Jordan, the Dead Sea and Wadi Araba on the west, it had no outlet to the sea until Abdullah…grabbed Maan and Akaba from the expiring kingdom of the Hijaz. Effectively, Transjordan was a strip of cultivable land 270 kilometres long with a width tapering from 80 kilometres in the north to nothing in the south, and flanked by a great deal of desert; with a population of 350,000 [apparently including the Ma'an and Aqaba districts in the south], one railway line and hardly any roads, no resources whatsoever, and no revenue except for a modest British subsidy. The capital and largest town of this backward and primitive kingdom was Amman – a drab and dusty place which could not even boast a glorious past. It was perhaps not altogether inappropriate that this one-horse town should serve as the capital of what was essentially a provincial backwater'.[22] Abdullah was ruler in name only. He was utterly dependant on the British, especially for cash and military support. Although he cultivated and generally enjoyed the allegiance of the tribes, their fealty sometimes proved fickle. The ultimate guarantor of his rule was his army, the British-officered Arab Legion, formed in 1923, and, from its creation in 1926 until its withdrawal west of the Jordan river in 1930, the Transjordanian Frontier Force, whose role was to police the desert and which was also British-commanded.

Transjordan did at least have a future, unlike the kingdom of Hejaz whence Abdullah had come. After his victory over the Hashemites at Turaba in 1919, Ibn Saud had turned his attention to others of his neighbours but in 1924 he renewed his onslaught against the Hejaz. In October that year King Hussain was forced to abdicate in favour of his eldest son, Ali, and went into exile. His initial refuge was Aqaba, which still formed part of the Hejaz. Ibn Saud's forces had already mounted raids deep into Transjordan, hitting Bani Sakhr villages a few kilometres south of Amman in 1922 and again in summer 1924. With Hussain's arrival in Aqaba, Ibn Saud threatened to attack there, prompting the British to transfer the fallen monarch to Cyprus. Soon after, the Wahhabis took Taif and Mecca and besieged King Ali in the port town of Jeddah. In a bid to salvage at least some part of the old kingdom, Abdullah, backed by the British, in May 1925 announced the incorporation of the Ma'an and Aqaba districts into Transjordan. The hapless King Ali had no choice but to acquiesce. Deeming further resistance futile, Ali abdicated on 20 December that year and went into exile in British-mandated Iraq where his brother Faisal had been crowned king in August 1921.

In 1923 London had recognised the existence in Transjordan of a government under Abdullah and acknowledged him as Amir but had said nothing about the status of his domain. An Anglo-Transjordanian agreement of 20 February 1928 went a step further and recognised the territory as an 'amirate', or principality. Transjordan's formal independence from the UK was agreed in a treaty signed on 22 March 1946 that also provided for 'perpetual peace and friendship' between the two while providing for continued British support for the Arab Legion and access to military facilities. On 15 May 1946 Abdullah's pliant government resolved that his title should be upgraded from Amir to King and this was endorsed by his equally pliant parliament on 22 May. In the same session, parliament voted to change the country's name to the Hashemite Kingdom of Jordan. Abdullah's coronation was staged three days later.

Palestine crisis

In Palestine, Britain's ultimately irreconcilable promises to the Jews and Arabs caused trouble almost from the start. The Balfour Declaration required Britain to encourage the creation of a Jewish 'National Home' in Palestine. In its earlier years, Zionists often portrayed the construction of this 'home' as entailing only the establishment in Palestine of a sizeable Jewish community whose members could live with dignity, free of the discrimination and pogroms they suffered in Europe. To admit to anything more might have inflamed Arab opposition to the extent of jeopardising the entire project. Beneath the gloss, however, the aim was nothing less than a Jewish state in which Arabs could at best be second-class citizens, and by the 1930s this goal was quite explicit. Initially, the outlook for Jewish statehood was unpromising. At the time of the Balfour Declaration in 1917 Palestine's Jewish population stood at around 50–60,000, the great majority of whom lived in Jerusalem. The Arabs totalled some 700,000, most of them settled peasant farmers in the well-watered northern part of the country but including some 70,000 *bedu* in the arid south.[23] The Arabs, over twelve times as numerous as the Jews, were the Declaration's 'existing non-Jewish communities' whose 'civil and religious rights' would supposedly be protected.

In the earlier years of the British mandate, only a few thousand Jews immigrated each year. The Arabs did not feel too threatened and generally the country was peaceful – although outbreaks of inter-communal violence in 1920 and 1921 offered a foretaste of what was to come. Far more serious were major riots in Jerusalem and Hebron in 1929 in which 133 Jews and 116 Arabs died – most of the latter at the hands of the police. Thenceforth the situation deteriorated inexorably as the trickle of Jewish immigrants turned into a flood with the rise of fascism in Europe. In 1930 fewer than 5,000 Jews arrived. In 1934 the figure was over 45,000 and in 1935 it rose to 66,000. The Arabs staged a general strike in 1936 and an armed rebellion in 1937–38. In 1937 a British commission of enquiry headed by Lord Peel concluded that the mandate was unworkable and recommended Palestine's partition into Jewish and Arab states. Further British efforts to square the Palestine circle were interrupted by the Second World War, after which the conflict escalated. The Zionists, now backed by the United States, demanded that Palestine's doors be thrown open to the survivors of Hitler's Holocaust. The Arabs saw no reason why they should pay the price for Europe's crimes. Arab-Jewish violence intensified while the British came under increasing attack from Zionist terrorist groups. In 1947 London declared its intention of relinquishing its mandate and handed the problem it had created to the newly-formed United Nations. On 29 November 1947 the UN General Assembly voted to divide Palestine into Jewish and Arab states with Jerusalem and its environs, including Bethlehem, to have international status. The UN vote, forced through by US pressure on smaller countries, was blatantly unfair. It gave the Jews almost 60 per cent of Palestine, including the most fertile areas, at a time when they formed only 30 per cent of the population and owned less than 8 per cent of the land area. The Palestinian Arabs rejected the UN resolution outright.

The partition vote triggered open war in Palestine. The divided, poorly-led and ill-equipped Palestinians, aided by armed volunteers from

Syria, were no match for the Zionists, whose aims were to seize as much territory as possible and to 'cleanse' that territory of as many Arabs as possible. On 14 May 1948 the last British troops departed and on the same day the state of Israel was declared. Already there were 300,000 Palestinian refugees. On 15 May units of the regular armies of Syria, Lebanon, Iraq, Egypt and Jordan entered the fray but, after some initial successes, failed to block further Israeli advances let alone recover territory lost earlier. Only the Arab Legion – whose British officers were under orders from London not to enter any part of Palestine reserved for the Jewish state by the UN – proved a match for the Israelis, expelling them from the Old City of Jerusalem and, with the Iraqis, holding the West Bank. Fighting continued until January 1949 and later that year Israel signed a series of armistice agreements with the Arab combatant states other than Iraq.

The Palestine war dramatically altered Transjordan's population, in number and structure. By May 1949 the West and East Banks had a combined population of 1.43 million of whom only 476,000 were Transjordanians. Of the Palestinian majority, 519,000 were refugees, most of them living in terrible conditions in tented camps, dependant on hand-outs from the UN. Of the refugees, around 100,000 were in the East Bank, mainly in Amman, whose population mushroomed from 50,000 in early 1948 to 120,000 by October 1950, in the north-western town of Irbid and in the Jordan Valley. The rest were in the West Bank, living amongst the native population of 433,000.[24] Of all the Arab states, Jordan alone granted Palestinians citizenship. The Israelis, quietly content that their state had been largely emptied of nearly 80 per cent of its Arabs, did nothing to help.

From his earliest days in Transjordan Abdullah had maintained discreet links with the Zionists. In later justifications, he insisted that he understood early the Zionists' power and their potential to cause the Arabs immense harm. Rather than indulging in politically correct but ultimately futile gestures of opposition, it was better to seek some form of accommodation with a force that was there to stay. At the same time, he was moved by a calculation that his impoverished domain might benefit from Zionist investment and expertise. Certainly his dealings with the Zionists were punctuated by demands for cash to replenish his meagre personal coffers. Although Transjordan had been excluded from the Palestine mandate's pro-Zionist clauses, Abdullah favoured Jewish settlement in his amirate.

He, and several leading Transjordanian families, negotiated land sales to the Zionists. Abdullah was already viewed by many Arabs as a British puppet. Although the deals were not finalised, his standing fell even further when the Arab press revealed details of their existence. Beyond doubt, however, the key motivation behind Abdullah's protracted dialogue with the Zionists was the hope that they might aid his territorial ambitions. In the earlier years of the dialogue, he tried to tempt them with the offer of autonomy within a unified Transjordanian-Palestinian kingdom, headed by himself – a proposal that the Jews politely declined. When partition entered the Palestine agenda with the 1937 Peel Commission, Abdullah was strongly in favour because Peel had recommended that the Arab parts of Palestine be merged with Transjordan. When war became inevitable, Abdullah quietly assured the British and the Zionists that his forces would not enter the areas allocated to the Jewish state by the UN, explaining that his objective was to annex those parts designated for the Arab state. His interlocutors raised no objections.

Abdullah's relationship with the Zionists has been chronicled in detail by Avi Shlaim in his gripping study *Collusion Across the Jordan*. In addition to his concerns about the dangers of Zionism, 'Abdullah's policy towards the Zionists was also governed by an expectation of gains – gains which, at least in part, could only be realized at the expense of the Palestinian Arabs', he writes. 'For Abdullah was shrewd enough to recognize at an early stage in the game that the force of Zionism, if rightly channelled, could turn out to be not a barrier but a help in fulfilling his ambition of a greater Transjordan'.[25]

Annexation

Following the Palestine war, Abdullah arranged some theatre to lend a mask of legitimacy to the course on which he was, in any case, set. Encouraged and assisted by the king and his government, some 3,000 delegates attended a Palestinian Congress in Jericho, just north of the Dead Sea, on 1 December 1949. They included mayors and military governors from the West Bank, notables from Transjordan, Syria and Lebanon and ex-supporters of the now-discredited Palestinian leader and Mufti, or leading religious notable, of Jerusalem, Hajj Amin Hussaini, who had consistently and fiercely opposed Abdullah's efforts to win hegemony over Palestine. The congress passed resolutions calling for the unification of Jordan and Palestine under Abdullah and ceding him authority to resolve the Palestine problem as he saw fit. Within days, the resolutions were ratified by Abdullah's government and parliament in Amman. On 11 April 1950 general elections were held embracing both banks of the Jordan. On 24 April a joint session of the upper and lower houses of parliament adopted a resolution declaring support for 'complete unity between the two sides of the Jordan and their union into one state, which is the Hashemite Kingdom of Jordan, at whose head reigns King Abdullah ibn al-Hussain'. In a glaring contradiction – at least from the Palestinian nationalist perspective – the resolution also reaffirmed an 'intent to preserve the full Arab rights in Palestine'. On 29 April 1950 the West Bank was formally annexed.

Although the Arab Legion's creditable performance had enabled him to pose as a champion of the Palestinians, Palestinian self-determination had been the last thing on Abdullah's mind during the conflict. To this day he is seen by many – probably most – Palestinians not as a realist who understood the limits of his power and did what he could to contain the threats from the British and the Zionists, but as a self-serving, land-grabbing traitor. Wilson records how one Palestinian at the time told the American consul in Jerusalem: 'The officials, the notables and the people rush forward to kiss His Majesty's hand, when actually many of them would rather break it'.[26] On 20 July 1950 more than his hand was broken. As Abdullah was entering the Al-Aqsa Mosque in Jerusalem for the Friday prayers a young Palestinian stepped out from behind the building's open door, raised a pistol and shot him behind his right ear at a distance of a few feet. Abdullah died instantly. Further shots were fired, one of which might have killed the king's grandson, Hussain, had it not been deflected by a medal on his uniform. Opening fire in panic, the king's guard killed not only the assassin but also some twenty innocent bystanders. The full circumstances surrounding Abdullah's murder have never been established. A hasty official investigation led to the trial of ten plotters, four of whom were executed. Although they were said to be linked to the king's old antagonist, Hajj Amin Hussaini, the evidence was far from conclusive. It was widely believed, however, that the murder was in revenge for Abdullah's collusion with the Zionists.

As a stopgap, Abdullah's son, Nayif, was appointed regent. On 6 September 1951 Nayif's elder half-brother, Talal, who had returned from Switzerland where he had been receiving treatment for schizophrenia, was crowned king. In August 1952 his worsening illness forced him to abdicate in favour of his son Hussain, who ascended to the throne, aged just eighteen, on 2 May 1953. If Abdullah had created Jordan's skeleton, it would be Hussain, in a reign that spanned nearly fifty years, who would provide the flesh.

Notes

1. Interview with author, Amman, 6 March 2003.
2. Interview with author, Amman, 6 March 2003.
3. Interview with author, Amman, 24 February 2003.
4. Wilfred Thesiger, *Arabian Sands* (Harmondsworth: Penguin Books, 1984).
5. Interview with author, Coulsdon, 22 August 2002.
6. Mary C. Wilson, *King Abdullah, Britain and the Making of Jordan* (Cambridge: Cambridge University Press, 1987), p. 37.
7. Philip Robins, *A History of Jordan* (Cambridge: Cambridge University Press, 2004), p. 15.
8. Peter Mansfield, *The Arabs* (Harmondsworth: Pelican Books, 1978), p. 218.
9. Wilson, *King Abdullah*, p. 44.
10. Ibid., p. 53.
11. Michael Asher, *Lawrence: The Uncrowned King of Arabia* (London: Penguin Books, 1999), p. 357.
12. Beverley Milton-Edwards and Peter Hinchcliffe, *Jordan: A Hashemite Legacy* (London: Routledge, 2001), p. xi.
13. T. E. Lawrence, *Seven Pillars of Wisdom: A Triumph* (London: Penguin, 2000), p. 359.
14. Interview with author, Umm al-Gathir, 2 March 2003.
15. Interview with author, Amman, 23 February 2003.
16. Interview with author, Amman, 24 February 2003.
17. Wilson, *King Abdullah*, p. 44.
18. Lawrence, *Seven Pillars*, p. 659.
19. Ibid., p. 359.
20. Wilson, *King Abdullah*, p. 3.
21. Kamal Salibi, *The Modern History of Jordan* (London: I B Tauris, 1998), p. 91.
22. Avi Shlaim, *Collusion across the Jordan: King Abdullah, the Zionist Movement, and the Partition of Palestine* (Oxford: Clarendon Press, 1988), p. 31.
23. Mansfield, *The Arabs*, p. 201; David Gilmour, *Dispossessed: The Ordeal of the Palestinians 1917–1980* (London: Sidgwick & Jackson, 1980), p. 21.
24. Wilson, *King Abdullah*, p. 190.
25. Shlaim, *Collusion*, p. 42.
26. Wilson, *King Abdullah*, p. 195.

CHAPTER 2

'Neither Democrat nor Demagogue': Jordan under King Hussain

THE FLOODLIT BILLBOARDS atop the Mirador café on Abdoun Circle (or roundabout, as the British would say) extol the wonders of the Hamondeh hairdressing salon and of Titto Bluni clothes. Across the roundabout, with its lawn, flowerbeds and date palms, stand the Dina Slim Centre, Marcell Beauty Centre, Lugino's Café, Pizza Hut and the Galleria Cinema, solid three-storey buildings faced with white limestone. Above them, framed by the hazy moonlit darkness of the October night, tower brightly-lit advertisements for Union Bank, which is 'Proud to Serve You', and for Sony Ericsson T610 mobile phones, which have 'Quickshare'. 'PASS IT ON', we are urged. On an adjacent rooftop a two-metre by six-metre backlit photo of a palm-fringed, white sand beach edged by a calm blue sea exhorts us to 'Discover the marvels of Mauritius, Maldives & Seychelles with Emirates Airlines'. The compelling rhythms of Western rock and popular Arabic music pound from the cafés. Shining limousines and occasional sports cars snake round the Circle, sometimes parking abruptly and haphazardly. The pavements bustle with young men and women, both sexes in tight jeans and equally tight T-shirts, mingling with no less westernised family groups enjoying a late evening stroll. No sign here of the austere Islamic fundamentalism now coursing through the region. At one table on the open-air terrace of the Mirador, laughing Jordanian teenagers, the girls' carefully styled hair streaked with high-lights, chat, drink tea, smoke *arghilas* – traditional water pipes – and tap their feet in time to the Egyptian and Lebanese love songs booming from the sound system. At another sits an Iraqi family, refugees perhaps from the then six-month-old Western occupation of their country. At others, Iraqi and Jordanian couples talk softly, some discreetly holding hands, their faces illuminated by the flickering tabletop candles. Downhill, past Murad Hair Styles, the Kinda Center – Body and Mind Care, Lubna Snack and Tareq Hair Styles – the yellow lights of Amman, now a sprawling city of well over two million people, stretch into the far distance.

A kilometre away, near the US and British embassies, business is brisk at the Blue Fig Brasserie, a favourite haunt of Jordan's gilded youth. Around the wooden tables, eyes and teeth flashing in the candlelight, huddle groups of teenagers locked in animated conversation, English phrases interspersed with Arabic, voices raised against the loud Arabic and Western hits. Black-clad young servers looking no different from their clientele dart between the tables. The Blue Fig offers a range of multi-national dishes, the designer menu cards declaring the cuisine 'a tribute to all the cultures of the world' and sporting the phrase 'Eat, drink and be merry, for tomorrow we die', which is attributed – wrongly – to Shakespeare.

The wealthy and fashionable Abdoun district with its imposing villas and diplomatic missions and its broad thoroughfares betrays no sign of Amman's origins as a 'drab and dusty…one-horse town', nor of Jordan's past as an 'insignificant patch of real estate which no-one seemed to want nor knew what to do with'.[1] The other end of Jordan's socio-economic spectrum lives 30 kilometres to the north, in the Baqa'a camp, a teeming, 1.4 square kilometre maze of breeze-block hovels that is home to over 100,000 Palestinians who are refugees three times over. Displaced in the 1947–48 Palestine war, they lived initially in camps in the West Bank. When Israel seized that territory in June 1967 they fled to camps in the Jordan Valley east of the river. In 1968, as the result of Israeli attacks on Palestinian guerrillas based in the camps, they fled again, to Baqa'a, sited in a broad valley on the main road to Salt. Like all the camps, Baqa'a was originally a tented settlement. First, the refugees replaced the tents with corrugated iron shacks, and then in turn by breeze-block dwellings. Today Baqa'a is the biggest Palestinian camp in Jordan and in the entire Middle East.

Aman Abu Taha al-Jouri is 37 and her family is from the village of Ajajah, near the West Bank town of Hebron. Her husband, now in his seventies, has not worked since 1985. They have five children aged from four to eight and depend on food aid and other hand-outs from the UN Relief and Works Agency for Palestine refugees (UNRWA). Their home, typical of Baqa'a, is a spartan L-shaped structure with a living room, small kitchen and two bedrooms, a small rectangular concrete yard lying between its two minuscule wings. The rooms have cracked walls and the corrugated iron roof is partly open to the sky. It rained heavily recently and the walls and floors are damp. The biggest items of furniture are two battered wardrobes. The family sleeps on rugs and blankets spread on the floor. Asked if she was hopeful about the Palestinians' future, Aman snapped: 'Where is there hope? What hope?'[2] Her husband, a stocky man with a walrus moustache who has a second wife by whom he has another seven children, is given to rhetoric. His family's poverty was nothing compared with the loss of their country. 'We want our country, even if we have to eat sand', he affirmed. His bitterness towards the states responsible for the Palestinian tragedy is intense. 'I want Israel, England and America to be destroyed', he declared.[3]

The Jordanians

The government claimed recently that Jordanians of Palestinian descent, formerly a clear majority of the population, had become a minority of 43 per cent.[4] The figure hinges on definitions and is open to serious question. Historically, Jordan was a part of Greater Syria and a crossroads between the provinces of the Ottoman Empire. Its settlements enjoyed commercial relations with the larger Syrian urban centres and the region's families intermarried widely. Merchant families from Damascus moved south to Jordan and particularly close links developed between the main East Bank towns of Salt, Irbid, Ajloun and Karak and their counterparts on the West Bank, Nablus, Jerusalem and Hebron. In the south and east, the *bedu* tribes moved freely across the open deserts. In the late nineteenth century small communities of Circassians and Chechens – non-Arab Muslims, respectively Sunni and Shia, fleeing Russian persecution in the Caucasus – settled in the territory. Amman began its life as a Circassian village adjacent to the old Roman amphitheatre. Early this century small numbers of Christian Armenians arrived, fleeing the Turkish massacres in their homeland. When Abdullah came in 1920 he brought with him several hundred Hejazis. In the north lived small communities of Druze, members of an esoteric Shia sect whose heartland lies in today's Syria and Lebanon. The mosaic also included Turkomans and Assyrians and even a small settlement of Bahais in the Jordan Valley.

The population was dramatically altered by the annexation of the West Bank and the influx of Palestinians after Israel's creation in 1948. By any definition, Palestinians became a clear majority of around two-thirds of the population although many of the refugees integrated with the East Bank population. The 1967 Arab-Israeli war prompted an influx of around 300,000 Palestinian refugees to the East Bank, but in 1988 Jordan disengaged from the West Bank (see p. 34), thereby losing perhaps 750,000 of its population. After the 1990–91 Kuwait crisis, when Jordan and the PLO were accused by the Gulf states of sympathising with Saddam Hussain, Palestinians with Jordanian nationality, many of whom had lived in the Gulf all their lives, were expelled *en masse*. Between 250,000 and 400,000 re-settled in Jordan.[5]

Against that background it is simply impossible to state precisely what proportion of Jordan's population is 'Palestinian'. The official statement that Palestinians had become a minority 'aroused lots of laughter here', said Dr As'ad Abdul Rahman, an Amman-based Palestinian political analyst and a former minister in the Palestine National Authority (PNA). 'It all depends on the definition. Is it the first generation of Palestinians? The present generation? Two generations back? Five generations back? I would estimate that Palestinians constitute between 40 and 80 per cent of Jordanians, depending on how many generations you include'.[6] What is not in dispute is that Palestinian refugees form a very substantial part of the population. In 2003 there were 5.48 million Jordanians.[7] The number of Palestinian refugees registered with UNRWA as at 31 December that year was 1,740,170. Around 80 per cent were, to varying extents, integrated with the wider society. One fifth lived in ten officially recognised and three unofficial camps, the latter best described as 'clusters of Palestinians', according to Charles Kapes, UNRWA's deputy director for operations in Jordan.[8] In addition, the southern port of Aqaba has a cluster of 16,000 unregistered refugees while perhaps 5,000 more live in the Karak area. Palestinians thus account for an absolute minimum of one third of the total population.

Kapes is married to a Jordanian of Palestinian extraction. Their baby boy's first name is Faris, a classic Muslim name. His middle name is Lawrence, after T. E.: 'We had to come to some sort of cultural compromise', explained the amiable 60-year-old New Yorker.

What Milton-Edwards and Hinchcliffe term the 'instinctive ambivalence' of East Bankers towards the Palestinians and *vice versa* is a defining feature of the kingdom. It is 'the great fault line of Jordanian society'.[9] The tensions, usually latent, have been aggravated by informal but nevertheless widespread discrimination against Palestinians in public sector employment. The kingdom was based on the East Bank, and Transjordanians have traditionally dominated the bureaucracy and military. The corollary is that Palestinian Jordanians predominate in the private sector and professions. Again, however, care should be taken with definitions. Most Palestinians who arrived before or in 1948, while not forgetting their origins and sympathising with Palestinian nationalism, have integrated and see themselves as Jordanians. Many of the 1967 refugees, in contrast, consider themselves as Palestinian first and foremost and as only temporary residents – and are often treated as such by Jordan's security agencies and police. The East Bankers, too, can be sub-divided into two broad groups. What have been termed the 'Transjordanian nationalists' or 'Jordanian nationalists' comprise 'those who, once the stigma of defeat and loss in 1967 had dissipated, were increasingly relieved to see the back of the West Bank',[10] considering that its inclusion in the kingdom had prevented the development of a coherent and unified state. In his seminal study, *Jordanians, Palestinians and the Hashemite Kingdom in the Middle East Peace Process,* Adnan Abu-Odeh (a former minister and adviser to both King Hussain and King Abdullah II) observes that Transjordanian nationalism, after lying dormant for some 40 years, 'resurged in 1970 as a product of the adverse triangular interaction among Jordan, Israel and the PLO'[11] (see pp. 32–3). It has since been the dominant trend amongst East Bankers, to the detriment of the Palestinians. In contrast, the 'Pan-Jordanians', largely comprising Jordanians of Palestinian origin whose families had settled in Jordan voluntarily, many of them before 1948, were '1950 Abdullahites' who 'believed in the unity of the two banks as the territorial basis of the Jordanian state, but with the centre of gravity of such a state remaining in Amman'.[12] Jordan's almost certainly irrevocable loss of the West Bank has – literally – cut the ground from under the Pan-Jordanians although they remain influential as advocates of the integration of Jordan's Palestinians within the kingdom.

In addition to its indigenous population, however defined, Jordan hosts large expatriate communities. 'We don't know the figure exactly: anything between 400,000 and 700,000', said Muhammad Halaiqah, deputy prime minister for economic affairs at the time of interview in late

2003. 'Egyptians would be a good 60 per cent and Iraqis probably 35 per cent'.[13] The bloody aftermath of the invasion of Iraq has prompted a steady influx of middle class Iraqis fleeing the violence and seeking education for their children. No-one knows their number for sure but by Spring 2005 it was being put at around 500,000.[14]

Religiously, Jordan is relatively homogeneous. Over 95 per cent of its people are Sunni Muslims, of whom perhaps 25,000 are of Circassian origin. Christians, mainly Greek Orthodox and mostly living in Amman, Karak, Madaba, Salt and Ajloun, account for around three per cent, although their numbers have been declining through emigration.[15] The Druze, numbering perhaps 20,000, are found in the north-eastern oasis town of Azraq and in Mafraq, Irbid, Amman, Zarqa and Aqaba. Some 2,000 Shia Chechens live mainly in the Jordan Valley and the south while around 800 Bahai live in their northern Jordan Valley village of Al-Adisiya.[16]

This ethnic and religious backdrop, a product of the country's peculiar origins and turbulent history, makes Jordanians' collective identity hard to pin down. National unity has been an overriding political imperative since the kingdom's establishment but the various elements of the population remain relatively distinct. 'Jordan is a mixture. There is ambiguity', said former Prime Minister Taher al-Masri.[17] He was echoed by the then information minister, Muhammad Afash 'Idwan: 'Jordan is a conglomerate. Jordan is the *bedu*, the city-dweller, the Palestinian, the refugee, the Circassian, the Christian, the Muslim, the Armenian. It's a melting pot'.[18] Most Jordanians define themselves in terms of their tribal or regional origins. 'I'm not a Palestinian', insists Al-Masri. 'I'm a Jordanian of Palestinian origin. My family originally came from Nablus and I was born there. But we became Jordanians even before the West Bank – East Bank union'.[19] 'I'm a Jordanian, from Salt', says Bassam Saket, head of the Jordan Securities Commission. 'My grandmother's father is a Turk who was the governor of Jaffa [in Palestine]'.[20] 'I'm from Amman but my family was originally from the Hejaz', declares Ibrahim Izzadine, president of the kingdom's media watchdog, the Higher Media Council.[21] 'I was born in Amman but both my parents came from Damascus', says Dr Abd al-Fatah al-Bustani, a leading dental surgeon.[22]

King Hussain

That Jordan now enjoys a relatively high degree of national cohesion despite the diverse origins, conflicting loyalties and uncertain identity of its people is a tribute above all to King Hussain. In the first half of his reign, however, it was often touch and go. When he succeeded to the throne, the shockwaves of the Palestine catastrophe were reverberating through the region. In 1949 alone three military coups had been staged in Syria. In 1952 Egypt's monarchy had been swept away by nationalist army officers including Gamal Abdul Nasser. The 1950s and 1960s were the heydays of a radical anti-Western Arab nationalism that demanded the liberation of Palestine, pan-Arab unity and socialism at home and non-alignment abroad. Jordan, with its restless majority Palestinian population and the longest Arab border with a truculent Israel, and surrounded by far more powerful radical Arab states, was at the heart of the turbulence. As the head of a regime that many accused of having sold out the Palestinians in 1948 and that relied on financial and military support from the United Kingdom and the United States – the two countries that, after Israel, were the most detested by the radicals – Hussain was an obvious target. Palestinians and nationalists – and most Palestinians at that time were nationalists – regarded him at best with ambivalence and at worst as little more than a lackey of their enemies.

King Abdullah had ruled as an absolute monarch, paying scant heed to his rubber-stamp parliament and treating his governments merely as executors of his decisions. Avi Shlaim records how, during a meeting with Israeli representatives in early 1949, within days of Israel's first general election, Abdullah had expressed approval that the Communists had not performed strongly, 'adding that Transjordan had no need for elections as he ruled and Parliament carried out his will'.[23] In his memoirs, he wrote warmly of Spain's fascist dictator, General Franco, whom he had visited in 1949. 'He is one of my greatest friends', affirmed the king. 'It seems to me that patriarchal rule by a single hand is preferable to other types of government'.[24] His son Talal's outlook was more liberal. In 1937 Sir Frederick Peake, the Arab Legion's commander, had denigrated Talal as being 'well in with the opposition and egging them on'. He was, opined Peake, a 'young man [who] talks most foolishly. He has been known to express very definite anti-English sentiments'. Peake had 'little doubt that he gives forth a lot of very dangerous ideas'.[25] The revised Constitution of 1952, which was the only major legislative outcome of Talal's brief and tragic reign, and which in amended form remains in effect today, included a range of clauses providing for democracy and respect for human rights. Reaffirming the regime's underlying authoritarian instincts, however, it qualified these by stipulating that they should be applied 'in accordance with the law'. Repeatedly, the monarchy was to exploit this doubtless intentional ambiguity by passing laws that effectively nullified the freedoms and rights supposedly guaranteed by the Constitution. Entirely unambiguous was the Constitution's affirmation of the monarchy as the undisputed fount of power. 'Executive power shall be vested in the King', it declared, confirming his role as supreme commander of the armed forces and his right to convene and dissolve parliament and appoint and dismiss governments. Article 30 stated flatly: 'The King is the Head of State and is immune from any liability and responsibility'.

Although an autocrat who never envisaged the monarchy relinquishing its core powers, Hussain was overtly despotic only when cornered – but in varying degrees he felt cornered for much of his reign. He appointed his first government, headed by the relatively liberal Fawzi al-Mulqi, in May 1953. A former ambassador to London, where he had assiduously cultivated a friendship with the then Prince Hussain, himself at the time a pupil at Harrow School, Al-Mulqi proved ineffectual. Panicked by the growing strength of the nationalist opposition, itself fuelled by bloody Israeli raids launched in retaliation for Palestinian guerrilla attacks across the border from Jordan, the regime turned to an older generation of politicians, who would dominate all the kingdom's cabinets in the period until October 1956. Al-Mulqi was sacked in May 1954 and replaced by Tewfiq Abu al-Huda, who had been premier twice under Abdullah and for the three years between Abdullah's assassination and Hussain's accession to the throne. Parliament was dissolved, and opposition newspapers were closed for six months. On 16 October 1954, the day of the general election, a demonstration in Amman turned into a riot. The Arab Legion was brought out to restore order, killing ten people in the process. It was a pattern that would be repeated down the years.

Key foci of opposition in the 1950s were the Baghdad Pact and the continuing British military presence in Jordan – both central facets of the inflammatory propaganda beamed relentlessly against Hussain's regime by Gamal Abdul Nasser's Voice of the Arabs radio station in Cairo. Conceived as a bulwark against Soviet expansion into the Middle East, the Baghdad Pact was a military alliance signed by Iraq, Turkey, Iran, Pakistan and Britain in 1955. Jordan, which had special treaty relations with and depended heavily on London, came under intense British pressure to join.

King Hussain favoured the move but in December 1955 the country was swept by five days of anti-Hashemite demonstrations and riots that were quelled only by the intervention of the Arab Legion and the imposition of a curfew. Hussain backed away from the Baghdad Pact, dissolved parliament and called a general election. In January 1956, however, his dissolution of parliament was ruled invalid by the courts because the relevant documents had not been signed by the interior minister as required. Further rioting erupted, to be quashed once more by the army. In a bid to bolster his frayed Arab nationalist credentials, in March 1956 the king fired Sir John Bagot Glubb – Glubb Pasha – the British officer who had been second-in-command of the Arab Legion since 1930 and its commander since 1939. The Arab Legion was meanwhile renamed the Jordan Arab Army although its old name remains in popular use until today. Shortly after Glubb's departure, Hussain dismissed the government, headed by Samir Rifa'i, that had been appointed only in January, dissolved parliament and scheduled new elections for October.

1956–58

The next crisis was already looming. In July 1956 Nasser nationalised the Suez Canal, leading to an invasion in October by Britain, France and Israel. Hussain refused Britain permission to use its military bases in Aqaba, Ma'an, Mafraq and Amman in its operations against Egypt. US pressure forced the aggressors to withdraw but the attack infuriated an Arab world already in nationalist ferment and Nasser emerged more popular than ever. The general election was held on 21 October, just a week before the attack on Egypt, and nationalists and Communists emerged as the biggest winners. Suleiman al-Nabulsi, the leader of the largest nationalist grouping, the National Socialist Front, was appointed as prime minister. In response to Suez, the new government severed diplomatic relations with France and resolved to abrogate the Anglo-Jordanian Treaty of 1946 that had formalised Jordan's alliance with – or, in the nationalists' view, subservience to – London. On 19 January 1957 Jordan signed an Arab Solidarity Agreement with Egypt, Syria and Saudi Arabia under which those states agreed to replace the £12 million annual subsidy that Jordan had hitherto received from Britain, and the Anglo-Jordanian treaty was terminated by agreement on 14 March.

At the same time, however, Hussain was moving to replace British sponsorship with American. In early 1957 President Eisenhower had pro-claimed his eponymous 'doctrine' that called for US financial and military support for Middle Eastern regimes threatened by 'international Communism'. The king's political pronouncements adopted an increas-ingly Cold War tone. Small matter that his most dangerous opponents were not the Communists but the radical nationalists. In March 1957 Nabulsi's government announced its intention to recognise Communist China and the following month declared plans to establish full relations with Moscow. With the king courting Washington and railing against Communism, the stage was set for a collision. The crisis deepened on 8 April when an army unit mounted Operation Hashim, a night-time manoeuvre that involved taking control of a series of major crossroads in Amman. Its ostensible purpose, according to differing accounts, was either to conduct a census of vehicles entering and leaving the city or to check the technical condition of the unit's own vehicles. Although the troops returned to barracks on Hussain's orders, he was shaken. 'The real idea [behind the deployment], by one account, was to intimidate the king's friends', wrote Hussain's biographer, Roland Dallas. 'The result was that the king immediately smelt a plot. He knew his back was against the wall...Daring moves were needed if he was to establish his authority'.[26] Two days later Hussain dismissed Al-Nabulsi and cast about for a more compliant premier.

There followed a dramatic episode that became known as the Zarqa Affair. Its details remain hazy to this day. According to the king's version, the chief of staff, Ali Abu Nuwar, an officer with nationalist sympathies whom Hussain suspected of having been behind Operation Hashim, on 13 April warned Said al-Mufti, a former prime minister who was in pole position to replace Al-Nabulsi, that any government he formed would have to be acceptable to the army and opposition. The king took this as a direct challenge from the military, and his fears were confirmed later the same day when news reached him of a rebellion at Jordan's main army base, in Zarqa, 25 kilometres north-east of Amman. Fearlessly, Hussain resolved to reassert control in person, driving to Zarqa and taking Abu Nuwar with him. Still according to the king's account, he arrived to find the base in chaos, with loyalists and rebels grappling with each other, but he confronted the troublemakers and quickly restored order. Abu Nuwar begged for mercy and was permitted to go into exile, travelling to Syria the next day. According to King Hussain, he had virtually single-handedly foiled a military coup. Abu Nuwar, however, always protested his innocence, insisting that Said al-Mufti had misinterpreted his position. Whatever the truth, Abu Nuwar was later pardoned and became Jordan's ambassador to France.

The Zarqa Affair was not the end of the crisis. Within days, a Syrian armoured column that had been deployed in Jordan to support the kingdom during the Suez crisis surrounded the northern town of Irbid, apparently on the order of Abu Nuwar's successor as chief of staff, General Ali Hiyari. Hussain countermanded the order and on 20 April Hiyari, too, fled to Syria. Two days later, a 'Patriotic Congress' of nationalists and leftists convened in Nablus, on the West Bank, and called for a union of Syria and Egypt, the reinstatement of dismissed army officers and a general strike. Nearby in the Mediterranean, meanwhile, the US Sixth Fleet was steaming eastwards in response to a plea for help from Lebanese President Camille Chamoun, who was embroiled in his own crisis with leftists and nationalists, and Eisenhower declared his commitment to the 'independence and integrity of Jordan'. On 24 April the government of Suleiman al-Khalidi, an ex-mayor of Jerusalem, who had been appointed only on 15 April, resigned. The same day Hussain replaced it with a cabinet of staunch loyalists headed by Ibrahim Hashim, who, like several other of Hussain's premiers, had occupied the same post under King Abdullah. With the king's opponents and supporters mobilising in the streets, Hussain took sweeping and decisive action to end the festering crisis. Early on 25 April he placed Jerusalem, Amman, Irbid, Ramallah and Nablus under curfew, arrested several hundred people, including army officers of doubtful loyalty, banned political parties and closed opposition publications. To underline its support for the king, Washington agreed a $10 million grant – the first in a long series that continue until now.

If in 1957 King Hussain was threatened from within, the following year he felt pressured from without. In February 1958 his two arch-enemies, Syria and Egypt, merged to form the United Arab Republic. The same month Jordan and its fellow Hashemite kingdom, Iraq, countered by forming an Arab federation. It proved short-lived. On 14 July Iraq's monarchy was toppled in a bloody military coup. Within days US marines landed in Lebanon to safeguard Chamoun's regime and British paratroopers flew to Jordan – through Israeli airspace – to guarantee Hussain's. The regime continued to be troubled by its radical neighbours and its domestic opposition but the combination of repression and the US–UK security umbrella ensured that no threat emerged on a scale that might threaten its survival – at least until the late 1960s.

Black September

Until now, there is disagreement as to why King Hussain allowed himself to be drawn into the disastrous Arab–Israeli war in 1967, in which Jordan lost the West Bank. There's no shortage of theories: that he felt he would risk a popular uprising if he failed to join Egypt and Syria; that he fatally miscalculated the Arab-Israeli balance of power; and that he anticipated superpower intervention to prevent a humiliating Arab defeat. Another factor, as Robins has pointed out, was simply 'the mercurial nature of Hussein's personality, especially at a time of crisis, operating in a highly individualised and uninstitutionalised domestic decision-making context'.[27] Whatever the truth, the conflict set the stage for an internal challenge far greater than those of the 1950s. The crushing Arab defeat in 1967 convinced the Palestinians of the futility of pinning any further hopes on the Arab regimes, however supportive their rhetoric, and that if they were to retrieve any of their usurped rights, it would have to be through their own efforts. The Palestine Liberation Organisation (PLO), originally formed in 1964 at an Arab summit as a compliant tool of the region's governments, attained an independent life in 1968 when Yasser Arafat and his Fatah organisation took over its leadership. Jordan, with its majority Palestinian population and its long border with Israel, was the natural operational centre for the PLO and its constituent guerrilla groups. In defiance of Jordanian policy, the Palestinians mounted attacks into Israel and the occupied West Bank, prompting bloody reprisal raids, and by the late 1960s the PLO had established a 'state-within-a-state' in the kingdom. Heavily-armed guerrillas roamed the streets, scornful of local sentiment and local authorities alike. 'They were out of control,' recounts Dallas. 'By one reckoning there were more than 50 factions, mostly reporting to nobody but themselves. Many financed themselves by holding up shopkeepers, demanding contributions to the cause. One group broadcast Marxist slogans from a minaret to mark Lenin's birthday. Arafat lacked both the military means and the political will to bring the groups under his control'.[28]

For King Hussain, already under pressure from his advisers to rein in the guerrillas, the final straws came on 6 September 1970, when George

Habbash's Popular Front for the Liberation of Palestine (PFLP) hijacked three Western aircraft to Dawson's Field, an airstrip near Zarqa, and on 15 September, when Palestinian guerrillas took over the northern city of Irbid and installed a 'people's government'. King Hussain declared military rule and on 17 September the Arab Legion attacked the Palestinians in Amman. Fierce fighting in the capital quickly spread to other towns. Three days later a Syrian armoured column entered Jordan in support of the guerrillas. Underlining the ambivalence of Israeli-Jordanian relations, the Israelis signalled their readiness to use their air force against the Syrian armour, which lacked air support, although in the event, the Syrians were beaten back by the king's forces. In November Hussain ordered the Palestinians still in Amman to relocate to the hill country around Ajloun and Jerash in the north. The tide had turned in the fighting and they had little option but to comply. In June 1971 the Legion attacked and by mid-July, after intense and bloody battles, the guerrillas had been crushed. Many escaped into Syria and thence moved to Lebanon, upsetting that country's delicate ethnic balance and contributing to the eruption of its own civil war in 1975. Some even fled across the River Jordan into Israel. 'By 15 July', wrote Robins, 'there was only one state left in Jordan'.[29]

Its defeat in Jordan did not spell the end of the PLO. Against Jordanian objections, an Arab summit in the Moroccan capital of Rabat in October 1974 declared it 'the sole legitimate representative of the Palestinian people' and approved the establishment of 'an independent national authority…in any Palestinian territory that is liberated'. The following month Arafat addressed the UN General Assembly in New York, which passed a resolution affirming its support for Palestinian self-determination. Until then, the touchstone of efforts to resolve the Arab-Israeli conflict had been UN Resolution 242, passed in the wake of the June 1967 war. This had called for Israel to withdraw from 'areas occupied' in the fighting and had affirmed the right of 'every state in the area' to live in peace. It had been reaffirmed in Resolution 338 that ended the October 1973 Arab-Israeli war, in which Jordan had played only a minor role by sending units to support Syria. Neither 242 nor 338 mentioned the Palestinians or their plight. The Rabat resolutions effectively challenged Jordan's annexation of the West Bank and King Hussain paid them lip-service only – a key factor in Jordan's often strained relations with the PLO in the subsequent years – but the die was cast.

On 31 July 1988, as the first Palestinian *intifada*, or uprising, raged in the occupied territories, and following the decision of an Arab summit in Algiers in June 1988 that Arab aid for the Palestinians under Israeli occupation should be channelled through the PLO rather than Jordan, King Hussain formally severed Jordan's 'legal and administrative ties' with the West Bank. One view is that Jordan was simply bowing to the inevitable. Another is that the move was 'a gambler's throw of the dice, made from a position of weakness and intended to bring about a dramatic improvement in King Hussein's position *vis-à-vis* the West Bank'.[30] Hussain was not relinquishing Jordan's claim to the West Bank. Rather, according to this explanation, he expected that the PLO would be unable to capitalise on the move and that a West Bank populace would turn to him anew in the absence of any viable alternative. It was 'not...a sporting admission that the best man had won and that man was Arafat', wrote Robins. Hussain's 'intention was to set a trap, to hand the PLO "a poisoned chalice".'[31] If this interpretation is correct, the king's decision was a grave miscalculation for it was he, not Arafat, that was ensnared in the trap. Within six years, a Palestine National Authority (PNA) headed by Arafat would be formed as the precursor to a sovereign Palestinian government, and Jordan's control of the West Bank would be just a matter of history.

Kuwait crisis

The final major crisis of King Hussain's reign was prompted by Saddam Hussain's invasion of Kuwait in August 1990. During the 1980s Jordan had developed an intimate alliance with Iraq. Amman was Baghdad's staunchest supporter in its 1980–88 war with Iran. After the closure of Iraq's Gulf ports, Jordan, via its Red Sea port of Aqaba, had become the main conduit for Iraqi-bound arms and other goods and a major export route for Iraqi oil. Iraq had become by far the biggest market for Jordanian industrial and agricultural products, and Jordan's main supplier of oil, which was provided on highly concessionary terms. Good relations with Iraq had become a vital Jordanian national interest. With the invasion of Kuwait, the UN imposed comprehensive trade sanctions on Iraq, and Washington and its Gulf allies set about creating a broad military coalition to liberate Kuwait. Jordan was in an impossible position: it was closely allied to the US and enjoyed warm relations with its fellow conservative monarchies in the Gulf; but it was also close to Saddam's Iraq, and the sanctions threatened to destroy its economy. Public opinion was another critical factor. Jordan's large Palestinian community had little time for the Kuwaiti royal family. Many had relatives working in Kuwait and were well aware of the discrimination suffered by Palestinians there.

In this period, meanwhile, Saddam enjoyed close relations with the PLO, and his standing in their eyes was boosted immeasurably when he explicitly linked Kuwait's fate to Palestine's. Contrasting the West's impatience to liberate Kuwait with its protracted acquiescence in Israel's occupation of Arab lands, he offered to evacuate Kuwait if Israel would withdraw from the occupied Palestinian territories, and he threatened to respond to any attack on his forces in Kuwait by bombarding Israel with rockets tipped with chemical weapons. Jordanians, and particularly Palestinian Jordanians, strongly backed Iraq, and the launch of Jordan's democratisation project a year earlier (see p. 38) meant that they could vent their feelings freely. King Hussain was acutely aware that siding with the Americans and Kuwaitis could cause a popular explosion at home, with possibly dire consequences for his regime. He tried to steer a middle course, offering himself as a mediator. Although not recognising Kuwait's annexation as Iraq's 'nineteenth province', he declined to condemn Baghdad by name, declined to join the anti-Iraq coalition and dragged his feet on the implementation of sanctions against Iraq. For Washington and Kuwait, this was not good enough. 'What was different about this conflict', observed the American scholar Laurie Brand, 'was that the international community had defined away neutrality: any state that was not with the coalition, as constructed by the United States, was depicted as being pro-Iraqi. Unlike past conflicts, in this case there was no middle ground'.[32]

Jordan suffered severely from the conflict and its doomed efforts to remain neutral. Up to 400,000 Jordanians of Palestinian origin who had lived and worked in Kuwait were expelled after the conflict in retaliation for Amman's perceived pro-Iraqi stance. A flow of remittance income that had been a pillar of the economy was thereby abruptly halted while the employment and other needs of the returnees were a heavy burden. The UN sanctions closed the crucial Iraqi market and forced Jordan to seek oil elsewhere on harsher financial terms. Aid from the US and Gulf declined. Payments from a UN fund to compensate states affected by the crisis did little to offset Jordan's losses, which came at a time when the economy was already in deep recession for other reasons. Jordan's Central Bank estimated that in 1990 alone the Kuwait crisis cost the kingdom $1.5 billion – equivalent to 35 per cent of its 1989 gross domestic product (GDP).[33] Starting in 1992, Jordan distanced itself from Iraq; but only with its peace treaty with Israel in 1994 did Amman manage to rehabilitate itself in US eyes, while a rapprochement with the Gulf states was not achieved until the late 1990s.

Peace with Israel

In 1979 Egypt's President Anwar Sadat had broken Arab ranks by signing a bilateral peace treaty with Israel and in September 1993 the PLO itself made peace with the Israelis by signing the Oslo Accords, providing for an Israeli evacuation of the Occupied Territories and the establishment there of an independent Palestinian state. Jordan came under intense US pressure to emulate Sadat but declined. After Oslo, however, Hussain – who in 1963 had revived his grandfather Abdullah's tradition of discreet contacts with the Israelis – felt free to take the plunge. An important motive was surely to rehabilitate himself in the eyes of a US he had antagonised during the 1990–91 Kuwait crisis. On 26 October 1994 the Jordanian premier Abd as-Salam al-Majali and his Israeli counterpart Yitzhak Rabin met on the border in the Wadi Araba, south of the Dead Sea, and signed a full peace treaty. An immediate tangible result was a dramatic boost in US aid. Jordanian analyst Ali Kassay records: 'The United States declared Jordan a non-NATO strategic ally, wrote off its debt, and raised aid levels progressively from a minimal amount to a point where Jordan became in less than a decade the fourth largest recipient of US economic and military assistance in the world: $1 billion over three years'.[34] In April 1995 Jordan and Israel exchanged ambassadors and tourist and other commercial exchanges began. In May 1996, however, the hardline Likud bloc, dedicated to continued colonisation of the Occupied Territories, won power in Israel under Binyamin Netanyahu. Israeli obduracy caused the Oslo Accords to founder, thereby thrusting the Jordanian–Israeli peace into icy stagnation. Matters hit a new low in September 1997 when Mossad, Israel's foreign intelligence service, attempted to assassinate Khalid Misha'al, the leader in Jordan of the radical Palestinian Islamist group Hamas. The agents, posing as Canadian tourists, sprayed poison into Misha'al's ear but were then apprehended by his bodyguards. An incensed King Hussain demanded that Israel immediately supply the antidote and insisted that he would release the hit-squad members only in exchange for the Gaza-based spiritual leader of Hamas, Shaikh Ahmad Yassin, who was then in an Israeli jail. The Israelis complied. Misha'al's life was saved and Yassin flew to Amman for medical treatment before returning home.

The plaudits won by the king for his decisive handling of the Misha'al affair notwithstanding, the Jordanian public had deep reservations about his peace treaty with Israel. Critics, and there were many, argued that it would merely encourage the Israelis in their foot-dragging over implementing the Oslo Accords and that the time for peace should be *after* the Palestinians had achieved a measure of justice, not before. For the king, desperate to rebuild relations with the Americans after the Kuwait crisis, the peace treaty – and he wanted a warm peace – took precedence over all else. Correctly anticipating the sustained protests that the treaty and subsequent attempts to 'normalise' Jordanian–Israeli relations would arouse, in 1993 he sharply constrained a democratisation programme that he had launched in 1989 following riots linked to the dire state of the economy (see below). Democracy was welcome as a tool for reasserting the regime's control but less so when it might threaten the central plank of its foreign policy.

Mainly because of Israel's continued truculence towards the Palestinians and partly because of the consequent resistance to normalisation within Jordan, the kingdom's relations with Tel Aviv have remained anything but normal. In April 2004 I tried to interview the Israeli ambassador to Amman. Repeated telephone calls to several embassy numbers were handled by answer machines and not returned. I then went to the embassy, a limestone-faced structure in the up-market Rawabih district of western Amman, just downhill from the Happy Days Kindergarten. It was ringed with steel barriers and men of the interior ministry's paramilitary Amn al-Am, or Public Security Directorate, with their distinctive blue-grey camouflage uniforms, armed with automatic rifles. An officer politely explained that no-one was in the embassy. From other sources, I learned that the ambassador's residence was equally deserted. Fearing reprisals, the entire Israeli diplomatic establishment had departed without fanfare following Israel's assassination on 22 March of Hamas' leader, Shaikh Ahmad Yassin. On 17 April, two days before I visited the heavily guarded embassy, the Israelis had murdered Yassin's successor, Abdul Aziz al-Rantisi.

'Defensive democracy'

Jordan's incorporation of the West Bank from 1950 to 1988 and its Palestinian majority have made the Palestine question at once an internal and foreign issue. The kingdom's heavy reliance on foreign donors – initially the UK and later the US, the oil-rich Gulf states and international financial institutions – and on remittances from Jordanians working in the Gulf has also blurred the distinction between domestic and foreign affairs. In the 1970s the kingdom enjoyed an economic boom, but this was replaced by a deepening recession in the 1980s as Western aid declined and aid and workers' remittances from the Gulf slumped because of the collapse of world oil prices. The crunch came in 1988, when the Jordanian dinar precipitously slid in value against the US dollar. In view of the kingdom's heavy dependence on imports, the result was runaway inflation that had devastating consequences for the large part of the population already living on the bread line. By early 1989 Jordan was unable to meet repayments on its foreign debts and had no option but to seek emergency funding from the IMF, which obliged on condition that Amman institute an austerity programme. Prices of basic commodities were hiked in April that year, sparking riots that began in Ma'an and quickly spread to other southern towns and villages. The unrest was fundamentally different from past upheavals that had been linked to the Palestinians and urban nationalists. The East Bank, and especially its south, was the traditional heartland of support for the monarchy.

Although he started his reign on a liberal note, Hussain would soon set democracy aside in favour of stability and regime survival. The dramas of the 1950s had been trials of strength between the monarchy and parliament. Since 1957 political parties had been banned, general elections had been carefully managed and none had been held since April 1967. Martial law had been imposed partially in 1957 and fully during the 1967 war. As under Abdullah, parliament and governments had become mere creatures of the king. After the Ma'an riots, Hussain suddenly displayed a penchant for democracy, appointing a new government which he instructed to end corruption and nepotism and, crucially, to restore parliamentary life. Elections were held in November 1989 that were acknowledged to be free and fair. Over half the seats were won by conservative Islamists, leftists, pan-Arabists, liberals and reformers (see Chapter 12).

After more than two decades of ruling virtually as a dictator, why did

Hussain suddenly embrace democracy? The consensus is that the 1989 elections were an exercise to legitimise the regime at a time when the Ma'an riots had revealed a clear crisis of confidence. '"Defensive democracy" was very much the order of the day', explain Milton-Edwards and Hinchcliffe. 'The monarch had survived tremendous political upheavals and threats to his rule. He had responded to these threats with a variety of political strategies and tactics designed to shut out political participation in the affairs of the country. However, by 1989 the failure of other political strategies linked to economic recession may have propelled him to accept a new option'.[35] But this is only part of the explanation. Crucially, the Jordan of 1989 was not the Jordan of 1957 or 1970. Radical pan-Arab nationalism had been discredited by the disaster of June 1967. The Palestinians had abandoned hope of liberating all their homeland and were ready to settle for independent statehood in the West Bank and Gaza Strip. Communism was on the retreat and the Soviet Union was collapsing. By the late 1980s none of Jordan's main political currents was posing a challenge to the established system. 'With regard to the monarchy, the formerly radical Palestinians, Ba'athists, Communists and others had moderated beyond recognition in comparison with earlier periods', observed Virginia University's Ranjit Singh. 'Simply put, there would not have been a free parliamentary election in 1989 had the king faced the level of radical mobilisation and influence he confronted in 1957. Hussain's decision to resume electoral politics in 1989 coincided with an absence of significant challenges to his authority. Whatever other factors may have inspired Hussain, liberalisation would not have been a meaningful option if this necessary condition had not first been met...It is highly unlikely that the King would have risked a fair election in 1989 without this shift in the domestic balance of power'.[36]

National Charter

Having restored parliamentary life, Hussain's next step, in April 1990, was to appoint a 60-member royal commission to draft a National Charter setting out his vision of a liberalised and democratic Jordan. The commission, whose members were chosen to represent all shades of opinion, was chaired by Ahmad al-Obeidat, an ex-prime minister and former director of the General Intelligence Department (GID) – the main Jordanian intelligence agency and a key tool of repression since its formation in 1964.

Divided into eight chapters covering matters as diverse as democracy, the economy, foreign relations, education, the media and the Jordanian-Palestinian relationship, the Charter was ratified in June 1991 by a 2,000-member National Congress, also appointed by the king. Although not legally binding, the document has since been a central point of reference for Jordanian political developments. Affirming that 'the democratic option is the most efficient and appropriate means of fulfilling the aspirations of the Jordanian people', the Charter called for 'political, party and intellectual pluralism', 'social justice', 'respect for human rights' and 'the supremacy of the law'. It identified 'respect for the mind, belief in dialogue, recognition of the right of others to disagree, respect for the opinion of others, tolerance, and rejection of political and social violence' as 'basic characteristics of Jordanian society'. Consequently, there would be 'no compulsion in religion or recourse to fanaticism, sectarianism or regional bias'. Political parties would be allowed, providing 'their objectives are legitimate, their methods are peaceful and their statutes do not violate the provisions of the Constitution'. It would be unacceptable for party leaders and members to have 'structural or financial affiliation ... with any non-Jordanian' and for parties to act 'upon instructions or directions from any foreign state or body'. All parties would be required to 'rely on local, recognised, declared and specified Jordanian resources'. On the media, the Charter affirmed that 'freedom of thought and expression, and access to information' were a 'right' but that the media should operate 'on the principles of freedom, national responsibility, respect for the truth and regard for the values of the Arab and Islamic nation'. Freedom of access to information should be guaranteed by the state 'to the extent that it does not jeopardise national security or the national interest'. It was stipulated that the media 'must be committed to the service of the country as a whole' and 'must not be used to propagate the particular philosophy of any political party or group'.

While much of the National Charter was commendable as a blueprint for a liberal democracy, it was plain that the new order would have limits, and that these limits would be defined by the existing establishment. It was highly significant that, at a time when Jordan had a fully-functioning parliament, a charter on democracy had been drafted on the king's initiative by an unelected commission and ratified by an unelected congress. Also significant was that representatives of opposition trends had helped draft it, thereby allowing themselves to be co-opted by the establishment.

Walking a tightrope

Martial law was lifted in July 1991 and in 1992 a Political Parties Law was promulgated that allowed the opposition to function legally, albeit within constraints that assured their loyalty to the system. Over twenty political parties were formed, ranging from the Muslim Brotherhood-dominated Islamic Action Front (IAF) to several Communist and Ba'athist groups (see Chapter 12). For decades, political parties had been banned and forced to operate clandestinely while parliament had been marginalised. Even in the new democratic Jordan, the establishment made clear its determination to retain ultimate control. Perhaps unsurprisingly, both parties and parliament would remain very much on the political sidelines. Although the media was kept on a tight leash, a Press and Publications Law issued in 1993 relaxed some of the controls and led to a flowering of the media. But the new journals, and especially the weeklies that were platforms for the opposition, soon fell foul of the authorities (see Chapter 14), with the media's trenchant criticism of the 1994 peace treaty with Israel as a particular bone of contention. The government of Abd as-Salam al-Majali issued a new and highly restrictive press law in 1997 while parliament was in recess. Further press laws were issued in 1998 and 1999 but failed fully to undo the damage. In line with the wider retreat from democracy during the 1990s, stemming mainly from the king's determination to minimise opposition to his peace treaty with Israel, Hussain decreed a new electoral law just before the November 1993 elections and after the outgoing parliament, by far the most representative in Jordan's history, had stood down. The new law inaugurated the so-called 'one man, one vote' system (see Chapter 12), which was blatantly designed to strengthen the monarchy's traditional support base at the expense of Islamist and secular candidates with political programmes that extended beyond parochial issues. The tactic worked, with oppositionists winning only 26 seats in the 1993 poll. In protest at the new system, the Muslim Brotherhood – which, as the regime had calculated they would be, had been the biggest losers – boycotted the 1997 elections. The resultant parliament was not even nominally representative.

The switch to democracy in 1989 sparked a rapid rise in the number of Jordanian non-governmental organisations (NGOs). In the five years up to 1989 the number registered with the ministry of social development and the ministry of culture, the two main regulatory agencies for NGOs, increased 24 per cent, from 391 to 477. In 1989–94 there was a 67 per cent rise, to 796. Most of the kingdom's NGOs are charitable organisations but cultural NGOs, many of them dealing with quasi-political subjects, grew fastest in the early 1990s. In 1989 they more than trebled in number, from 42 to 156.[37] In this arena, too, the regime displayed ambivalence, officially encouraging NGO activity as part of its drive to encourage civil society in the new democratic Jordan while at the same time quietly ensuring that matters did not get out of hand. NGOs are regulated by Law 33 of 1936, as amended in 1956, 1965 and 1966. Each NGO must register with a ministry, which must approve the organisation's proposed activities before giving permission for it to operate. The NGO must submit a detailed annual report to the ministry, which has sweeping powers to intervene in the NGO's financial and other affairs. Ministry officials attend internal NGO elections and must approve the results. Crucially, Law 33 forbids NGOs from expressly political activities and this requirement was reinforced by the 1992 Political Parties Law, which forbids 'the use of the premises, instrumentalities and assets of associations, charitable organisations and clubs for the benefit of any partisan organisation'. In addition, volunteer workers in NGOs and board members must be approved by the *mukhabarat* (the GID – General Intelligence Department) and by the Public Security Directorate. The state has frequently used its wide discretionary powers against NGOs it deems to have overstepped the mark, dissolving them or intervening to reorganise their leadership and structure. In 1995 eleven charitable societies were closed. In 1996 eighteen were dissolved and in January 1997 alone five were shut down.[38]

During the decades when parties were banned and parliament was dormant, Jordan's professional associations retained a relatively high degree of independence and functioned as important political arenas. In the 1970s they had been dominated by leftists and nationalists but, in tune with the wider trend in Jordan, Islamists assumed increasing influence during the 1980s. With the 1989 democratisation, the associations – especially those for engineers, lawyers and medical professionals – emerged as strident opponents of key regime policies, in particular spearheading a campaign against the normalisation of relations with Israel. Although the regime did not act on its threats to shut them down, it subjected them to heavy pressure to refrain from overtly political activity, insisting that the agitation arose from unrepresentative minorities within the associations. In 1995, for example, King Hussain, criticising the associations for their stance towards the peace treaty with Israel, declared that 'the minority will not monopolise the leading posts in these unions and professions. This minority discusses things which it does not have the right to discuss at the expense of duty and the basic role it should play'.[39] Despite the pressures, the professional associations, of which there are now 14 with a membership of over 100,000,[40] continue as a major opposition political force second in influence only to the Islamists.

In domestic affairs, 1989–93 was a watershed. Before, no attempt was made to disguise the regime's authoritarian essence. In the period since – both under King Hussain and his successor, King Abdullah – the political establishment, with the monarchy at its centre, has walked a tightrope. On the one hand it has tried to maintain a semblance of liberalism in order to appease local opinion and preserve the kingdom's image with foreign donors increasingly preoccupied with notions of 'good governance'. On the other, it has sought to prevent the opposition from mounting any significant challenges, especially to the peace treaty with Israel. Writing in 2002, Quintan Wiktorowicz, of Rhodes College in Memphis, put it admirably:

> More than ten years later, citizens of Jordan's 'new democracy' still experience substantial limitations to political freedom. Despite a series of relatively free and fair elections, the legalisation of political parties and the boisterousness of parliament, the regime continues to limit opposition and dissent. Demonstrations, civic organising, the press and other modes of political participation are circumscribed by lingering authoritarian practices that are temporally juxtaposed with institutions of procedural democracy. This repression, however, is not typified by the overt, brutal forms of physical coercion that characterised the martial law period; rather it is what may be termed 'embedded authoritarianism' – social control projected through a complex array of administrative procedures, legal codes, and informal regulative practices designed to constrain opposition without resorting to violence. In embedded authoritarianism, the primary agent of control is the bureaucracy, not the *mukhabarat*, the military or totalitarian instruments…Wrapped in the rhetoric and sanctity of democracy, the Jordanian regime can no longer afford blatant repression. Instead, power and control are embedded in bureaucratic processes, masked beneath the veneer of visible democratic institutions and practices'.[41]

Death of a symbol

On 7 February 1999, in the 45th year of his reign, King Hussain died after a long struggle with cancer, prompting a spontaneous outpouring of national grief rare in a region where rulers are more often feared than loved. Dallas records: 'Funeral flags flew over Amman. Jordanians sobbed and shouted their grief. The depth of feeling expressed was akin to that after a death in the family'.[42] Just two weeks before his death, and for reasons that remain the subject of speculation (see Chapter 11), Hussain had named Abdullah, his 37-year-old, half-British eldest son, as his heir apparent, passing over his younger brother Hassan who had been Crown Prince since 1965. Abdullah, who had been commander of Jordan's Special Forces and who was married to Rania, a Palestinian Jordanian who had been amongst those who returned from Kuwait after the 1990–91 crisis, succeeded to the throne the day his father passed away.

King Hussain was no ceremonial monarch. Throughout his reign, he was the source of virtually all Jordanian policy to the extent that he came to personify the state. 'The king was a special case', wrote Dallas. 'He had become identified with Jordan; he was its emblem'.[43] In the West, he enjoyed an enviable image as a charismatic, jet-setting action man who loved fast cars and motorbikes and piloted his own aircraft. His reputation was if anything enhanced by his fabled penchant for glamorous women: he married no less than four times. He was the 'plucky little king' who had survived at least nine documented assassination attempts and countless rumoured plots. Standing back from the myth, Hussain was also an autocrat, and an impulsive one at that, who surrounded himself with a coterie of sycophantic and self-serving advisers and indulged a passion for foreign policy at the expense of more mundane domestic affairs. He suffered 'a lifelong macro-economic illiteracy'[44] that played a major part in the kingdom's economic collapse in the late 1980s. At times of crisis, opponents were detained in their scores and, especially after the 1970–71 civil war, maltreatment and torture were rife. But while constitutional and legal safeguards of democratic and human rights were stretched to the limit and beyond, they were never quite abandoned entirely. There was little of the systematic, institutionalised brutality of the neighbouring Ba'athist regimes in Syria or Iraq. If Hussain was certainly no democrat, he was also no demagogue. And, as well as being decisive and ruthless, he was often magnanimous. Many of his foes would later be rehabilitated to re-emerge as loyal members of the political establishment. 'For King Hussain, it was never personal like it was with Saddam or Hafiz al-Asad', playwright Nabil Sawalha told me. 'He was a very tolerant and compassionate man. He could be very tough when he felt that the system – the Hashemite monarchy – was threatened. But he was never gratuitously cruel or sadistic'.[45] It was this, perhaps above all else, that distinguished Hussain from most of his fellow Middle Eastern rulers.

Notes

1   Beverley Milton-Edwards and Peter Hinchcliffe, *Jordan: A Hashemite Legacy* (London: Routledge, 2001), p. 36.

2   Interview with author, Baqa'a Camp, 27 February 2003.

3   Interview with author, Baqa'a Camp, 27 February 2003.

4   Andrew Jeffreys (ed.), *Emerging Jordan 2003* (London: Oxford Business Group, 2002), p.11.

5   Interview with Muhammad Halaiqah, Deputy Prime Minister for Economic Affairs, Amman, 5 October 2003.

6   Interview with author, Amman, 24 February 2003.

7   *Hashemite Kingdom of Jordan Statistical Yearbook 2003* (Amman: Department of Statistics).

8   Interview with author, Amman, 22 April 2004.

9   Beverley Milton-Edwards and Peter Hinchcliffe, *Jordan*, p. xiv.

10 Philip Robins, *A History of Jordan* (Cambridge: Cambridge University Press, 2004), p. 135.

11 Adnan Abu-Odeh, *Jordanians, Palestinians and the Hashemite Kingdom in the Middle East Peace Process* (Washington, DC: United States Institute of Peace Press, 1999), pp. 240–1.

12 Philip Robins, *A History of Jordan*, p. 135.

13 Interview with author, Amman, 5 October 2003.

14 Email communication with Joost Hiltermann, Director of Middle East Project, International Crisis Group, Middle East Regional Office, Amman, 21 April 2005.

15 US Library of Congress, Federal Research Division, *Jordan: A Country Study* (Washington, DC: Library of Congress, 1989).

16 Ibid.

17 Interview with author, Amman, 5 October 2003.

18 Interview with author, Amman, 24 February 2003.

19 Interview with author, Amman, 5 October 2003.

20 Interview with author, Amman 6 March 2003.

21 Interview with author, Amman, 20 July 2003.

22   Interview with author, Amman, 7 October 2003.

23   Avi Shlaim, *Collusion across the Jordan: King Abdullah, the Zionist Movement, and the Partition of Palestine* (Oxford: Clarendon Press, 1988), p. 397.

24   King Abdullah of Jordan, *My Memoirs Completed: "Al Takmilah"* (London and New York: Longman, 1978), p. 60.

25   Mary C. Wilson, *King Abdullah, Britain and the Making of Jordan* (Cambridge: Cambridge University Press, 1987), p. 131.

26   Roland Dallas, *King Hussein: A Life on the Edge* (London: Profile Books, 1999), p. 67.

27   Philip Robins, *A History of Jordan*, p. 124.

28   Roland Dallas, *King Hussein*, p. 131.

29   Philip Robins, *A History of Jordan*, p. 132.

30   Ibid., p. 163.

31   Ibid., pp. 163–4.

32   Laurie A. Brand, *Jordan's Inter-Arab Relations: The Political Economy of Alliance Making* (New York: Columbia University Press, 1994), pp. 285–6.

33   Marcus Bouillon, 'Walking the tightrope: Jordanian foreign policy from the Gulf crisis to the peace process and beyond', in George Joffé (ed.), *Jordan in Transition 1990–2000* (London: Hurst & Company, 2002), p. 10.

34   Ali Kassay, 'The Effects of external forces on Jordan's process of democratisation', in George Joffé (ed.), *Jordan in Transition 1990–2000* (London: Hurst & Company, 2002), p.55.

35   Beverley Milton-Edwards and Peter Hinchcliffe, *Jordan*, p. 58.

36   Ranjit Singh,'Liberalisation or democratisation? The limits of political reform and civil society in Jordan', in George Joffé (ed.), *Jordan in Transition 1990–2000* (London: Hurst & Company, 2002), pp. 76–7.

37   Quintan Wiktorowicz, 'Embedded authoritarianism: bureaucratic power and the limits to non-governmental organisations in Jordan', in George Joffé (ed.), *Jordan in Transition 1990–2000* (London: Hurst & Company, 2002), p. 114.

38   Ibid., p. 118.

39   Renate Dieterich, 'The weakness of the ruled is the strength of the ruler: the role of the opposition in contemporary Jordan', in George Joffé (ed.), *Jordan in Transition 1990-2000* (London: Hurst & Company, 2002), p. 140.

40   Figures supplied by fax by the Union of Professional Associations, 13 July 2003.

41   Quintan Wiktorowicz, 'Embedded authoritarianism', p. 111.

42   Roland Dallas, *King Hussein*, p. 284.

43   Ibid., p. 280.

44   Philip Robins, *A History of Jordan*, p. 97.

45   Interview with author, Amman, 23 February 2003.

CHAPTER 3

'Bread before Freedom': Jordan under King Abdullah II

ALTHOUGH AT 37 he was much older than his father had been when he had succeeded to the throne, Abdullah was politically inexperienced. As the monarch's eldest son he had lived at the heart of the regime and had assisted his father at official functions and sometimes acted as his personal envoy to foreign governments. But above all he was a career soldier who had little feel for the machinations of the kingdom's fractious political elite. He readily concedes that the initial months were 'a major learning curve', explaining: 'I've been a soldier all my life'.[1] He did, however, come to the throne with an overall strategy. 'Before he passed away, my father said he had this ambition to do some dramatic reforms, which were political, social and economic', King Abdullah told me. 'My point of view was that we had to start on the social and economic. It was so much better to do political reform on a full stomach than on an empty one'. Bread before freedom, in short. He has held fast to this strategy, showing much greater interest than his father in the economy, accelerating the kingdom's economic liberalisation and privatisation programmes and encouraging measures aimed at positioning Jordan as a player, albeit minuscule, in the global economy. While proclaiming from the start his commitment to further democratic reforms, he has placed these firmly on the back-burner. In his first four years, commented the International Crisis Group (ICG) in 2003, the new king had 'shown an overriding penchant for regime stability that placed economic progress and Jordan's integration into the global market squarely before the need to open up the political system'.[2]

Initially, King Abdullah's inexperience was on full display. For his first prime minister, appointed in March 1999, he chose Abdur Rauf ar-

Rawabdah, an illiberal, die-hard East Banker whose government rapidly became steeped in allegations of nepotism and corruption. In Jordan, however, chiefs of the Royal Court have wielded as much, if not more, power than prime ministers (see Chapter 11). As his first Royal Court Chief, Abdullah appointed Abdul Karim al-Kabariti, a former prime minister and 'an impatient liberal'[3] whose outlook was much closer to the king's. The first period of Abdullah's reign was dominated by an acrimonious and paralysing rivalry between Ar-Rawabdah and Al-Kabariti. Their relationship 'soon degenerated into a running exchange of petulant jibes, over such issues as women's rights, press freedoms and economic liberalisation', observed Robins, commenting that Abdullah's appointment of such intractable opposites had been 'either incoherent confusion or a misguided attempt to replicate his "all things to all men" foreign policy [see p. 63] at home'.[4] One year into his 'learning curve', an increasingly exasperated king acted. In January 2000 Al-Kabariti was replaced by Fayez Tarawneh, who had been King Hussain's last prime minister, and in June 2000 Ar-Rawabdah was replaced by Ali Abu Ragheb, a US-educated businessman-turned-politician and strong supporter of the International Monetary Fund's prescription for Jordan.

Parliament suspended

King Abdullah and his new prime minister may have professed liberal intentions but regional developments soon intervened to change the domestic agenda. In September 2000 the second Palestinian *intifada* erupted, sharpening pre-existing tensions over Jordan's relations with Israel. A National Coalition for the Support of the *intifada*, linking 16 political parties and 14 professional associations, spearheaded a campaign of support for the Palestinians that included large and often angry street protests. Although the regime was never under threat, security became the overriding concern for king and government. Abdullah's Letter of Designation to Abu Ragheb had instructed his government to formulate 'a modern elections law that gives everyone the opportunity to free and fair competition to represent the various sectors of society with its various political and cultural colours'.[5] On 24 July 2001, however, the king delayed the general election scheduled for November. The pretext was the need for extra time to implement new administrative and other procedures related to the new electoral law, but the real factor was fears over the *intifada*-linked turmoil. The delay was then extended in the light of the 'difficult regional situation': the continuing *intifada*; the 11 September 2001 attacks on the US and President Bush's resultant launch of his 'war on terrorism', starting with the invasion of Afghanistan; and, from late 2002, the first impending and then actual US-led invasion of Iraq. A violent confrontation between Islamists and security forces in the southern town of Ma'an in late 2002 (see p. 50) surely confirmed the authorities in their view that the time was not yet ripe for elections.

The absence of the legislature did not mean an absence of new laws. On the contrary. In 2001–3 over 220 'temporary laws' were issued by royal decree, many with grave consequences for democracy and civil liberties. October 2001 saw the promulgation of amendments to the penal code that introduced harsh penalties for publishing items that could damage national unity, incite crimes or hatred, or damage the dignity or reputation both of individuals and the kingdom as a whole. A public gatherings law required organisers of demonstrations to obtain a permit three days in advance and made them personally liable for any damage to property that might occur. A state security court law was issued denying the right of appeal to people convicted of misdemeanours. A municipalities law gave the government the right to appoint the head and half the members of municipal councils whereas previously all members, except those in the Greater Amman Municipality, had been elected for four-year terms. Critics insisted that both the suspension of parliament and the temporary laws were unconstitutional. It is hard to disagree (see Chapter 13).

'Jordan First'

Having suspended parliament and while engaged in what one critic called 'a massacre of legislation',[6] the king chose to reaffirm his commitment to democracy. In October 2002 the government launched a 'Jordan First' campaign. According to the monarch's website, www.kingabdullah.jo, the campaign was intended 'to strengthen the foundations of a pragmatic, democratic state', to emphasise 'the pre-eminence of Jordan's interests above all other considerations' and to 'spread a culture of respect and tolerance and integrity and fortify the concepts of parliamentary democracy, supremacy of the law, public freedom, accountability, transparency, and equal opportunities'. The real intention, apparently, was to encourage Jordanian national sentiment and therefore unity by refocusing public attention on domestic issues at a time when it was riveted by the crises over Iraq to the east and in Palestine to the west. In echoes of the National Charter exercise in 1990–1, a royal commission was appointed to draft a Jordan First document containing recommendations for action. Unveiled on 18 December 2002, the document was largely a re-statement of the National Charter, and it was framed in language that suggested that the entire exercise was, as much as anything else, intended as an opportunity for the expression of loyalty to the monarchy and the established system. Jordan First, it declared, was 'not merely a slogan raised or an objective uttered'. Rather, it was 'the shining link and efficacious bond that enwraps all Jordanian patriots, who see in their belonging to their homeland a gateway to their loyalty to their nation'. The document called for a strengthening of democracy, personal liberties and press freedoms and for measures to improve women's status in society. It urged greater efforts to achieve social justice, especially by reducing poverty and unemployment. It recommended reforms to improve the efficiency of the courts and reiterated the National Charter's call for the establishment of a constitutional court. The sole recommendation to have been implemented to date has been the establishment of a six-seat quota for women in parliament (see Chapter 12). Apart from that, the only tangible legacy of the Jordan First campaign are roadside placards throughout the kingdom displaying the national flag – horizontal black, white and green-stripes with a red triangle containing a white, seven-pointed star – raised high by outstretched arms alongside the words *Al-Urdun Awalan* ('Jordan First'); and the colourful metal lapel badges still worn by some, on which the flag flutters from a mast formed by a white number one.

Upheaval in Ma'an

While the Jordan First Document was being drafted in Amman, serious violence erupted in the southern town of Ma'an that rudely belied the document's portrayal of Jordan as a cosy and stable community moving confidently into the future under the benevolent guidance of a revered monarchy. An isolated and conservative community 210 kilometres south of Amman that had been a traditional stronghold of support for the monarchy, Ma'an had already acquired a reputation for instability. It had been the scene of the first of the April 1989 riots that had prompted Jordan's democratisation programme, and further riots had spread there from the other southern towns of Tafila and Karak in August 1996 following a sudden sharp rise in the price of bread. The immediate spark of the November 2002 violence was an attempt by police to question a local Islamist militant, Muhammad Shalabi, also known as Abu Sayyaf. It was thought that he might have information relating to the 28 October 2002 murder outside his Amman home of Lawrence Foley, an American citizen working for the US Agency for International Development (USAID). Shalabi resisted, was wounded by police gunfire but managed to escape and took refuge in his father's house, where he was protected by about fifty of his supporters. The episode quickly escalated, first into gun battles between the local police and the Islamists and then into intense street battles involving thousands of army and Special Forces troops supported by armoured cars and helicopters. The militants were subdued but in the process six people died, many more were wounded, 150 people were arrested and much property was damaged.

Until now, the authorities depict the violence as a simple case of a government clampdown on a lawless gang of armed thugs and smugglers. Plainly it was much more than that. An incisive report on the episode by the International Crisis Group (ICG) stressed that the causes were multiple and complex, and in large measure unique to Ma'an: 'Nowhere else has there been the same devastating combination of a sharp reversal of a traditional regional role; sustained economic distress; weak political leadership; negligible civil society and private sector investments; isolation from the national mainstream; a culture of arms possession; inconsistent law enforcement policies; and repeated interventions by the police and security forces which many among the local population see as unwarranted punishment, harassment and humiliation'.[7] The report nevertheless insisted that Ma'an was not so different from the rest of the south. 'Jordan's most urgent area of concern is the South, where, with the exception of Aqaba – and unlike the rest of the country – negativity and cynicism are widespread', said the ICG. 'To many in south Jordan, the future holds little hope for either them or their children'.[8] But the ICG went on to stress that it did not end there, for many of the issues at stake were relevant throughout the kingdom: 'inadequate popular participation, political representation and government responsiveness; economic distress in the face of rapid change and dislocation; uneven law enforcement and arbitrary security tactics; and anger at developments in the occupied Palestinian territories and Iraq'.[9] The small group of armed

Islamists in Ma'an may have been a strictly local feature, but 'since 1989 Ma'an has served as a warning sign, an indicator that socio-economic tensions and deficiencies in the political system can breed extremism, lawlessness, rebellion and violence'.[10] The ICG report concluded: 'Ma'an has become something of a litmus test for Jordan – a test of government policies, national institutions, the private sector and civil society. There has been a collective failure of all four to date, and time is running short'.[11] King Hussain had been shocked by the April 1989 riots in Ma'an. Abdullah was no less taken aback by the November 2002 explosion although he seemed open to independent advice, taking personal delivery of the ICG report amid much publicity.

When I visited the town in April 2004 with my assistant, Riham Baqa'in, the authorities were still jumpy. Special permission for the visit was required of the information ministry, which instructed that I should first report to the local governor's office, a newly-built complex at the town's northern entry. There, Abdullah Beek, the deputy governor, politely enquired of my plans, showing special interest in whether I intended any 'political interviews', of which he plainly disapproved. Mischievously, I asked him why he was so worried, to which he sturdily maintained that he was concerned only because of 'the regional situation'. Presumably, he meant that, as a Westerner, I might encounter hostility from the townspeople because of anger over Iraq and Palestine. Smiling, I replied that the 'regional situation' also existed in Amman, Salt, Karak, Azrak and other parts of Jordan that I had visited without any indications of official concern for my safety. We left the building accompanied by a soft-spoken man in a black leather jacket who said that he was not from the *mukhabarat* but a civilian police detective from Amman; he remained with us throughout the visit to Ma'an.

The mood of this isolated little desert town, with its single main street and shabby, yellow limestone buildings, was hard to gauge. People seemed sullen, but this may have been the result of the sandstorm kicked up by the hot, dry *khamsin* wind from the south that gathered strength all that day. It's hard to look cheerful with sand in one's mouth, eyes and nose and discarded plastic bags of various hues flying through the air. Few people were in the streets but again that was because of the weather. Many of those that did brave the storm were dressed traditionally, the women in Islamic *hijab* – headscarf and long-sleeved coat extending to the shins or below; older men in *thawbs* – ankle-length gowns – and red-and-white-checked *keffiyas* wrapped around their faces against the dust. Younger men wore jeans and sweaters, and one sported a battledress jacket, black slacks, sandals and a red-and-white *keffiya*. The main street, divided by a narrow central reservation with date palms, boasts small fruit and vegetable shops and a series of tiny restaurants. I can recommend the outstandingly tasty filafal and humous sandwiches in fresh, unleavened bread at Al-Zahra ash-Shamiya (The Damascus Rose) restaurant. Incongruously in this stronghold of conservative Islam, a women's clothing shop displayed a mannequin clad in a white mini-skirt that would pass muster in Paris. In Amman, an acquaintance had joked that 'every other person in Ma'an is a *mukhabarat* agent'. But the only overt sign of security – other than my guardian detective – was a navy blue Public Security armoured car parked by a roundabout on the town's southern edge where the main road comes in from Mudawara, near the Saudi border.

Iraq crisis

In late 2002, Ma'an was not the only issue on King Abdullah's mind. In Washington the ultra-conservative Bush Administration had decided to invade Iraq for reasons that were in part highly questionable, in part simply fantastical – and entirely confused. Saddam Hussain, it was claimed, had stockpiled weapons of mass destruction (WMD) that threatened the West; he was a brutal dictator whose people needed liberating; he was linked to Usama bin Laden's Al-Qa'ida organisation that had perpetrated the 11 September attacks. So-called 'regime-change' in Baghdad was the US prescription. In London, Prime Minister Tony Blair, more mindful than Bush of the need to cast at least a glance at international law, claimed that an attack on Iraq was unavoidable because Saddam had defied UN resolutions requiring him to dispose of his WMD. Jordan's two key Western allies were hell-bent on invading Iraq. Like other regional leaders, Abdullah was well aware that the US and UK's case for war was deeply flawed and quietly did his best to dissuade them from an adventure that he suspected would end badly for them; that he was certain would further destabilise a region already in uproar because of Israel's repression of the Palestinians in the occupied territories; and that he feared would cause particular turmoil in his own domain, which depended on subsidised Iraqi oil and whose people were solidly behind Saddam. He was ignored.

Like his father at the time of the 1990–91 Kuwait crisis, Abdullah was in a cleft stick. He was under intense pressure from his key Western backers to join what Bush liked to call the 'coalition of the willing' but knew that to do so might unleash forces at home that could threaten his throne. He tried – successfully as it turned out – to have it both ways. While expressing dismay at the conflict and, before hostilities started in March 2003, urging a peaceful solution, Jordan joined the US-led coalition. But its sole officially acknowledged contributions were to accept the stationing of Patriot anti-missile batteries on its territories, ostensibly for its own protection but in fact for Israel's, and to send two army field hospitals to occupied Iraq. Less publicly, Jordan allowed US and British Special Forces to operate from remote bases in the desert near the Iraqi border. A similar formula had been adopted over the earlier US invasion of Afghanistan, when Jordan, a declared US ally in the 'war on terrorism', had kept out of the fray except for the provision of a hospital. It was enough to satisfy both the US and UK, on the one hand, and domestic opinion, on the other. Although angry demonstrations were staged in Amman and other towns, heavy security ensured that these did not spiral out of control. Luckily for Amman, the war proved short-lived. Had it been more protracted, the regime might not have got off so lightly. Jordan has since forged financially rewarding links with post-Saddam Iraq, although relations turned distinctly uneasy with the Shia victory in Iraq's January 2005 elections (see Chapter 16).

Within two weeks of the end of the main fighting in Iraq, Abdullah moved swiftly to bolster his standing at home by scheduling for 17 June the general election that had been delayed since 2001, latterly because of the 'difficult regional situation'. Next, the government partially repealed the oppressive temporary law amending penal code provisions relating to the press that had caused outrage on the part of the media and pro-democracy activists. Addressing public concerns over Palestine, Jordan was meanwhile pressing for action on the so-called Road Map project that President Bush had formally announced in June 2002 and the European Union, Russia and the UN had endorsed later that year. The project provided for an Israeli withdrawal from the West Bank and Gaza Strip and the establishment of a democratic and liberal Palestinian state by 2005, with progress depending on the Palestinians and Israelis meeting a series of preordained interim objectives. The first post-war summit on the Road Map was held in Aqaba on 4 June 2003. The problem was that the Road

Map's success depended on 'the good faith efforts of the parties, and their compliance with each of the obligations' en route to the final destination of 'a final and comprehensive settlement of the Israel–Palestinian conflict'.[12] Whatever shortcomings existed on the Palestinian side, Ariel Sharon's Israel was simply not in the business of collaborating in the establishment of a Palestinian state. To the dismay of Jordan and the other parties to the accord, in subsequent months the Israelis repeatedly sabotaged progress by attacking Palestinian militants, provoking suicide bombings in revenge that in turn led to further Israeli assaults. By early 2004 the Road Map was in tatters.

The Jordanian election in June, two weeks after the Aqaba summit, went smoothly, with no sign of the Islamist revival that had been feared would be a consequence of the Iraq conflict. Despite threatening to boycott this election as it had the 1997 poll because of the one-man, one-vote electoral law, the Islamic Action Front participated, winning 17 seats (see Chapter 12). Five independent Islamists also won seats. Although, as always, the traditional urban and tribal notables formed a comfortable majority, the Islamists again constituted by far the biggest opposition group. King Abdullah hailed the elections as 'a new page' for the kingdom.[13]

Islamic revival

Muhammad Abdullah Amira, a large, dignified man with a thick, bushy beard, works as a cargo-receiving officer in Aqaba port and lives with his wife and three children in a modest apartment in the town's *Wahdat ash-Sharqiya* (Eastern Units) area. His family originates in the West Bank town of Nablus but moved to Amman in the 1930s. He has lived in Aqaba for seventeen years. Amira wears a full-length robe termed a *thawb* in classical Arabic and a *dishdasha* in colloquial, and a close-fitting white cap: an *udhunsur* in classical and a *tarqiya* in colloquial Arabic. He is a *khatib* – a preacher who rotates between the 25 of Aqaba's fifty mosques and prayer areas that offer Friday sermons. He estimates that over 60 per cent of Aqaba's population goes to Friday prayers and about 10 per cent perform their five daily prayer sessions in the mosques. As a devout Muslim, Amira is one of the latter. An adherent of the mainstream Salafi current of Sunni Islam, he considers himself 'a true Muslim'. He agrees that many Jordanians sympathise with the extremist Islamism of Usama bin Laden but insists that few would actually move from words to action. The support for Bin Laden is 'not deep, and just a matter of emotions'.[14]

Abd as-Salam al-Fandi, 31 and married with a baby daughter, is the Imam of the Ahmad bin Taimiyah Mosque in Badr al-Jadid village, in the hills 13 kilometres west of Amman. On Fridays the mosque, built in 1993 and named after a renowned cleric from Harran, near Urfa in what is now south-eastern Turkey, who died in 1328, is packed with 150 men while rather fewer women worship in a separate prayer room. What does Islam mean to this placid farming community? 'For most people, Islam is praying, fasting, performing the *hajj* pilgrimage, giving *zakat* alms, and so on', he said.[15] Nevertheless, while most are not involved with explicitly political Islam, they feel that their religion – and hence their way of life – is threatened by an aggressive and rapacious West. 'People believe there's a war with the West', says Al-Fandi. 'It's not a fight over borders but a battle over the existence of Islam'. He adds: 'It's not only about armed conflict but also about economics – control of oil, like in Iraq – and about how the West imposes its decisions'. Islam's stance is defensive: 'Muslims have rights. We don't attack, we just defend', insisted Al-Fandi. That was the background for people's sympathy for Usama bin Laden. 'People here hate the US for what it has done, and this makes them like Bin Laden: an eye for an eye, an ear for an ear'. He chuckles: 'Now a lot of people name their children Usama'. To counter this tendency, embarrassing for a state solidly behind Washington's 'war on terrorism', a law was passed in October 2002 stipulating that names should 'not violate religious or social values, nor disturb public order'. An accompanying list of forbidden names included Usama bin Laden and, bizarrely, the names of the former Israeli prime ministers Binyamin Netanyahu, Yitzhak Rabin and Golda Meir. The website *Islam-online* reported on 13 October 2003 that civil registry records showed that 'scores of people named their newborns after Bin Laden and former Iraqi President Saddam Hussain' but that only two people had been named after Rabin and Netanyahu. The report did not record whether any Jordanians were named Golda Meir.[16]

Al-Fandi's point about Muslims feeling pressured by the West was also made, albeit slightly differently, by Bassam Saket, chairman of the Jordan Securities Commission, the body that regulates the Amman stock exchange: 'We have our own culture and heritage, and we want to keep them', he said. 'We respect other people's heritage. But Bin Laden is not a Muslim. He's a killer who attacks innocent people. We are against him'.

Extremist Islamism owed its rise not so much to local religious or political dynamics but to aggressive Western policies. He insisted: 'You [in the West] are creating, throughout the Arab world, so many new graduates of Bin Laden'.[17]

'Jordanian society at large is becoming more Islamist', said former prime minister Taher al-Masri. 'You see it in the number of new mosques being built, in how crowded the mosques are. You see it through [liberal, secular] people, who are very careful to consider Islamic sensitivities: not to drink alcohol in public as they did in the past. People I know whom I never imagined would do such a thing now go to the mosque to pray'.[18] He stressed, however, that Islamism as an expression of culture should not be confused with overtly political Islamism. The former was gaining strength but the latter appeared to have peaked, he said, noting that the Islamic Action Front's portion of the vote had changed little between the 1989, 1993 and 2003 elections. His assessment is shared by Baker al-Hiyari, assistant director of Amman's Royal Institute for Inter-Faith Studies, a body sponsored by Prince Hassan that runs research and publications programmes focusing on Christian-Muslim relations. 'Political Islam has stabilised while cultural Islam is growing', he said, although noting that cultural Islam was nevertheless largely a reaction to external political forces. 'You may not be religious but religion underpins your value system, and any negative impact on that makes you feel threatened', he explained. 'Muslims feel threatened in this part of the world'.[19]

Nowhere in Jordan is this threat felt more than in the Palestinian camps, where Islamism has taken its greatest strides. The Palestinians long ago tired of the Arab governments' empty slogans of support. Now they have grown weary of the paralysis and corruption of the late Yasser Arafat's Palestine National Authority (PNA), the embryonic government that since 1994 has had limited powers of autonomy in the West Bank and Gaza Strip. In the Baqa'a camp, 30 kilometres north of Amman, the mood is sullen and angry. Adel Hamdan, aged 42, whose family is from Jaffa, has lived in Baqa'a since 1968 and is director of the local office of the Department of Palestinian Affairs, a government agency attached to the prime ministry. 'Feelings are pessimistic', he said, because since the 1993 Palestinian-Israeli peace treaty – the so-called Oslo Accords – that created the PNA, 'nothing has changed'.[20] Many Jordanian Palestinians – and perhaps a majority in the camps – have embraced fundamentalist Islamism of one shade or another, inspired by Lebanon's Hizbollah, whose guerrillas kicked the Israelis out of Lebanon, and by their own Hamas and Islamic Jihad, whose suicide bombings in Israel are applauded here. At least the Islamists act rather than talk, they feel. In a small grocer's shop near Baqa'a's bus and taxi station I encountered Awwad Youssef, 31, whose family is from the Deir az-Ziban district, near Hebron on the West Bank. What was his estimate of the proportion of the camp's residents that supported activist Islam? Awwad, who works for an Islamic charity, the Jamia'at al-Markaz al-Islam (Islamic Centre Society), did not hesitate: 'They are all Islamists'.[21]

For the monarchy, which derives part of its legitimacy from its descent from the Prophet Muhammad, conservative Islam has been a traditional wellspring of support. The Jordanian branch of the Muslim Brotherhood (Al-Ikhwan al-Muslimoun), a fundamentalist Sunni organisation founded in Egypt in 1928, has loyally backed the regime since the days of the first King Abdullah. In 1957, when political parties were banned, the Brotherhood remained legal on the grounds that it was not a party, as such. 'The abiding reality of mosque–state relations was that the Islamists and the king [Hussain] needed each other even though, at times, they might exchange cross words', writes Dallas. 'The king needed an organisation of conservative, gentlemanly Muslims as a buffer against Islamic and Palestinian extremists. The Brotherhood needed the king as an insurance policy covering its continued existence as a political and religious force'.[22] The Ikhwan's explicitly political wing, the Islamic Action Front, was formed only with the passage of the Political Parties Law in 1992, and functions as a loyal opposition. While certainly anxious to keep conservative Islam's influence within manageable limits, the regime enjoys a good working relationship with its representatives. Extremist Islamists take a very different line from the Ikhwan, viewing the Hashemite state as part of an unholy alliance against Islam headed by the US and with Israel as a key member. For its part, the regime has targeted extreme Islamism relentlessly, seeing it as the major threat to the kingdom's stability. Not for nothing did Jordan become a committed US ally in the 'war on terrorism', and the authorities' uncompromising stance was underlined in the Ma'an incident in November 2002 (see p. 50). At the same time, however, the regime understands what is obvious but what Washington apparently fails to grasp: that extremist Islamism is fuelled by unjust and aggressive Western and Israeli policies towards Palestine and the wider Arab and Islamic worlds. The simple message from the imam of Al-Badr al-Jadid village and from the *khatib* of Aqaba is one that the West would do well to heed.

The official stance towards Hamas, which has no particular quarrel with Jordan, has been ambivalent, reflecting the need to tread a narrow path between the organisation's wide support amongst Jordanian Palestinians and insistent US and Israeli demands for coercive action. King Hussain had allowed Hamas to work politically in the kingdom. In August 1999, however, mounting pressure from the US and Israel prompted the government to close Hamas' Amman offices, arrest a dozen of its members for questioning and issue arrest warrants for five of its top officials in Jordan, including its local leader, Khalid Misha'al (the target of a botched Israeli assassination attempt in 1997; see Chapter 2). One was deported to Yemen, of which he was a national. The other four were taken into custody but by November a deal had been struck, under which charges against them were dropped, and they were deported to Qatar, whose amir had agreed to give them refuge. Again under US and Israeli pressure, Jordan on 15 September 2003 froze the assets of six leading Hamas figures, sparking a wave of protests. Within days the decision was rescinded.

Human rights

Nothing touches the essence of the Jordanian system more than the National Centre for Human Rights, established in 2002 to investigate complaints and to raise public awareness of human rights. It is headed by Ahmad al-Obeidat, former prime minister – and ex-head of the *mukhabarat*, the feared General Intelligence Department (GID) that has a dark reputation for human rights violations. I put it to him that some might see a contradiction between his past and present posts. 'I fully understand this point of view', replied Al-Obeidat. 'But Jordan has its own circumstances, its own characteristics'.[23] That an ex-GID director should now head a human rights body echoes a more basic contradiction: that a state that has not hesitated to abuse human rights when deemed necessary should sponsor an agency committed to defending those same rights. The system's impulse to co-opt and control is irrepressible. Parliament is revived, but required to function as an adjunct to the regime. Laws and the Constitution are declared inviolate but are designed to safeguard the established system and, when found wanting, are twisted to order. Press freedom is acclaimed, but it must be 'responsible' freedom that does not challenge the *status quo*. And it's all done – at least publicly – in a manner so gentle, polite and measured that it takes a constant effort of will to maintain a grip on the underlying reality. None of this means that the National Centre for Human Rights is ineffective; or that Al-Obeidat himself, who is credited with ending the GID's worst abuses and who was at the forefront of the post-1989 democratisation, is anything but a man of sincerity and integrity. But the system cannot be understood without grasping the subtle ways in which it moves to have its cake and eat it, to be at once democratic and undemocratic, benevolent and despotic.

Just weeks before the proclamation of the law establishing the National Centre for Human Rights, after all, the authorities had shut down the Jordanian Society for Citizens' Rights (JSCR), an NGO that had been formed in 1998. The government claimed that the JSCR had transgressed the rules governing NGOs (see Chapter 2). The JSCR's ex-Chairman, Dr Fawzi Samhouri, a 52-year-old dentist whose family originates in Lydda, now in Israel, has no doubt that the real reason for the closure was that his society was treading on too many establishment toes. The JSCR was conducting three main campaigns: on behalf of the 1,000 Jordanians whom the authorities have refused to allow back into the country; against the withdrawal of nationality from people living in the West Bank in 1988, when Jordan severed its ties with the region; and for the upper house of parliament to be elected rather than appointed. 'These were all red lines that people are not supposed to cross', said Samhouri. He is unconvinced that the new Human Rights Centre will prove effective, suspecting that it will be loathe to act forcefully against the authorities because its board is government-appointed and government-funded. 'Let's wait and see', he said. 'I hope that I'm wrong, but I'm not optimistic'.[24]

Certainly there is no shortage of issues to engage the Centre for Human Rights. The US State Department's *Country Reports on Human Rights Practices – Jordan 2003*, released in February 2004, states flatly: 'Members of the security forces committed human rights abuses'.[25] Conceding that the government's respect for human rights 'improved in some areas' during 2003, the report affirmed that 'many problems remained'. These included 'police abuse and mistreatment of detainees, allegations of torture, arbitrary arrest and detention, lack of transparent investigations and of accountability within the security services, denial of due process of law stemming from the expanded authority of the State Security Court and interference in the judicial process, infringements on citizens' privacy rights, harassment of members of opposition parties, and significant restrictions on freedom of speech, press, assembly and association'. Dr Hisham Bustani, a leading pro-democracy campaigner, has provided a graphic account of systematic beatings of detainees in police stations and in the Juweida prison, on the edge of Amman, that he witnessed in 2002 after being arrested for helping to organise demonstrations against the normalisation of relations with Israel and in support of the Palestinian *intifada*.[26] Anti-corruption campaigner Toujan Faisal, who was the only woman MP in the 1993-97 parliament, says that she was subjected to psychological torture during a 100-day detention in Juweida in 2002.[27] Theirs are not isolated cases.

In fairness to the system, it must be said that most Jordanians, most of the time, live in freedom from the shadow of state repression that darkens much of the rest of the region. The Public Security Department and the GID generally tread lightly. Torture and abuse of detainees does not appear to be part of the culture of the security apparatus. 'The track record of Jordan and the regime is good on issues related to physical abuse, to the tendency to be brutal and to exercise the nasty habit of making your enemies disappear', said Dr Labib Kamhawi, a British-educated Jordanian Palestinian businessman based in Amman who was formerly president of the independent Arab Organisation for Human Rights in Jordan.[28] But simply to compare Jordan with its neighbours and let the argument rest there would be to let the system off too lightly, local campaigners insist. 'It's not like other repressive countries', said Sa'eda Kilani of the Amman-based Arab Archives Institute, which conducts research on media and other issues related to democracy. 'But I prefer comparisons with countries that are better than us. Why compare ourselves with the worst when we should be comparing ourselves with the best?'[29] Labib Kamhawi, who is from Nablus but is banned by Israel from entering the West Bank whence he was deported in 1972, and whose father was a member of the PLO's Executive Committee, agrees: 'They have been much more civilised than their counterparts in the region. But it's no excuse to say that we have a heavy-handed, security-orientated political system that is both non-democratic and anti-democratic at the same time but, well, it's less bloody than Syria or Iraq'.[30]

Terrorism

As a US-allied state that has made peace with Israel and has supported the Western interventions in Iraq and Afghanistan, Jordan is a tempting target for Islamist terrorists. 'I'll be quite honest with you. We're in a state of war', said King Abdullah in mid-2004. 'I hate to say it, but we're picking up terrorist groups [at a rate of] one every two weeks. We've just picked-up two Saudis and a Yemeni who were going to blow up the training centre [for Iraqi police cadets; see Chapter 16]'. The threat, he predicted, 'will probably be with us at least for the next couple of years'. Islamist terrorism in Jordan dates back to the early 1990s, when an estimated one thousand Jordanians who had fought against the Soviet Union in Afghanistan returned home. The arrest in mid-1991 of some 100 members of a group styling themselves the Prophet Muhammad's Army was an early manifestation of the kingdom's own 'war on terrorism', and the years since have been punctuated by actual or attempted terrorist attacks and crackdowns by the regime. The first major incident during King Abdullah's reign was Lawrence Foley's murder (see p. 51). In August 2003 a truck bomb exploded outside the kingdom's embassy in Baghdad, killing 17 people and wounding many more. No group claimed responsibility but it seems likely to have been perpetrated by Islamists. Potentially far more devastating would have been the planned suicide attack on the GID headquarters in Amman, foiled by the authorities in April 2004. According to the highly alarmist official account, the assault, using trucks fitted with ploughs and loaded with explosives and deadly chemicals, could have created a lethal gas cloud that might have killed as many as 80,000 people. Six Jordanians and two Syrians were arrested in a series of raids while four others were killed in a shoot-out with security forces in Amman. Twenty tons of chemicals, including, it was claimed, blistering agents, choking agents and nerve gas, were seized, along with three trucks. In a televised confession, one of those arrested said that he had been acting on orders from Abu Mousab al-Zarqawi, a Jordanian whom the US accuses of being a key figure in Al-Qa'ida who has masterminded many attacks in Iraq, where he is based. Earlier in April, the State Security Court had sentenced Al-Zarqawi and seven others to death for Foley's murder. US officials, however, questioned whether the Amman plotters had intended to create a toxic cloud, noting that the seized chemicals included large quantities of sulphuric acid, which increases the blast of explosives.[31] Although small comfort to the Jordanian authorities, it may be that the plotters had planned a series of major conventional bombings, and news reports said that, as well as the GID building, their intended targets had included the prime minister's office and the US embassy.

Although there have been no organised Palestinian guerrilla attacks against Israel from Jordan since the late 1960s, lone gunmen do occasionally wreak havoc. In November 2003 a truck driver from Zarqa opened fire on a group of Ecuadorean tourists who had just crossed into Israel from Aqaba. One was killed and several were wounded. It was horribly reminiscent of an atrocity in March 1997 when a Jordanian military driver, said to be mentally deranged, had seized a soldier's gun and fired on a group of Israeli schoolgirls on a field trip to an island in the Jordan river, killing seven and wounding six others. Israeli diplomats within Jordan, however, are targets for Islamist terrorists. In November 2000 Israel's deputy consul in Amman was wounded when a gunman opened fire on his car. Responsibility was claimed by two previously unheard-of groups, the Jordanian Islamic Resistance Movement for Struggle and the Group of the Holy Warrior Ahmad al-Daqamsah, the latter named after the schoolgirls' killer.

Foreign affairs

Jordan's location at the hub of a volatile region is one key to understanding its foreign policies. Three others are its conservative, Western-orientated monarchical regime; its meagre resources and a consequent perennial dependence on foreign aid; and its majority Palestinian population whose views, generally more radical than those of East Bankers, the government has always had to take into account. The interplay of these factors has frequently produced paradoxes. While officially at war with Israel until 1994, Jordan cultivated a discreet *modus vivendi* with its western neighbour that included secret meetings between King Hussein and Israeli leaders. In the 1980s Amman enjoyed an intimate relationship with Saddam Hussein's nominally radical nationalist Iraq and paid a heavy price for its stance in the 1990–91 Kuwait crisis (see Chapter 2), but in 2003 it backed the US-led operation to topple Saddam. Jordan's basic orientation towards the West and other pro-Western regional states notwithstanding, the kingdom's foreign policy has been markedly pragmatic. The regime has displayed what Milton-Edwards and Hinch-cliffe describe as 'a persistent desire to be all things to all men within the region as well as on the international stage'.[32] Muhammad Halaiqah, deputy prime minister at the time of the interview, put it another way: 'We speak to the Israelis. We speak to the Egyptians, to the Palestinians, the Syrians. We used to speak to Saddam. Now we speak to the new Iraqi regime. We speak to everybody. We are always open and forth-coming'.[33]

A constant of Amman's international relations has been its close ties with the UK and US. Jordan owed its creation to the British and until the 1950s London paid the kingdom's bills and supplied and ran the army. After the 1957 crisis, the UK's position was increasingly supplanted by the US. Although officially non-aligned internationally, Jordan in practice was firmly part of the West and established diplomatic relations with the Soviet Union only in 1963. Until today, the US and to a lesser extent the UK constitute the ultimate guarantors of the monarchy's wellbeing. Prior to the East Bloc's collapse, it suited a beleaguered Amman to portray itself as a bulwark against 'Communism'. Jordan's real worry, especially in the 1950s and 1960s, however, was not so much 'Soviet expansionism' as the threat of radical Arab nationalism – and the radical regional states, headed by Nasser's Egypt, mirrored Jordan in being nominally non-aligned but effectively allied to Moscow.

Following the toppling of Egypt's monarchy in 1952, Jordan was the target of a sustained campaign of subversion by Cairo, to which King Hussain responded regionally by bolstering ties with the fellow Hashemite regime in Iraq. In July 1958, however, the Iraqi monarchy was ousted in a nationalist army coup while in December that year Syria, Jordan's northern neighbour, merged with Egypt to form the United Arab Republic. Jordan was left dangerously exposed, with openly hostile regimes in two of its three immediate Arab neighbours and in its near-neighbour Egypt. On the basis of the adage 'my enemy's enemy is my friend', these developments prompted a rapprochement with the monarchy's historic antagonists, the Saudis (see Chapter 1), who were also key targets for the radicals and for whom Jordan 'came to constitute a security belt'.[34] The collapse of the Egyptian-Syrian union in September 1961 brought little respite to Jordan, for in March 1963 radical Ba'athists seized power in Damascus – just a month after a Ba'athist coup in Iraq.

Despite its essentially collaborative relationship with Israel, Jordan took part in the 1967 Arab-Israeli war, for reasons that remain uncertain (see Chapter 2). The kingdom's defeat was swift and costly. The West Bank, whose incorporation within Jordan had been the first King Abdullah's prime objective in the 1948 Palestine war, was lost to the Israelis while the emasculated kingdom had to cope with a new flood of refugees. A major consequence of the 1967 war was the rise of the Palestinian guerrilla movement, based in Jordan. This in turn led to King Hussain's 'Black September' assault on the Palestinians (see Chapter 2) which caused his vilification throughout the region. Apart from its immediate implications for Jordan, the 1967 war dramatically exposed the yawning gulf between the rhetoric and realities of radical pan-Arab nationalism. Thereafter, especially in Egypt and Syria, the radicals gradually lost ground, easing the regional political environment for Amman. In November 1970 the more pragmatic, military wing of the Syrian Ba'ath, led by Hafiz al-Asad, ousted the extremist civilian wing that had seized power in 1966. A month before, Nasser had died and been succeeded by the far less ideological Anwar al-Sadat. Rather than propagating revolutionary ideals and forging Arab unity at the expense of regimes like Jordan's, the priority for Asad and Sadat was to rebuild their armed forces with a view to recovering their lost territories. In October 1973 the Syrian and Egyptian armies launched simultaneous attacks against the Israelis. King Hussain was not informed of the plans for war although Asad and Sadat had taken the precaution of improving relations with him in advance. In September 1973 the three met in Cairo and within weeks both Egypt and Syria restored diplomatic relations with the kingdom. Cairo had cut ties in 1972 after Hussain had proposed a bilateral peace plan with Israel providing for the West Bank and Gaza Strip to be included in his kingdom. Syria had broken relations in 1971 in protest at the king's crackdown on the PLO. In the 1973 war, Jordan's role was confined to the last-minute despatch of an armoured unit to support the Syrians. Although militarily the Israelis eventually prevailed, the Arabs performed creditably. The 1973 conflict was hailed in the region as a victory that had restored Arab pride.

Ever since Israel's creation in 1948, non-recognition of the Zionist state had been an axiom of Arab politics. Officially at least, Jordan subscribed to the pan-Arab stance, shunning separate negotiations with the Israelis and participating in the Arab economic boycott of Israel. In November 1977

Arab solidarity was shattered by Anwar al-Sadat's surprise visit to Jerusalem to inaugurate talks that culminated, via negotiations at the US presidential retreat at Camp David in Maryland, in the signature of an Egyptian-Israeli peace treaty in March 1979. This provided for an Israeli withdrawal from Sinai and for limited autonomy for the Palestinians in the Gaza Strip and the West Bank under joint Egyptian, Israeli and Jordanian authority. As so often in regional affairs, Jordan had to tread a tightrope. Although not hostile to Sadat, and under intense pressure from the US to join the Camp David process, Jordan also had to take account of Syria and Iraq. Both vehemently opposed the agreement, arguing that it did not meet minimum Palestinian demands and therefore would not bring lasting peace, and that an Israel with its southern front secured would more readily strike elsewhere. Perhaps above all, Amman had to consider the potential financial consequences of siding with Sadat. Arab summits in Khartoum in 1967 and Rabat in 1974 had agreed millions of dollars in aid for the frontline states, including Jordan. A summit convened in Baghdad in November 1978 to co-ordinate the Arab response to Camp David pledged to punish Egypt by isolating it diplomatically and politically if it signed the Camp David treaty. It also pledged budgetary support for ten years for Syria, Jordan and the PLO, with Jordan's share set at $1.2 billion annually. In line with the summit resolutions, Amman severed political and economic relations with Cairo but its boycott was unaccompanied by the vituperation that characterised the Syrian and Palestinian positions towards Egypt.

Following Black September, Jordan's relations with the PLO had been poisonous. With Camp David, King Hussain and Yasser Arafat found themselves in the same camp, leading to a rapprochement. Relations nevertheless remained uneasy because of well-founded Palestinian suspicions that Jordan had not abandoned its aspirations to speak for the Palestinians and to recover the West Bank, despite Amman's formal acceptance of the 1974 Rabat summit resolutions affirming the Palestinians' right to self-determination and declaring the PLO to be their sole representative. To be fair to Jordan, its uncomfortable relations with the PLO derived in large measure from Israel's – and therefore Washington's – refusal to recognise or deal with the PLO directly. All the major initiatives to resolve the Palestinian-Israeli conflict, from Camp David in 1978–79 to the Reagan Plan in 1982 and the Madrid Peace Conference in 1991, envisaged some form of Palestinian autonomy in a West Bank associated to a lesser or greater extent with Jordan, and all assigned Jordan a key negotiating role.

After 1973, Jordanian-Syrian relations improved steadily. Syria was becoming embroiled in the Lebanese civil war, it was engaged in a deadly feud with the rival Ba'athist regime in Baghdad and it was deeply concerned by Sadat's severance of Egypt's close links with Moscow and his concomitant rapprochement with the US. Damascus needed all the regional friends it could find. In June 1975 Hafiz al-Asad had even paid a state visit to Amman, where a possible Syrian-Jordanian merger was discussed. After 1979, however, relations nose-dived. King Hussain had declined to join a Syrian-sponsored Steadfastness and Confrontation Front formed in 1978 to counter Camp David and linking Syria, the PLO, South Yemen, Libya and Algeria. Although Syria and Jordan both opposed Camp David, Damascus correctly perceived that Amman's opposition was only lukewarm. Damascus was also suspicious of an improvement of Jordan's ties with its arch-enemy, Iraq, that had started in 1978. The Iran–Iraq war started in September 1980, Syria siding with Iran, and Jordan with Iraq. The Syrian regime was meanwhile facing a violent internal rebellion spearheaded by the Muslim Brotherhood, which, not without reason, it accused Jordan of supporting. In 1981 Jordan cut diplomatic relations with Syria, accusing it, also not without reason, of plotting terrorist attacks against senior officials. Ties were not restored until 1986 and relations have since ranged from correct to collaborative.

During the 1980s a close alliance with Iraq, driven above all by economic factors, was the central plank of Jordan's regional foreign policy (see Chapter 2). Cairo saw the Iraq–Iran war, in which Baghdad enjoyed strong support from Saudi Arabia, Kuwait and the other Gulf states, as an opportunity to re-enter the Arab fold and it became an important supplier of labour and weaponry to Iraq, with Jordan acting as the key conduit. In September 1984 Jordan took the next logical step by restoring diplomatic relations, thereby paving the way for Cairo's reha-bilitation in the Arab world – a process that had been rendered more palatable to Arab opinion by Sadat's assassination in October 1981 and his replacement by the less stridently pro-Western Husni Mubarak. Although Syria's response to the Jordanian move was loud and angry, Damascus did not go so far as to reverse a thaw in its relations with Amman that had started earlier that year with efforts to revive bilateral economic ties. In February 1989 the Iraqi-Jordanian-Egyptian axis was formalised by the creation of the Arab Co-operation Council, which also included North Yemen.

Jordan's disengagement from the West Bank in July 1988 sounded the death knell for its claim to the territory (see Chapter 2). Since then, and especially since the signature of the Oslo Accords in September 1993 and its own signature of a peace treaty in 1994, Jordan has played second fiddle to the PLO on the Palestine issue, its role having been largely confined to supportive efforts to secure progress on Oslo's implementation. In view of Jordan's large and probably majority Palestinian population, such progress has always been the key to a normalisation of Jordanian-Israeli relations. In 1996, however, the right wing Likud bloc under the extreme nationalist Binyamin Netanyahu came to power in Israel with a programme that amounted to a rejection of Oslo. With the Palestinians in the occupied territories under renewed pressure, the Jordanian-Israeli peace went into deep freeze. The victory of the Labour Party under Ehud Barak in the May 1999 Israeli elections eased the political climate but failed to bring any real progress. The result, in September 2000, was the eruption of the second *intifada*, far more bloody than the first, that continues until now. The return of Likud, under another hardliner, Ariel Sharon, in the February 2001 elections and his re-election in January 2003, precluded any thaw in Jordanian-Israeli relations. One important consequence of the Jordanian-Israeli peace treaty, however, was that it brought a full restoration of amicable ties between Amman and Washington after a protracted estrangement stemming from King Hussain's failure to join the anti-Iraq coalition in the 1990–91 Kuwait crisis. Jordan's stock in Washington has since risen further because of its enthusiastic support for President Bush's 'war on terrorism', its endorsement of the invasion of Afghanistan, its support – albeit limited and cautious – for the US-led invasion of Iraq in 2003 and its backing for the Road Map project that was intended to revive the moribund Palestinian-Israeli peace process (see p. 54).

Jordan has always been close to the UK but a more recent feature has been a drive to cement ties with other European states. Increased aid has been a key objective but the Palestine question has also been high on the agenda. Jordan considers Europe to have a better grasp of the issue than the US and is keen for Europe to play a bigger role in Middle East peace efforts. A former minister explained: 'Politically, we are aligned with the US. Historically, culturally, economically, emotionally, psychologically, we are allied to Europe. It's next door. It's our depth. They're our neighbours. We need the support of the US, but on the Palestine issue we are more comfortable with European policies'.[35] In addition to repeated trips to London, King Abdullah had by spring 2004 paid visits to France, Spain, Italy, Germany, Belgium, Norway, Ireland, Austria, Sweden and Switzerland. Jordan signed a Co-operation Agreement with the European Union in 1977 and this was superseded by a wide-ranging Association Agreement that came into force in May 2002. While also visiting the US frequently, the king did not ignore Russia, travelling to Moscow for talks with President Putin in November 2001 and again in July 2002.

Wasta

'Jordanian citizens and foreign investors should rest assured that corruption will not have any foothold in Jordan thanks to the relentless efforts of the Anti-Corruption Unit and the other concerned departments', declared King Abdullah in February 2000, during a visit to the GID's Anti-Corruption Unit. 'Corruption is a red line, and we will not be lenient with anyone trying to tamper with public funds or abuse his public position for personal gain or to harm the image of the nation or to obstruct the course of our work towards attaining a higher standard of living for all citizens'.[36] Such exhortations are routine. In his Letter of Designation appointing Ali Abu Ragheb as prime minister in 2000, King Abdullah called on the new government to work for an end to 'all forms of administrative bloating, negligence, corruption, abuse of public posts, nepotism, cronyism and whimsical decisions' as a means of creating a society of equal opportunities.[37] He raised the issue again in a speech opening parliament on 1 December 2003, reminding MPs of their duty to combat 'corruption, favouritism and wasta'.[38]

Arising from the central role of family and tribe in Jordan, wasta – the use of personal connections and influence for advancement or gain – permeates the system, as elsewhere in the region. Whether it is a high-level official appointment or major commercial contract that is at stake or the speedy issue of a lowly official permit, Jordanians turn first to an intricate network of informal family and other contacts to secure their objective. Almost everyone denigrates wasta as a major obstacle to the development of a fair society where positions are attained on merit, and a serious distortion of an economy supposedly based on competition. Yet almost everyone relies on *wasta*. In a survey conducted in 2000 by the Arab Archives Institute, 87 per cent of respondents stressed the importance of eliminating *wasta*, which they saw as a form of corruption. But over 90 per cent believed that they would be using it.[39] It is both a cancer at the heart of the system and the glue that holds it together. Stories abound of bizarre instances of *wasta*. 'The General Director of the Television Corporation recollected that a then prime minister reached out to him in order to appoint some acquaintances of his in the TV Corporation', relate Sa'eda Kilani and Basem Sakijha in their fascinating study of the phenomenon, *Wasta: The Declared Secret*.[40] 'Two hours later a bus carrying 20 people arrived'. The passengers informed security men at the main gate that they had been sent by the prime minister himself to meet with the general director. Puzzled, the latter at once contacted the premier, politely asking how he could be expected to employ so many people. 'This is not important', the study quotes the prime minister as retorting. 'Just appoint them, quickly'. They were all appointed. Kilani and Sakijha note that the prevalence of *wasta* says much about citizens' confidence in the formal structures of their state. 'If rights are usurped', says their report, 'it is *wasta* and less so the judicial system, the media and parliament that can restore [those] rights'.[41]

'I don't use *wasta* myself', King Abdullah told me, explaining: 'You use *wasta* to get something from me because you're my friend: you come to me and ask for something. I don't have to ask for anything because I'm at the top of the system'.[42] Confirming that 'people try to use *wasta* because of their connection to me', he said that 'a prime example' were appointments at the Royal Court. 'I get individuals who come to me and say, "Please put my son in the Court". I say, "Well, he must go through the application and testing procedures. If he's up to standard, then he gets accepted". [The individual might retort] "But I'm the head of this tribe", and I'm like, "Yes, I'm sorry, but I'm not a sort of social security net"'. Reiterating his unrelenting hostility to *wasta*, he declared: 'The only way you can fight it is to try to be the example yourself, and the same thing goes for the government'.

Wasta is separate from, though related to, more conventional forms of corruption motivated by financial gain. Jordan suffers less from the sort of petty corruption found in neighbouring Syria, where poorly-paid officials expect tips merely to do their routine work and where traffic police make more money from bribes than from their salaries. 'I've lived here twelve years and I've never bribed a traffic policeman', said Omar Almetwaly, proprietor of Aqaba-based Jordan Sinai Hotels & Tours, who runs a magnificent silver convertible 1996 Collector Edition Chevrolet Corvette with a 5.7 litre engine and a top speed of 300 kilometres per hour. 'I've never seen a policeman get bribed. I've never heard of one taking a bribe. It doesn't exist here. [If you tried to do it] you'd be in trouble'.[43] Many in Jordan's large bureaucracy are nevertheless open to bribery, while spectacular cases of financial corruption at high levels of government periodically emerge, to the surprise of no-one, further eroding public confidence in the state. Samih Battikhi, the head of the GID at the time of the king's February 2000 visit to the Anti-Corruption Unit, was himself sentenced in July 2003 to eight years' imprisonment for his involvement in a bank-loan fraud, although the sentence was halved by his successor at the GID, Sa'ad Khair. He was also ordered to repay $24 million to the defrauded banks.

For all the official determination to eliminate *wasta* and corruption, the task will not be easy. 'The king wants a clean society', said Muhammad Halaiqah, former deputy prime minister for economic affairs. 'Our legislation, our procedures, are in that direction. But it's going to be a lengthy struggle because one has to fight the culture. In a small country like Jordan we are like a family, and everybody thinks he's a relative of the other'.[44] Or, as Oliver Schlumberger, of Germany's Tübingen University, has put it more pithily: 'A social norm cannot be wiped out as if it was a stain on the carpet'.[45]

The economy

Jordan is small. Most of its territory is desert and it suffers acute water shortages. It has no oil. Agriculture, largely confined to the better-watered highlands of the north-west, accounted for a mere 3.3 per cent of gross domestic product (GDP) in 2002.[46] Jordan has large reserves of phosphate rock and potash is extracted from the highly saline Dead Sea. Although potash, phosphates and related fertilisers and chemicals account for one quarter of exports, the mining and quarrying sector as a whole accounts for only 2.7 per cent of GDP. Manufacturing, with a 14.7 per cent share of GDP, includes large phosphate and potash-based fertiliser and chemical plants, although most establishments are modest, often family-run, ventures engaged in light industrial activities like textiles and food processing. Service activities such as trade, finance, transport and

Jordan: Key economic indicators

	1998	1999	2000	2001	2002	2003
Annual growth rate of GDP at constant prices (%)	3.0	3.1	4.1	4.9	4.8	3.2
Per capita GDP at constant prices ($)	1,490	1,491	1,509	1,539	1,569	1,574
Inflation (%)	3.1	0.6	0.7	1.8	1.8	2.3
Annual growth rate of exports at current prices (%)	−1.8	1.6	3.7	21	21	8.3
Annual growth rate of imports at current prices (%)	−6.7	−3.3	23.7	5.0	3.5	10.8
Trade balance at current prices ($ bn)	−2.02	−1.9	−2.7	−2.5	−2.2	−2.5
Remittance income (net) ($ bn)	1.34	1.46	1.65	1.82	1.94	2.02
Balance of payments at current prices ($ mn)	120	405	949	−30	330	992
Budget deficit at current prices ($ mn)	418	198	169	219	284	87
Net domestic debt at current prices ($ bn)	1.2	1.2	1.3	1.6	1.9	2.4
Foreign debt at current prices ($ bn)	8.7	8.8	8.5	8.1	7.5	7.6
Total debt at current prices ($ bn)	9.9	10	9.8	9.7	9.4	10

Source: *Hashemite Kingdom of Jordan, Statistical Yearbook, 2000*, also for 2001, 2002 and 2003 (Amman: Department of Statistics).

communications are together by far the biggest component of the economy, accounting for 46 per cent of GDP in 2002. 'Government services' – essentially the bureaucracy – accounted for a further 14.7 per cent. Closely reflecting the GDP figures, 3.6 per cent of Jordan's labour force in 2003 were engaged in agriculture and 12.4 per cent in industry while 74.9 per cent were engaged in services, including the civil service and armed forces.[47] For the most part, however, Jordan's service sector, comprising some two thirds of the economy and dominating employment, is essentially non-productive in the sense of directly generating wealth. Yet the kingdom's average per capita income compares favourably with those of other regional non-oil states with far richer resource bases. In 2003 it stood at $1,811[48] – similar to the figures for Algeria and Morocco and about 50 per cent higher than in neighbouring Syria.

That incomes are so high in relation to the economy's productive base reflects a heavy dependence on revenues from abroad. One of Jordan's key assets is its strategic location, which has allowed it to attract large flows of foreign military and other aid. As Laurie Brand has observed: 'Whether as a key land link in British imperial designs in the early period, or as a pro-Western buffer between the Arab states and Israel, Jordan's geographic location in the Eastern Mediterranean and as a country bordering Israel, Saudi Arabia, Iraq and (nearly) Egypt has given it an importance of which most small and natural resource underendowed states could only dream'.[49] In 1973–88 foreign loans and grants, mainly from the US and the Gulf states, accounted for between 22 per cent and 55 per cent of annual government revenues.[50] In 1999–2003 foreign grants (not including $1.1 billion in emergency US economic and military aid agreed in May 2003 to help Jordan offset the impact of that year's crisis in Iraq) ranged between $280 million and $963 million annually, accounting for between 11 per cent and 29 per cent of total government revenues.[51] Brand has argued persuasively that the pursuit of 'budget security' (i.e. foreign aid) is the key factor shaping Jordanian foreign policy, going a long way to explain the notable pragmatism of the kingdom's international stances.[52]

The kingdom also has a well-educated labour force, a large proportion of which has sought work abroad. Remittances from these workers, many of them in the Gulf states, form a crucial pillar of the economy. The kingdom's limited productive base means that its balance of trade in goods is in chronic deficit, in 2001–03 averaging $2.4 billion annually.[53] In sharp contrast, the balance of trade in services is routinely in credit, averaging $2.2 billion in 2001–03.[54] This was almost entirely the result of remittances, averaging $1.9 billion annually in 2001–03.[55]

Jordan's heavy reliance on foreign aid and workers' remittances makes it highly vulnerable to adverse developments abroad, as was most strikingly demonstrated during and after the 1990–91 Kuwait crisis (see p. 35). 'Each time we get up to breathe, there's a hit on the head', said Muhammad Halaiqah, deputy prime minister for economic affairs at the time of the interview. 'Every ten or fifteen years there's a major happening in the region which confuses your plans. We never had a good ten or fifteen years to plan ahead'.[56] The intimate relationship between the domestic economy and foreign affairs often makes it hard to separate the two.

Although Jordan's regime is pro-Western and has always officially advocated free market economics, the state has traditionally been the major force in the economy, owning the largest productive enterprises and employing much of the labour force. Since early 1989 a liberalisation programme has been under way, initially launched as a condition of receiving emergency aid from the IMF following the acute economic crisis in 1988–89 (see p. 38). The aims have been to reduce current account and budget deficits, thereby allowing a reduction in debt and a recovery in foreign exchange holdings. State enterprises in areas such as telecommunications, transport and energy have been partly or fully privatised or restructured as the prelude to privatisation. A general sales tax, now accounting for about half of government revenues, was introduced in 1994, replacing an unwieldy consumption tax. Price controls have been lifted and efforts made to restrain government spending, including by lifting subsidies on basic commodities. Under King Hussain, the regime embraced the IMF's prescription cautiously, fearing the potential social and political consequences. That its fears were well-grounded was dramatically underlined in 1989 and 1996, when price rises for basic commodities sparked serious rioting in Ma'an and other southern towns (see p. 38 and 51).

King Abdullah, apparently more convinced than his father of the benefits of reform, has accelerated the programme and widened it to include measures aimed at integrating Jordan into the global economy. The kingdom joined the World Trade Organisation in April 2000 and in October that year became only the fourth country, after Israel, Canada and

Mexico, to sign a Free Trade Agreement with the US. In June 2001 a free trade accord was signed with the European Free Trade Association (EFTA), which links Switzerland, Liechtenstein, Iceland and Norway, and Amman signed an Association Agreement with the EU in May 2002. In January 2003 Jordan, Egypt, Tunisia and Morocco – all states with EU Association Agreements – agreed to form a sub-regional free trade area to facilitate trade with Europe. Already in the 1990s Jordan had become a partner in the US Qualifying Industrial Zones (QIZs) scheme involving the designation of duty-free zones for the manufacture of goods destined for the US. Jordan's first QIZ was designated in 1998 and by mid-2004 it had ten more. Jordan had also been one of eleven Arab states that in 1998 signed the Arab Free Trade Agreement providing for the establishment of a free trade area by 2008.

Fifteen years after the launch of Jordan's economic reform programme, no clear and sustained pattern of improved performance has yet emerged (see p. 72). Expressed in constant prices, GDP expanded at an average annual rate of 3.5 per cent in 1995–99.[57] At 4.3 per cent, the equivalent figure for 2000–2003 was little better. But GDP gains are seriously eroded by population growth, even though Jordan's population is now expanding at an average annual rate of 2.8 per cent compared with 4.8 per cent per year in 1961–79 and 3.3 per cent in 1998–9.[58] Today's per capita GDP, adjusted for inflation, is not much different from the $1,521 of 1995.[59] Inflation, rampant in the late 1980s as a result of the Jordanian dinar's collapse, is now under control, although it has been rising steadily since 1999. Exports increased by over one fifth in both 2001 and 2002 although the rate of increase fell sharply in 2003. But higher exports have been offset in part by rising imports and no sustained reduction in the trade balance has occurred. Likewise, although the balance of payments has generally stayed in surplus, it remains highly vulnerable to the vicissitudes of foreign aid. Much of a $992 million surplus in 2003 was accounted for by a major influx of funds from the US related to that year's crisis in Iraq. Although the kingdom's debt burden has eased over the past decade, it remains very heavy, with domestic and foreign public debt still accounting for 101 per cent of GDP in 2003.[60]

For all the rhetoric about the need to roll back the state, government spending as a proportion of GDP stood at 23 per cent in 2002, unchanged from its level during the 1990s.[61] The government is still the kingdom's biggest employer by far, accounting for around half the labour force if the approximately 100,000 members of the armed forces and interior ministry's paramilitary forces are included. This is the same proportion as in the early 1990s[62] and indeed as in the 1970s.[63] Jordan's second biggest employer is UNRWA, with a staff of 6,400 in 2003.[64] For all the talk of 'good governance' and 'transparency', *wasta* and other forms of corruption remain widespread (see p. 69).

The benefits and disbenefits of the economic liberalisation programme can be debated, and hotly. What is certain is that it has signally failed to improve the lot of a substantial proportion of Jordanians. Higher prices because of sales tax rises and the lifting of subsidies have hit the worse-off disproportionately. An official survey in 1997 showed that one third of the population lived below the poverty line, with 12 per cent in abject poverty.[65] The situation has since almost certainly worsened. Unemployment remains chronic. Officially, the rate averaged 14.5 per cent in 2003[66] but the real figure is estimated at around 25 per cent.[67] In some of the Palestinian camps it is estimated at well over 30 per cent.[68] Still rapid population growth means that around 60,000 young people enter the labour market each year,[69] ensuring that unemployment and poverty will persist for the foreseeable future, constituting a major potential source of unrest.

'I'll tell you frankly', said Dr Halaiqah, who has been a leading figure in Jordan's economic reform programme. 'We liberalised. We privatised. We downsized. We did all the "izeds" in Jordan. Or the "ions" – liberalisation, privatisation, whatever. But the focus in the past ten years was on the economic front and very little was done on the social front. We did not do enough'.[70] Mazen al-Ma'aytah, president of Jordan's Trade Union Federation, insisted that the economy had been 'in recession' since the late 1980s, although he blamed the regional situation rather than the government. Echoing the despair felt by many Jordanians at the bottom of the pile, he affirmed: 'We have no real hope: only promises and waiting'.[71]

Notes

1   Interview with author, Amman, 29 June 2004.
2   International Crisis Group (ICG), *The Challenge of Political Reform: Jordanian Democratisation and Regional Instability* (Amman and Brussels: ICG, 8 October 2003), p. 3.

3   Philip Robins, *A History of Jordan* (Cambridge: Cambridge University Press, 2004), p. 202.
4   Ibid., p. 202.
5   www.kingabdullah.jo.
6   International Crisis Group, *The Challenge of Political Reform*, p. 7.
7   International Crisis Group (ICG), *Red Alert in Jordan: Recurrent Unrest in Maan* (Amman and Brussels: ICG, 19 February 2003), p. 13.
8   Ibid.
9   Ibid.
10 Ibid.
11 Ibid., p. 14.
12 US State Department, *A Performance-Based Roadmap to a Permanent Two-State Solution to the Israeli-Palestinian Conflict* (Washington, DC: Office of the Spokesman, 30 April 2003).
13 Nicholas Pelham, 'King's supporters win big majority in Jordanian poll', *Financial Times*, 19 June 2003.
14 Interview with author, Aqaba, 1 March 2003.
15 Interview with author, Badr al-Jadid, 22 July 2003.
16 www.islam-online.net.
17 Interview with author, Amman, 6 March 2003.
18 Interview with author, Amman, 5 October 2003.
19 Interview with author, Amman, 19 April 2004.
20 Interview with author, Baqa'a camp, 27 February 2003.
21 Interview with author, Baqa'a camp, 27 February 2003.
22 Roland Dallas, *King Hussein: A Life on the Edge* (London: Profile Books, 1999), p. 251.
23 Interview with author, Amman, 6 March 2003.
24 Interview with author, Amman, 5 October 2003.
25 US State Department, *Country Reports on Human Rights Practices 2003 – Jordan* (Washington DC: Bureau of Democracy, Human Rights and Labor, 25 February 2004).
26 Interview with author, Baqa'a camp, 21 July 2003; and Hisham Bustani, 'Inside Hell: 5 Days in Al-Jweideh Prison', www.arabtimes.com/reader/english08, 22 April 2002.
27 Interview with author, Amman, 24 February 2003.
28 Interview with author, Amman, 23 February 2003.
29 Interview with author, Amman, 21 July 2003.
30 Interview with author, Amman, 23 February 2003.
31 www.cnn.com/2004/WORLD/meast/04/26/jordan.terror.
32 Beverley Milton-Edwards and Peter Hinchcliffe, *Jordan: A Hashemite Legacy* (London: Routledge, 2001), p. 95.

33   Interview with author, Amman, 5 October 2003.
34   Laurie A. Brand, *Jordan's Inter-Arab Relations: The Political Economy of Alliance Making* (New York: Columbia University Press, 1994), p. 88.
35   Interview with author, Amman, October 2003. The interviewee requested anonymity.
36   'King: Jordan combating all forms of corruption, will not allow anyone to abuse its laws', *Jordan Times*, 22 February 2000.
37   King Abdullah, 'Letter of Designation to HE Mr Ali Abul Ragheb', 19 June 2000, www.kingabdullah.jo.
38   King Abdullah, 'Speech from the Throne Opening the First Session of the 14th Parliament', 1 December 2003, www.kingabdullah.jo.
39   Sa'eda Kilani and Basem Sakijha, *Wasta: The Declared Secret* (Amman: Arab Archives Institute, March 2002), p. 17.
40   Ibid., p.18.
41   Ibid., p. 22.
42   Interview with author, Amman, 29 June 2004.
43   Interview with author, Aqaba, 28 February 2003.
44   Interview with author, Amman, 5 October 2003.
45   Oliver Schlumberger, 'Transition to Development?', in George Joffé (ed.), *Jordan in Transition 1990–2000* (London: Hurst & Company, 2002), p.243.
46   *Hashemite Kingdom of Jordan Statistical Yearbook 2003* (Amman: Department of Statistics).
47   Ibid.
48   Ibid.
49   Laurie Brand, *Jordan's Inter-Arab Relations*, p. 42.
50   Ibid., p. 48.
51   *Hashemite Kingdom of Jordan Statistical Yearbook 2003*.
52   Laurie Brand, *Jordan's Inter-Arab Relations*.
53   *Hashemite Kingdom of Jordan Statistical Yearbook 2003*.
54   Ibid.
55   Ibid.
56   Interview with author, Amman, 5 October 2003.
57   *Hashemite Kingdom of Jordan Statistical Yearbook 2002* and *Statistical Yearbook 2003*.
58   *Hashemite Kingdom of Jordan Statistical Yearbook 2003*.
59   Ibid.
60   Ibid.
61   Ibid.
62   Laurie Brand, *Jordan's Inter-Arab Relations*, p. 73.
63   Beverley Milton-Edwards and Peter Hinchcliffe, *Jordan*, p. 86.
64   Interview with Charles Kapes, Deputy Director, UNRWA Operations,

Jordan, Amman, 22 April 2004.

65   Dalya Dajani, 'Jordan continues to fight poverty, but challenges still lying ahead', *Jordan Times*, 20 July 2003.

66   *Hashemite Kingdom of Jordan Statistical Yearbook 2003.*

67   'The EU's relations with Jordan', www.europa.eu.int.

68   Interview with Charles Kapes, Amman, 22 April 2004.

69   *Middle East Economic Digest,* Vol. 48, No. 42, 15-21 October 2004, p. 6.

70   Interview with author, Amman, 5 October 2003.

71   Interview with author, Amman, 22 July 2003.

CHAPTER 4

Abdullah bin al-Hussain – King

LIKE HIS FATHER, King Abdullah exudes nervous energy. He speaks freely, fast and earnestly, often using terminology borrowed from corporate America. He talks of 'learning curves', 'best practices' and 'pushing the envelope', each point leading into the next in a bubbling stream of consciousness.[1] But at its core, the energy is highly focused. As well as knowing whence he came, he knows where he wants to go. He is fiercely attached to what he terms his 'vision': a strategic view of Jordan as a stable, relatively liberal and largely democratic state based on solid, self-perpetuating institutions and wedded to free market economics. There is no aspect of this vision on which King Abdullah does not have an opinion, usually detailed, and, while expressing distaste for micro-management, he is ready to 'step in', as he puts it, whenever he feels it's necessary – which is rather often. Again in the mould of his father – and indeed of his great-grandfather, Abdullah I – this is very much a hands-on, can-do monarch, driven in part by a self-confessed streak of impatience. He perhaps lacks something of the common touch for which King Hussain was renowned. In the aftermath of the Ma'an confrontation (see p. 50) he did not visit the troubled southern town to listen to the complaints of ordinary people – as his father likely would have done. A soldier by profession, he appears most comfortable in the company of fellow military men. This does not mean that he is aloof or cold. If he were, his passion might be less convincing, or at least less evident. His warmth is genuine, and therefore his charm too.

Warmth should not be confused with weakness. King Abdullah is single-minded and determined, even ruthless. He does not hesitate to sideline those, from prime ministers to courtiers, whom he deems to lack sufficient attachment to his 'vision', and privately he is contemptuous of forces – notably fundamentalist Islamists – that he sees as being diametrically opposed to it. By temperament, the king favours dialogue and consensus, but within limits. Democracy lies at the centre of his vision, but not if it entails a parliament and government dominated by 'extremists'. A free press is laudable, but not if it undermines the 'national interest'. But it is he who defines the national interest. As with any autocratic ruler, regime maintenance is King Abdullah's over-arching priority, to be ensured if necessary by his state's coercive core, the army and General Intelligence Department. Brute force, however, is very much a last and reluctant resort.

The king's preoccupation with economic development and higher living standards arises largely from a benign concern for his people's welfare, and he's no stranger to the poor. 'I spent almost 20 years in the army and so had a great affinity for what the soldier suffers in the sense of what his family goes through', he told me. 'Most people join the armed forces because you get three meals a day, with meat in two of them, which most people in the cities don't understand'. But he also calculates that dealing effectively with poverty and unemployment will raise the monarchy's standing and thus bolster its security. 'People say, "why are you pushing economic reform?" Well, if people are happy, they're going to be happy with the king', he explains. 'If they're not going to be happy, then I've got a problem. If you want the Hashemite House to survive, and I have a responsibility to make sure that happens, it has to survive by being able to adapt into a modern context. Moving society forward is our survival at the same time'. Political and social reforms can come later, he argues, his thinking again coloured by questions of regime security. With the 'extremists' having been deprived of political ammunition over the economy, 'the moderates, the overwhelming majority' will be able to dominate the phase of political and social change. Charming he may be, but King Abdullah is also a hard-nosed politician who knows where his interests lie.

A large part of the disarming charm is a personal modesty. The impressive public relations machine surrounding the king portrays him as a father figure to Jordanians, but it hasn't gone to his head. There's none of the offensive profligacy of some of the Saudi royals, and none of the relentless and ultimately absurd personality cult of rulers such as Syria's Hafiz al-Asad or Iraq's Saddam Hussein. 'When people come and say,

"Your Majesty, we're loyal to you", I say, "Look, that doesn't do anything for me,"' he explained. 'I'm trying to change the issue from *wala'a* ['loyalty'] to *intima'a* ['belonging']'. What matters to him is not so much the monarch as an individual but the monarchy as an institution, a concern underlined by his decision that the coins and notes in a recent re-issue of the national currency should carry not just his own image but also those of his forebears. King Abdullah presents not so much as a monarch but as an approachable, plain-speaking, down-to-earth and even slightly self-effacing professional army officer.

Punishing schedule

Given his punishing schedule, it's as well that the king possesses such energy. Five days a week, he typically rises at 7.30–8.00 a.m. and goes straight to the gym to work out for an hour before breakfast, concentrating on cardiovascular exercises three days weekly and on weight training the other two days. Early morning workouts were standard in the army but, on succeeding to the throne, he stopped taking regular exercise and became 'very fatigued and kind of depressed'. He recalled that inserting workouts into his agenda had been his 'biggest fight with protocol' at the Royal Court. After the gym and breakfast, he works in 'the house', checking and signing papers or drafting speeches, before embarking on his public schedule. For the first five years of his reign, 'the house' was the Bait al-Baraka ('House of Blessing') Palace, a modest structure (at least by the standards of Middle Eastern potentates) set in beautiful gardens on a hilltop in the Hashimiya district on the north-western outskirts of Amman. It stands close to the compound of the Bab as-Salam ('Gate of Peace') Palace, named after one of the entrances of the Great Mosque in Mecca and which was the final home of King Hussain and Queen Noor, who continues to live there today when not in her Aqaba palace (see p. 88). In mid-2004, however, the king and queen moved into a new home, the Bait al-Urdun ('House of Jordan') in the Hummar district, not far from Hashimiya.

Meetings and audiences with all manner of Jordanians, from tribal notables to ordinary citizens, account for around 60–70 per cent of King Abdullah's working week (see Chapter 11). Much of the rest of his time is taken up by 'government problems'. At the start of his reign, he explained, he had had to devote much time and energy to such matters 'because to push the economic and social reforms one had to change the mind-set of the government'. Although much had been achieved, the successes had been 'nowhere near our expectations'. As a result, he said, 'I've had to step in with a bit of micro-managing'. In one instance he had had to intervene to streamline the implementation of labour regulations relating to Qualifying Industrial Zones (see p. 75). He had recently become personally involved in efforts to ease congestion at Aqaba port. 'I physically went there to meet with the port director, with the head of the Aqaba Special Economic Zone Authority [ASEZA – an autonomous agency charged with developing Aqaba and its hinterland], with the governor [of Aqaba Province], with the dock workers and the truck drivers, asking them what were the problems and trying to unplug them', he explained. 'It's kind of fire brigade work, I guess'.

Unemployment is a major area of concern. 'It's not being tackled stringently enough, so I'm having to step in with ideas and thought groups on how to engage vocational training more, and how to get the poor off the streets and into training and jobs', said King Abdullah. One project on which he was working was for a form of national service for surplus applicants to the military, to be implemented in collaboration with the private sector. Usually, between 8,000 and 14,000 people apply to join the armed forces each year but 56,000 had applied in 2004. It was, the king continued, 'a shocking number' that highlighted the presence of a large pool of unemployed who genuinely wanted to work. 'I was asking myself what I was going to do with 56,000 people', he recalled. 'I knew I couldn't take them into the armed forces'. He added that, as a former soldier, he firmly opposed military conscription. In his view, conscript armies are 'a waste of time'. The proposal is for surplus applicants to undergo three months of basic military training and then to spend nine months attached to private enterprises, with the government paying half their salaries and meeting medical and other social security costs. Those with aptitude would be selected for specialist vocational training and would hopefully go on to find permanent employment in the private sector.

King Abdullah has much faith in the discipline and self-respect that can result from military training, virtues that he sees as being of great value to the wider society. 'You get two brothers', he explained. 'One goes to the army, the other goes to the government, but the one that goes to the government sits behind a desk, drinks coffee and hardly does any work.

His brother who joins the army, he's cleaning the toilets the minute he wakes up. He's on the parade field all day. He's working very hard in very difficult conditions and by the time he gets in at 9 o'clock at night, if he's not doing guard duty, he's exhausted. But he's happy, he's proud and he's motivated'. A form of national economic service for surplus army applicants would 'get the discipline into the workforce, [whose] work ethic is low'. Although Jordan's armed forces are overwhelmingly dominated by East Bankers of *bedu* origin, with Palestinian-Jordanians grossly under-represented, King Abdullah lauds the military as an important vehicle for forging national identity and unity and feels that this would be another benefit of the proposed new national service scheme. Boot camp, he said, was 'a social equaliser' that brought together 'people from different sectors of society that would never [normally] exchange with each other'.

The king's government-related work can take novel form. Like his father before him, he occasionally ventures out incognito, disguised with the help of wigs and fake beards, to test the public mood or to check the performance of public agencies. 'It's been about six months since I last did it', said King Abdullah. 'I've been everything from an Egyptian worker to a shaikh.' He added that he would make such forays more often but for the need for ever more elaborate disguises. 'I'm working on using more upscale plastics', he disclosed. 'But that's more complicated because you need a couple of long sittings'. These undercover missions are not conducted randomly. They originate with complaints to the Royal Court by citizens. 'We'll send people incognito to investigate and, if there's a major problem, usually it's dealt with by the appropriate minister or government official', explained the king. 'If we feel that it hasn't been addressed promptly, then I'll physically go myself because the best argument I can have with a minister or official is that I was there and this is what happened'. One target was a government tax office which was in chaos. 'I actually went into one official's office and stole a whole bunch of people's tax files and walked out with them', he recalled. 'Later that day I called the director. He said, "Everything's fine". And I said, "No, and I'll send you the reports that I actually stole from your office. I was there". He couldn't say anything then. He was like, "Er…no, I knew you came", and he tried to put a positive spin on it. And I said "No, that's not the way it is"'.

A regular feature of a typical royal week is an 'army day', usually involving major exercises. 'I'll go meet the senior officers, listen to the plan, [learn] if it's defensive or offensive operations', said the king. 'Hopefully, if it's offensive, I'll actually go down to the battalion and sit on the battalion commander's tank or the company commander's tank and just enjoy smelling diesel fumes again, just to see from the company level the way the attack goes, and what the soldiers are up to'. This, he revealed with boyish enthusiasm, was his 'funnest day' of the week.

Family

Despite his official duties, the king takes pains to maintain as near-normal a family life as possible. Meals are important foci of family life. 'Luckily, we've just moved into a new house where the kitchen/dining room is communal', he said. 'I miss [the children] for breakfast but I wait for them to come back for lunch. [Queen] Rania and I have lunch with them, and we usually have dinner together'. Wednesday nights are reserved for family dinners, with all members helping prepare the meals. 'I love cooking', he disclosed. Was he good at it? 'I like to think I am', he replied, adding that he was honorary chairman of a chef's association that had recently been formed on his initiative. Queen Rania was 'an expert on desserts', he noted. 'I usually do the main courses and she does the desserts'. The two older children (see p. 165) assist with tasks such as chopping vegetables. The king particularly enjoys *tapanyaki*, a Japanese meat dish with rice, and Cajun and Thai cuisine.

Thursday nights – the start of the Muslim weekend - involve 'dinner with friends, or maybe we catch a few movies'. Fridays and Saturdays in summer are usually spent in Aqaba, where the family has a four-bedroomed house near the beach, close to the Israeli border and 150 metres from a palace that was the southern home of his late father and Queen Noor, who still uses it when in town. 'Friday is invariably on the beach with the kids, but always there's a big Friday barbecue where we experiment with different styles of cooking - fish, ribs and so on', said the king. 'It's kind of open house, so whoever's down there comes for Friday lunch. I get all my friends to take a station and cook. Everyone comes in to help'. Boat trips into the Gulf of Aqaba are a feature of the weekends but most of the time is spent 'playing on the beach'.

King Abdullah's hobbies include scuba-diving, collecting ancient weapons and motorcycling. 'I drive a Harley, which I used to commute to work on [when in the military]', he said. 'And then a friend of mine got me a very nice Honda, which is another beautiful bike. My father got me a Harley with a sidecar and if the kids are around [we go out] with my wife and two daughters in the jump seat and my son behind me'. When he was younger, he had also been a sports car enthusiast. 'Sadly, I've now lost that enjoyment because I've got a guard car in front of me and another one behind', he said. 'But with motorcycles I'm allowed a bit more flexibility, I get away with it a bit more'. Another hobby that absorbs King Abdullah is making model armoured vehicles, using a technique he learned from a friend in San Diego. 'It's a weird system that employs plastic kits which you then convert into bronze in a foundry', he explained. 'I bought a couple of these models two and a half years ago and I loved them. I then convinced my friend to come to Jordan and he taught me how to do them. I have a workshop with all the welding and sanding equipment. I lose two or three hours very easily working on a model'. It's a hobby about which the queen is somewhat dubious. 'A lot of it involves soldering and fire, so my wife is not all that convinced it's safe', laughed the king. He also enjoys shooting: 'Whenever I get the chance I go down to the range just to keep up my military skills'. Hiking is another pursuit. 'I love taking my son, who is a bit older now, and my younger brother, Ali, who's very much into nature, to different parts of the country', said the king. Was his enjoyment of hiking hampered by the presence of a large security entourage? 'When you go out where there's nobody, they're less worried', he said. The king used to be a keen parachutist. Was it true that he had had to sacrifice this pastime because of safety fears since becoming king? 'That's what they keep telling me', he responded. Who tells him this? 'Everybody around me', he said, adding that the officer who had replaced him as commander of Jordan's Special Forces 'has hung my parachute up on his office wall just to tease me'. It appears, however, that the king plans to rebel. 'I think one of these days I'll jump', he said, 'but it will be with a foreign army, before my protocol people figure it out'. He recalled that he had once quietly planned a jump in the United States with the collaboration of the then US chief of staff, 'but my protocol people found out and raised an issue, and the American government panicked'.

King Abdullah's week

The hectic pace of the royal lifestyle can be gauged by King Abdullah's programme in September–October 2004. On the evening of Monday 27

September, after attending military exercises, conducting four private audiences and attending a joint birthday party for his two daughters, he flew to Paris, arriving at midnight. The following morning he conferred with President Chirac for an hour before flying to Rome. On the Wednesday he lunched with Italian Prime Minister Silvio Berlusconi and then gave an interview to the Rai 1 television station. After a series of private meetings he dined with Italy's 83-year-old President Carlo Ciampi before returning to Amman. On the Thursday morning he conducted three private audiences and then met with participants in a paramedics training workshop. 'As commander of the Special Forces, I had a problem with the level of paramedics that we had in the army', he said. 'So I created a nucleus of combat paramedics, and I've now formed a civilian version'. Stressing the urgent need for enhanced skills in this area, he commented: 'At present, Jordan's paramedics are basically glorified stretcher-bearers'. The king went on to Zarqa to lunch and confer with local notables. Key topics of discussion were unemployment and the pollution caused by the city's industries, which include Jordan's only oil refinery. Zarqa, he noted, had been the kingdom's major military centre, and he had 'moved all the army bases out and spread them around the country'. The former military area covers 22 square kilometres. 'All its buildings have been demolished and I'm in the process of finding funding to build a brand new city, which will alleviate the [local] poverty', he said. In the evening, the king flew to Aqaba, where he spent the following day with his family. On the Saturday he inaugurated the Aqaba Gate shopping mall and checked on progress at the new Intercontinental Hotel that was scheduled to open in January 2005. He went on to the port to preside at the official hoisting of a gigantic flag of the 1916 Arab Revolt (see Chapter 1). Comprising a red triangle at the hoist imposed on three horizontal stripes, black over green over white, the banner forms the basis of the kingdom's national flag, which sports the same red triangle and stripes although with the green and white transposed and with a seven-pointed white star on the triangle representing the seven verses of the *Fatiha*, the opening *sura*, or chapter, of the *Qur'an*. The new Aqaba flag, measuring 60 metres by 30 metres, is the same size as that adorning the Royal Court compound in Amman (see p. 155), and jointly they head the world's flag-size league table. At 133 metres, however, the Aqaba flagstaff, seven metres taller than its Amman counterpart, is the highest in the world. In the evening the king returned to Amman. On Sunday 3

October, in quick succession, he met with members of the Royal British Defence Academy, held private audiences, conferred with a delegation from the sultanate of Brunei, with which the kingdom has warm ties, presided at a meeting to discuss ways of upgrading Jordan's media and attended a dinner.

On the Monday morning the king attended military exercises in which the Special Forces demonstrated new parachuting techniques. He then conferred with Iraq's interim prime minister, Iyad Allawi and conducted some audiences, before flying to London. The next morning he met with Tony Blair for discussions on Iraq, the Israeli-Palestinian conflict, 'the moderate Islamic message that we're trying to promote' and bilateral economic relations. 'It was very good', said King Abdullah. 'I think this was the best of all the meetings I've had with him'. There followed my interview with the king. On the Tuesday he held a series of private meetings and conferred with representatives of six leading British television production companies to discuss their possible involvement in an ambitious project for a new Jordan-based satellite channel. The station would seek a younger audience than the existing Qatar-based Al-Jazeera and Dubai-based Al-Arabiya stations by focusing on quality entertainment programmes, he explained, adding: 'You want to attract a younger audience by entertaining shows first, and then get the right political and news content'. From London, King Abdullah, who was accompanied by Queen Rania, flew to Berlin to meet German Foreign Minister Joschka Fischer and President Horst Kohler, the latter a former president of the International Monetary Fund (IMF), upon which the kingdom's fortunes have recently depended so heavily. He then opened a major exhibition at the city's Altes Museum entitled 'Faces of the Orient: 10,000 Years of Art and Culture from Jordan', which was scheduled to move to Bonn in 2005. He departed for Amman late that evening, arriving at 1 a.m. on Friday.

During Abdullah's years in the army, wrote Milton-Edwards and Hinchcliffe, 'Hardly anyone ever considered him as a likely candidate for the throne. He certainly was never groomed for this responsibility'.[2] At the start of his reign, commentators habitually pointed to his political inexperience, asserting that this might make him almost a prisoner of the same small coterie of advisers that had surrounded his father. His weak command of classical Arabic was invoked as telling evidence of his unreadiness for power. These early critics now stand confounded. Serious questions may certainly be asked about the efficacy of his economic policies, and about the extent of his commitment to meaningful democracy and public freedoms. What is not in doubt is that Abdullah is very much his own man, energetically driving Jordan towards a future defined by his 'vision'. Six years after becoming king, he seems very much at ease in his role – and his Arabic is now well up to scratch.

Notes

1   Interviews with King Abdullah were conducted in Amman on 29 June 2004 and London on 5 October 2004.
2   Beverley Milton-Edwards and Peter Hinchcliffe, *Jordan: A Hashemite Legacy* (London: Routledge, 2001), p. 119.

CHAPTER 5

Barjas al-Hadid – Tribal Shaikh

SHAIKH BARJAS SHAHER SAIL AL-HADID, tribal chief, member of parliament, former airforce officer, father of the mayor of Amman and owner of four thoroughbred Arabian horses, is, in the *bedu* manner, merely a first amongst equals. Good-humoured, short and plump, with a neatly trimmed moustache and rich brown eyes that are at once smiling and penetrating, he carries his authority lightly. But behind the amiable, even jovial, exterior lie years of experience – and the hard political clout that comes with the headship of a 25,000–30,000 strong tribe and easy access to the kingdom's highest decision-makers.

One of perhaps 15 such figures in Jordan, Shaikh Barjas, born in 1936, is a pillar of the East Bank establishment whose family and tribe have offered the ruling family unstinting loyalty since Prince Abdullah arrived in Ma'an in 1921 to claim Transjordan for the Hashemites. When not engaged on parliamentary, family and private business, Barjas spends his time mediating tribal disputes and interceding to advance the interests not only of members of his Hadid *ashira* (tribe or, more strictly, clan) but of anyone else who appeals for his assistance. To watch Barjas at work from his sumptuous three-storey mansion at the highest point of Jabal Hadid, Amman's highest hill, is to glimpse a world as old as the tribes themselves, where contacts and influence, trust and honour, hospitality and generosity often count for as much as and sometimes more than formal state structures and procedures.

Barjas' dress is as traditional as his loyalties. In summer his *keffiya* is white, in winter red-and-white checked, and is held in place by a black *aqal*, a double-ringed rope head-piece. He wears a beige *thawb*, or robe, covered by a light brown *abaya* cloak trimmed, as befits one of his social rank, with gold braid, or *qasab*. The braid, improbably made in Paris, alone cost $210. It is matched by a large gold watch gleaming on his left wrist.

The Hadid tribal history, and hence Barjas' family history, is inter-twined with the story of Jordan. 'We took part in the Arab Revolt with Prince Faisal, and we fought against the French in Syria', says Barjas with pride. 'We fought at the battle of Maisaloun [see p. 7]. My father and cousin and many from our tribe were there'.[1] His father, Shaher, and his cousin, Minwer, both went to Ma'an in 1921 to pledge allegiance to Prince Abdullah, with whom they subsequently enjoyed a warm relationship. 'King Hussain was born in 1935', relates Barjas. 'For the first three months of his life he had a wet nurse who was a Hadidi. When my father died in 1947 – when I was only nine years old – King Abdullah insisted that he be buried in the royal family's cemetery, above the Raghadan Palace in Amman'. Barjas' loyalty to the monarchy is on plain display in his splendid living room with its twin reception areas, each boasting multi-coloured carpets and sofas and armchairs upholstered in blue with a pattern of silver flowers. On one wall are framed colour photographs of King Hussain and the present King Abdullah, both in smart business suits. On a small coffee table stands a colour photo of King Abdullah in military uniform. When he speaks of Jordan's present and past kings, Barjas does so with unashamed respect.

Noble birth

Although Barjas' father was also the shaikh, or head, of the Hadid, the title is not necessarily hereditary. 'Sheikhdom is not rigidly defined or auto-matically inherited, but sheikhs normally belong to families from which previous sheikhs have come', noted the American anthropologist Linda Layne in her study of Jordanian national identity and tribalism, *Home and Homeland*. 'Noble birth is only one of the many traditional criteria for tribal leadership. Personal characteristics such as bravery, generosity, charisma, and leadership abilities are important attributes of a sheikh...In the past, a tribal sheikh acted as a spokesperson for the tribe when dealing with sheikhs from other tribes or with Ottoman authorities. These sheikhs also mediated disputes within and between tribes, and their homes served as meeting places for community decision-making'.[2]

Shaikh Barjas' manifest wealth derives from his family's ownership of large tracts of land. 'When I need funds, I just sell some land', he explained, adding that he donated his MP's salary to the needy. His mansion may be magnificent but it is much more than an expression of personal wealth. It reflects not just his own prestige but that of the Hadid tribe as a whole. 'Size is a sign of status in both tents and houses and sheikhs had, and continue to have, larger tents than ordinary tribesmen', noted Layne. 'These tents serve as a sign of the sheikh's status and by extension that of the tribe'.[3]

The Shaikh's wife, Noof Salim Khair, known as Umm Nidal ('mother of Nidal'), aged 58, has a family history as privileged and eminent as his own. Her parents were from a major landowning family in Amman, which sits astride the Hadid's traditional territory. Her mother's father was the city's mayor in Ottoman times. Barjas and his wife have four sons and two daughters, all of whom live in Amman. Nidal, aged 43, is the capital's present mayor; Muhammad, 38, a major in the *mukhabarat*, or intelligence service (the General Intelligence Department); and Hussam, 35, a businessman. The youngest, Hamzah, 22, is at university. One daughter, Arwa, 39, trained as a beautician while the other, Hala, 35, studied as a teacher.

Barjas' father was a military adviser to the first King Abdullah and Barjas' first career was in the armed forces. 'I wanted to be a fighter pilot', he recalled, sipping thick Turkish coffee. He learned to fly during a one-year stint at a military college in Cairo in 1957–58 but his dreams of flying fighters were ended after he was severely injured in a hard landing in a light aircraft, for which he needed six months of intensive treatment at the American University of Beirut (AUB) Hospital. 'After that, I stayed here in Jordan for one year recuperating', he said. 'I then applied to fly fighters but was rejected on medical grounds. They said I could fly transport planes but I declined. Instead, I worked on the administrative side at the Amir Faisal Military College until 1976, attaining the rank of lieutenant-colonel'. He left the air force because he wanted to serve the people, he said, adding: 'This is one of our traditions and I inherited this from my father'. In 1984-86 he served on Amman city council, and this was followed by eight years in the Senate, the appointed upper house of parliament. In 1997 he ran for election to the lower house and was returned with a thumping majority as an MP for Amman's Fourth District, a constituency for which he was re-elected in the 2003 poll.

Barjas is acknowledged as one of the kingdom's most skilful mediators and conciliators. 'If someone has a problem, he comes to me', he explained. 'If he is guilty of a crime, has a problem with his wife, whatever. Most are ordinary people. And they come from outside Jordan too, from Yemen, from Egypt – from everywhere'. In front and to the left of his mansion on Jabal Hadid, with its breathtaking view across the capital, stands a substantial *madafa*, or reception salon (literally 'place of hospitality'), where those seeking his help congregate. 'Every day at least 50 people come here. If I can help, I do. If not, I just apologise', he said. 'I'm exhausted all the time!' His activities take him throughout the kingdom, 'from Aqaba [in the south] to Ramtha [a village on the Syrian border in the north]', and he has also been despatched on sensitive missions abroad, twice to Iraq and once to Saudi Arabia. 'One of my trips to Iraq concerned some people who had been sentenced to death there, and whose families had asked me to mediate', he noted. That Barjas' fame has spread throughout and beyond Jordan is a tribute to his skills but another factor is the Hadid's affiliation with other tribes, both in Jordan and in neighbouring lands, with whose shaikhs Barjas maintains close links. As well as forming part of Jordan's Balqa tribal confederation (*qabila*), the Hadid are closely related to a 500,000-strong tribe in Syria and another in Iraq with over 50,000 members.

Honour

In a part of the world where the extended family and tribe are the fundamental social, economic and political units, and where *sharaf*, or honour, is everything, traditional mediation seeks to ensure that problems affecting individuals do not escalate into conflicts involving entire families and tribes. The values that make Shaikh Barjas and his fellow conciliators critical to the harmony of Jordanian society have been well-summarised in the US Library of Congress' country study of the kingdom: 'Slight or injury to a member of a tribal group [traditionally] was an injury to all members of that group; likewise, all members were responsible for the actions of a fellow tribal member. Honor inhered in the family or tribe and in the individual as the representative of the family or tribe. Slights were to be erased by appropriate revenge or through mediation to reach reconciliation based on adequate recompense'.[4] Tribal mediation complements but does not supplant the formal judicial and law enforcement process. 'We help the police and judges', explained Barjas. 'When there are problems between tribes, they go to the [provincial] governor and say: "We want Mr Hadid to help find a solution". It's solved tribally and this occurs throughout Jordan'. Typically, agreements reached as the result of mediation are set out in writing and promulgated in the name of God, the Prophet Muhammad and the king, with the mediating shaikhs as guarantors. Often, they are published in the newspapers.

One of his more celebrated cases involved a Japanese photographer returning via Amman from a trip to Iraq in May 2003, following the US-led invasion. An X-ray machine at Amman's Queen Alia airport detected a suspicious metal object in his suitcase. A security officer opened the case and discovered that the object was a rocket-propelled grenade (RPG) that the journalist had brought from Iraq as a souvenir. When the officer, a member of the 5,000-strong Sirhan tribe whose territory lies along the Jordanian-Syrian border, picked it up it exploded, killing him and wounding two others. The Japanese then revealed that he had given another RPG to a Jordanian friend. 'The officials went immediately to this friend's house and they found his children playing with the grenade', said Barjas. Tribal custom requires murder to be compensated by mutual agreement, failing which honour can be satisfied only by vengeance against the killer's family. Such so-called blood feuds can be grisly and protracted affairs involving a cycle of retaliation and counter-retaliation that sometimes passes from generation to generation. Manslaughter also requires compensation. Potentially, the death of the airport security officer could have triggered a blood feud. At the very least it required compensation. Either way, the matter was sensitive because it involved a national of a foreign state that is a major aid donor to Jordan. 'I received a call from Faisal al-Fayyez [then minister for the Royal Court who went on to become prime minister in 2003] saying that the king wanted me to go to the Sirhan tribe to solve the problem', related Barjas. 'The Sirhan believed that what had happened had been an act of God. It wasn't as if the Japanese had intended to kill the man. The Sirhan said that they didn't want anything from the photographer. King Abdullah gave the family money. The army also gave the family money, plus a monthly stipend, and accepted twenty Sirhan into the army. Possibly, the Japanese or the company he worked for also paid money to the family'.

In March 2004, Barjas was centrally involved in a case which certainly could have sparked a blood feud. 'There was a man who was making a sign for an Amman dentist, Dr Shibli Amari', recounted the shaikh, adding that the dentist had checked and treated the man's teeth for free. 'Subsequently, the man returned to burgle the dentist's house, killing him in the process. He stole $125 from the dentist's pocket and took various items from the house. He confessed to the crime'. Fearing retaliation, the killer's family made an approach to the dentist's relatives. In such cases, the mediation is conducted via representatives of the parties. The latter meet face-to-face only to formalise the final agreement. 'There was a big *jaha* [mediation, although *jaha* also denotes the delegation acting on behalf of a party to a dispute] involving a delegation from the thief's family while I, together with several MPs, represented the Amaris', recounted Barjas. 'The Amari family wanted the thief to die. In our religion, in the *Qu'ran*, it is stated: "The killer should be killed". Although the Amaris are Christian, they are Arab and therefore share much Muslim culture'. At the time of my final interview with Shaikh Barjas, the murderer was in custody awaiting trial. Whether the thief was executed would be for the courts to decide, and the families would accept their ruling, Barjas continued, explaining that the *jaha*'s purpose was solely to avert a feud between the families, not to influence the judicial process. It was agreed that for six months, pending the court's verdict, there would be no retaliation and that the accord could be extended for a further six months if more time were needed. After sentencing, a final settlement would be negotiated in which the thief's family would pay compensation and the two families would agree to have peaceful relations. 'Usually in such cases, the compensation is between $14,000 and $42,000', said Barjas, although he noted that it could be more.

A busy week

One of my interviews with Barjas, on a bright, sunny Saturday morning in October 2003, was devoted to reviewing his week. 'I've been working hard', he exclaimed with a smile. 'You should have been here half an hour ago. There were thirty people in the *madafa*!' His busy schedule meant that he had not seen much of his family. 'I saw my son Nidal, but it was only at a party, for five or ten minutes', he said. On the Monday he attended a meeting of his 14-member parliamentary group, the National Democratic Bloc (NDB - *Al-Kutlat al-Wataniya al-Dimuqratiya*). Like all parliamentary groupings other than the Muslim Brotherhood's political wing, the Islamic Action Front, the NDB is essentially non-ideological. Its members came from all parts of Jordan and included both tribal and non-tribal MPs, said Shaikh Barjas. They were linked by 'personal ties and a similar outlook', he continued. 'We all love our country. We all love our nation. We work for the benefit of this country. We know what are Jordan's strong points and weak points. We work with the king for the benefit of the country and the people. We are a poor country. We don't have oil. We don't have much water. The aim of King Abdullah, like King Hussain before him, is to bring investment to this country. He's working very hard'.

I put it to him that many Jordanians dismiss parliament as a supine talking-shop where rich men go to become even richer. 'We've heard these things but they're not true', insisted Barjas. 'There are no rich men in parliament. I don't know any rich people in parliament. Most of them live on loans. Most don't have cars. Sometimes the citizens are not the best judges. They don't have an accurate knowledge of the situation'. He fully supports the king's calls for the formation of modern, ideological parties: 'We need only two or three parties. Our population is 5.4 million and yet we have over thirty political parties! Why not two or three?' Barjas said that the problem was that the people did not trust politicians, whom they perceived to be corrupt and motivated by personal ambition. 'Presently, everyone wants to be the leader of a party', he explained. 'People vote only for the person, not for their views. That's how the system has traditionally worked'. He is optimistic that change will come, declaring: 'There are clean people who have not yet surfaced'. He nevertheless believes that Jordan's democracy is effective. 'If you heard how the MPs debate and curse the government, you wouldn't believe it!' Likewise, Barjas, who was a member of the Human Rights Commission that recommended the establishment of the National Centre for Human Rights, believes that human rights are adequately protected. 'In Jordan it's better than anywhere in the region', he said. 'The king, God bless him, always calls for respect for liberties. Abdullah has exceeded all expectations!'

On the Wednesday, Barjas spent 'about two hours' resolving a potential problem between the Atwan and Daboubi clans. 'A pedestrian had been killed in a car accident', he explained. 'This was an accident, not murder, and so there was no acrimony'. The police had put the driver in prison and Barjas was given all the police documentation showing that it had indeed been an accident. 'This avoided what could have been a major problem', he noted. 'If you go to the deceased's relatives in such a situation without the evidence, it can be a big problem'. In the Atwan-Daboubi case, no money was paid to the dead man's family, although they received $17,000 from the driver's insurance company.

The following day Barjas headed a *jaha* 'to ask a lady's hand in marriage'. The girl was from the Daboubi clan while the man was from the Dahaj. 'This is the normal practice here', he said. 'If someone wants to propose marriage, he sends people to ask her family for permission. Usually – as in this case – it's agreed beforehand. It's a matter of prestige. If a third party formally makes the request it enhances the reputation of the lady's family and it safeguards her own reputation'. The same day, he attended a lecture at the Hussain Medical Centre by an American plastic surgeon who had performed three operations in Houston on the shaikh's son, Hamzah. 'I sat with the doctor and invited him to dine with us', commented Barjas. 'Unfortunately he was only in Jordan for four days and didn't have time to visit'. Also on Thursday, Barjas visited the national news agency, Petra, 'on behalf of someone from the Bani Hassan tribe who wanted a job there'. The Bani Hassan, centred on Zarqa to the north-east of Amman and in and around the northern towns of Mafraq and Jerash, are Jordan's biggest tribe, with about 120,000 members. Such petty *wasta* takes up much of Barjas' time. When I arrived for one of my interviews with him, he was dealing with the case of a young woman who had come with two male relatives and who was seeking a job with the municipality, which is headed by Barjas' son, Nidal. After briefly hearing her case, Barjas delegated the matter to his adviser, assistant and friend, Abu Firas, who made a call on his mobile phone and then told the girl that she should contact a certain official in the city hall. She and her companions departed well-satisfied, profusely expressing their gratitude. In the evening, Barjas first had a medical check-up at central Amman's private Sartawi clinic. 'Everything was 100 per cent OK!' he said. He then met Himyar Abdullah al-Ahmar, a Yemeni member of parliament who was part of an official delegation visiting Jordan. 'His father is the speaker of the Yemeni parliament and five of his sons are MPs', noted Barjas. 'His tribe numbers about eight million people and eighty members of his tribe are MPs'.

On the Friday Barjas spent several hours celebrating the marriage of two members of his Hadid tribe, and then went to a *jaha* to resolve a potential conflict between the Ja'abari clan, which is centred on the West Bank town of Hebron, and the Sha'alan, a leading sub-group of the Ruwala, one of Arabia's most powerful tribes with some 200,000 members and a traditional territory extending across eastern Syria and into Jordan. 'A young Sha'alan boy threw a stone at Waheed Ja'abari's car, just for fun', recounted Barjas, noting that Waheed's father had been a parliamentarian and a leading shaikh. 'Ja'abari jumped out of his car and grabbed the boy, whose father, Asmar Sha'alan, responded by pushing Ja'abari'. At that moment, Ja'abari had suffered a heart attack and died. 'I was representing the Ja'abaris while Tail al-Fayez, a shaikh of the Bani Sakhr [another leading Jordanian tribe whose territory extends south and east of Amman] headed the *jaha* that came from the Sha'alan', said Barjas.

The final significant event of Barjas al-Hadid's week was a Friday evening meeting of the Umm Nuwara Society, a charity of which he is honorary president, that helps the poor of the Umm Nuwara district, on the eastern outskirts of Amman. The main topic on the agenda had been how best to distribute assistance in the run-up to Ramadan, the Islamic month of fasting, which was then nearing.

Palestine, Syria, Iraq

Shaikh Barjas takes a close interest in foreign affairs. In the preceding week, Israel had bombed Syria, the *intifada* had continued to rage in the West Bank and Gaza Strip and resistance to the occupation of Iraq had persisted. The Israeli raid – the first inside Syria for nearly 30 years – had been launched in retaliation for a suicide bombing in Haifa the previous day, claimed by the Palestinian Islamic Jihad organisation, that had killed 19 Israelis. The target was a camp near Damascus where, the Israelis claimed, Islamic Jihad militants had trained, although Syria insisted that the camp was disused. Shaikh Barjas condemned the raid as an example of 'Israeli arrogance and aggression, supported by the US, which gives them all their weaponry'. Such actions, he added, 'merely increase our hatred for the US'. He insisted that the *intifada* was 'entirely the result of Israeli aggression', explaining: 'The Palestinians are meeting violence with violence. They are resisting oppression and aggression'. This had been underlined, he said, in the Haifa suicide attack that had prompted the raid on Syria. The suicide bomber, a 29-year old woman named Hanadi Jaradat from Jenin in the West Bank, had mounted the operation in revenge for the killing of her brother and cousin by Israeli forces the previous June. 'Every Israeli action causes a reaction', observed Barjas, adding that the UK and the West generally were 'not on the right side' in the Israeli-Palestinian conflict.

Iraq was 'a war that won't end for 20 years', declared Barjas. US President George Bush and British Prime Minister Tony Blair had behaved atrociously. The pretext for the invasion had been the need to remove Saddam Hussain's arsenal of weapons of mass destruction. 'Hans Blix, the former head of the UN weapons inspection team in Iraq, had said that there were none and the inspectors had found nothing', said the shaikh. 'Yet you [the US and UK] sent our sons to their deaths'. Shaikh Barjas has a soft spot for the British and feels that they were led astray over Iraq. 'If the British people knew the truth about Iraq they wouldn't have allowed Blair and Bush to invade', he said. 'But the media is misleading them. We lived with the British for many years. Britain has a long history, and the British are very civilised people. The same goes for the Germans and the French'. The United States, in contrast, was 'only 250 years old' and its people were 'a mix...Greeks, Thais and so on'.

Shaikh Barjas al-Hadid highlights the paradox at Jordan's heart. In the official discourse, Jordan has embraced democracy and the transparency and good governance that feature so prominently in the rhetoric of the global economy. But the daily reality is of a deeply conservative system where social, economic and political relations are largely based on traditional norms, on patronage and *wasta*. To the new global capitalists, the system, riddled with inefficiencies, is anathema. From the leftist standpoint, it is profoundly exploitative. Yet for all its shortcomings, the system that produced Shaikh Barjas and that he helps perpetuate is the basis of Jordan's stability and indeed its very identity. And it is essentially benevolent, offering individuals security and informal channels for social and economic advancement in exchange for acquiescence in the *status quo*. In the end, it's a question of values and culture. Most Jordanians feel comfortable in a system that is part of their heritage and whose vitality rests on personal bonds. Conventional Western analyses, whether from a capitalist or socialist perspective, find much to criticise, but they miss the point.

Notes

1   Interviews with Barjas al-Hadid were conducted in Amman on 7 October 2003, 11 October 2003 and 18 April 2004.
2   Linda Layne, *Home and Homeland: Dialogics of Tribal and National Identities in Jordan* (Princeton, NJ: Princeton University Press, 1994), p. 41.
3   Ibid., p. 59.
4   US Library of Congress, Federal Research Division, *Jordan: A Country Study* (Washington, DC: Library of Congress, 1989).

CHAPTER 6

Rajai Khoury – Businessman

Dr Rajai Khoury, one of Jordan's leading businessmen, much prefers music to politics. 'I play piano and sing', he smiled. 'I could entertain you for an hour with songs such as Neil Diamond's "Love on the Rocks" and Billy Joel's "Honesty" '.[1] With his 16-year-old son Kais, he has written an Arabic version of "Don't Let Me Be Misunderstood", the 1960s hit by the British rock group, The Animals. Together, they have recorded the song in a studio, with a full backing group, although it was for sheer pleasure and they've not tried to publish it. When I asked him whether any local or regional events had particularly interested him in the previous week, he replied: 'No political event attracted my attention. As a matter of fact, I try to avoid politics as much as possible. I'm in business, not politics'. He believes strongly in the adage: 'Give unto Caesar what is Caesar's, and unto God what is God's'. That doesn't mean that he's indifferent to the major issues of the day. He is a Jordanian of Palestinian extraction, with relatives in the West Bank town of Ramallah, just north of Jerusalem, and he is heavily involved in commerce with Iraq. 'Of course we sympathise with the Palestinians and Iraqis, and we'd like to see them live a good life', he said. But these sympathies did not translate into political activity, and suffering was anyway not unique to the Palestinians or Iraqis. 'All tragedies in the world, of many kinds, affect people, affect me personally', explained Dr Khoury. 'I'd like to see the people of the world living a great life, at peace'.

I met Dr Khoury at his corporate headquarters, a white limestone-faced, four-storey building on Mecca Street in west Amman's Umm Uthaina district, near the Four Seasons Hotel. Throughout, the building has dark brown parquet flooring and each level is divided into individual offices by a series of floor-to-ceiling partitions, white plastic at their bases with windows above. 'Utilitarian', I scribbled in my notebook. Dr Khoury's office occupies a corner of the third floor and, although one of the biggest, is not much different from the others. Its main feature is his expansive, glass-topped dark wood desk, set parallel to the back wall in the corner where a window overlooks the street. Before it stand two black leather chairs, and more line the partition opposite. Born in Amman in 1959, Dr Khoury is of medium build and height and carries none of the excess weight often displayed by wealthy businessmen. Both his hair and his moustache are nut-brown and close-cropped, and his eyes are dark green, although today they appear grey: 'Because I didn't sleep well last night', he explained. His suit, shirt and tie are all of sober shades of dark blue. A methodical, organised man, he speaks slowly and carefully, looking me straight in the eye. His expression gives nothing away, in the manner of poker-players and canny businessmen the world over. But his slightly reserved and formal demeanour can suddenly evaporate when he touches subjects that amuse or enthuse him. Then, his eyes sparkle and his face lights up with an engaging smile.

Good life

Dr Khoury and his family own and run the G. M. Khoury Group, one of Jordan's biggest importing and wholesaling businesses, specialising in medicines and medical supplies but embracing other products too. While declining to give exact figures, he confirmed that its revenues were 'in the millions'. At times, trading conditions could be difficult, he said, but 'sometimes we make money'. Profits were 'sufficient to give us a good life, to have new homes, to travel, to go to restaurants and to send our kids to school and university'. The business, founded by Rajai's father, George, had humble origins. Born in the north Palestinian town of Nazareth in 1927, George Khoury arrived in Amman in 1948 as a refugee from the Palestine war. 'He'd finished his schooling and had just completed a business course at college', said Dr Khoury. 'He arrived in this country with nothing, took a small room and found a job as an employee in a pharmacy. He expected to go back home one day'. Soon after, he met and married another refugee, Nuha Jiryis. Her family, from Haifa, had owned land, property and a textile factory, all of which they had lost, and had fled to Lebanon before moving to Amman a few years later. In 1952 George established his own business, G. M. Khoury Drug Store, related Dr Khoury. It quickly secured a series of agency agreements with major pharmaceutical companies that were seeking 'an enthusiastic, hungry Jordanian who could do the business for them'. The first was the UK's May & Baker, which would later become part of the French-based multinational Sanofi. Second came Germany's Bayer. 'When he started, my father was doing everything by himself', said Dr Khoury. 'The business grew, and today it is a group with ten companies and 200 employees'. His father is now semi-retired although he continues to take a close interest in the group.

Apart from Rajai, George and Nuha had two sons, Ramsey and Rafiq, and a daughter, Taroub. All are closely involved in the business, whose companies are divided into three main groups. Group 1, overseen by Ramsey, now aged 46, includes MedEast Import & Consultancy Agency (MED.I.C.A.), which specialises in medical supplies and consumer goods; Mass Marketing & Distribution, which imports consumer goods and food items duty-free and sells them to duty-free shops at Jordan's borders; Al-Hafs Company, which imports food products including juice concentrates from Denmark's Coro Food and the top-selling Power Horse energy drink, produced by Austria's S. Spitz Company; and Lion Electronics, which holds the agency for Olympus digital cameras. Ramsey is also Honorary Consul for Ireland, and the entrance to the G. M. Khoury Group's headquarters building is graced by an oval plaque bearing the state's national coat of arms, a yellow harp on an azure background. It's something of a family tradition. In his day, George was Honorary Consul for Norway. Group 2, for which Rajai is responsible, includes the original company, G. M. Khoury Drug Store, which is, he said, 'one of the leading pharmaceutical importers in Jordan, representing the best multinationals, including Pfizer, the world's No 1 pharmaceutical company, and selling to pharmacies around the kingdom'. The company includes a dental equipment and materials division which is managed by Taroub, aged 43. Global Health, established in 2004, operates specialist warehouses in Jordan's airport duty-free zones for use by pharmaceutical manufacturers supplying both Jordan and the wider Middle East. It is managed by Muna Joudeh, a family friend who has been employed by the group for eight years. Also in Rajai's group are Mass Pharma and Najat Pharma–Iraq, recently formed partnerships with Iraqi businessmen. Registered in the duty-free zone at Amman's Queen Alia International Airport, both supply Iraq, which has been a major market for the G. M. Khoury Group since the early 1990s. Group 3, overseen by Rajai's younger brother, 41-year-old Rafiq, comprises 3R Pharmaceutical and Cosmetic Industries Company, which produces and packs medicines, cosmetics, toiletries and household products under licence for the Jordanian and Iraqi markets; and Imea, which supplies a range of goods to several countries in the region.

Rajai and his brothers and sister may divide managerial responsibilities but they share ownership. 'All of us, including our father, are partners in all these companies', said Rajai. Although the group's companies are all privately held, he foresees a time when they might go public. Noting that he and his brothers and sister were 'the second generation', he explained: 'A third generation will come into the business, and for that it might be best to have public shareholding companies'.

Palestine

Although the family hails from Palestine, Dr Khoury is adamant that his group does not favour Palestinians when recruiting staff. 'We don't look at whether they are of Palestinian or Jordanian origin, whether they are Christian or Muslim. It makes no difference', he said. 'When we employ people, we look at their qualifications and experience. And we train them well so that they give us the best performance. And if they are loyal and excel in the business, we move them up to higher positions within the company'. He has no idea about the ethnic or religious breakdown of his workforce. 'We really don't care. If someone walks into my office looking for a job, if I'm impressed with him, I'll employ him. I even employed a Bulgarian lady for a year. She was very impressive and did a great job for me. You'll find some Jordanians who are impressive and some Palestinians who are impressive'. But didn't Palestinian-origin Jordanians form the majority of the private sector labour force while East Bankers dominated in the public sector? 'Maybe it was like that for the first generation [of Palestinians]', he replied. 'But now it's changing. The private sector is now much more integrated. Everyone goes to the same schools, they study at the same universities, they intermix and intermarry. The third generation, such as my children, hardly know the difference. They don't even think about it'.

The 'second generation' of Khourys is eminently well qualified to manage their business. Rajai attended the private Bishop's School in Amman, graduating in 1978. 'It had a British headmaster and was one of our best schools at that time', he recalled. He went on to the University of Texas at Austin, gaining a B.Sc. in pharmacy in 1982, the same year obtaining a licence to practise from the Texas Pharmacy Board. In 1982 he enrolled at the University of the Pacific, in Stockton, California, to study for a Doctor of Pharmacy (Pharm.D.) degree, gaining the qualification in 1984. He then returned to Jordan to undertake his two-year military service. Following three months of basic training he was posted first to the King Hussain Medical Centre and then to the Queen Alia Cardiac Centre, both in Amman. He joined the family business as managing director of G. M. Khoury Drug Store in 1986. His brother, Ramsey, holds a BBA degree in finance and marketing from the University of Texas at Austin and a Master's degree in business administration from Houston's Rice University. Rafiq has a BBA from Saint Edward's University, also at Austin. Having gained a B.Sc. in physical education from the University of Jordan and a Master's degree in education from Framingham State College near Boston, Taroub completed a correspondence course for a Canadian dental assistant's diploma after joining the family business.

Rajai married Lina Marto, a graduate in law from the University of Jordan, in 1988. She is from a Jerusalem family that traces its origins to southern Turkey, whence many Christian Arabs were forced to flee religious and ethnic persecution in the 1920s. 'They are Greek Orthodox Assyrians who couldn't stay in Turkey because of the problems between Christians and Turks, so they escaped to Jerusalem', explained Rajai. 'Then they moved here because of the hostilities in Palestine in 1948. They were twice refugees'. Lina's family prospered in Jordan. Her late father owned a large agricultural supplies business while a cousin was a minister of finance and deputy governor of the Central Bank. In addition to their son, Kais, they have two daughters, Tamara, aged 13, and Christina, 6. All three attend the private and prestigious Baccalaureate School in the Hummar district of north-west Amman, whose yearly fees range from $2,500 at kindergarten level to $8,800 for 12ᵗʰ grade students, plus a one-off $850 enrolment fee. 'I'm a lucky father because they're all doing well', declared Rajai. He hopes they will eventually join the family business although he won't pressure them to do so. 'Of course we give them the liberty to be educated according to their liking, and even to live abroad if they want to', he said. 'This world is global today. There's no such thing as "come home, son" or "come home, daughter". They will do whatever they want'.

Hedging bets

In the Middle East, religious affiliations are more than a matter of faith, for religious groups largely define themselves in terms of their culture. The Khoury family, while not especially religious, is Roman Catholic. At a time when Islamic fundamentalism is sweeping the region, its Christian communities – some of the oldest in the world – feel beleaguered. Their sense of insecurity varies in cause and intensity from one country to another. The Maronite Christians' defeat in the 1975–90 Lebanese civil war prompted a wave of emigration – the latest in a series from Lebanon dating back a century. Thousands of Christians have fled Iraq since the invasion in 2003. Saddam Hussein's regime, although vicious, had at least been secular. The bitter and violent campaign of resistance to the US-led occupation has been spearheaded by extremist Islamist factions who are both anti-US and anti-Christian. The threat to Iraqi Christians was dramatically underlined by a succession of church bombings in 2004. Even the Christian minorities of Syria and Jordan, whose physical security is not a live issue, have been shrinking through emigration. Of those that remain, the wealthier are hedging their bets. Writing of Syria's Christians in his compelling account of the plight of the Eastern Christians, *From the Holy Mountain*, British writer William Dalrymple noted that they had 'watched with concern the Islamic movements which are gaining strength all over the Middle East, and the richer...have all invested in two passports (or so the gossip goes), just in case Syria turns nasty at some stage in the future'.[2]

It's more than just gossip. Rajai Khoury and his immediate family hold Canadian citizenship. So does his brother, Rafiq. Ramsey, who is married to an American, holds a US passport. To meet the residency criteria for Canadian citizenship, Rajai and his family spent much of 1997–2001 in Toronto. He explained the move in terms of the benefits to his children, stressing that it did not signify any lack of commitment to Jordan. The spell in Canada had 'helped the kids develop a closer affinity with the Western way of life', he said. But had not citizenship been the key consideration? 'That's for sure', he responded. Canadian citizenship was 'not important, but helpful', he explained. It would 'facilitate a better future for our third generation, if they want to live in the West. It gives them the option to live where they want, in Canada or Jordan'. At the same time, he stressed: 'We are not worried about our future as Jordanians. On the contrary, we feel very safe living here. We feel that we are in a kingdom that offers the best security of any Arab country. In the Arab world, Jordan would be our No. 1 choice as a place to live. For myself, I have no intention of living in Canada. I've never had any intention other than to live here'. It had been more a question of creating options. 'You live in this world only once, and you have to make the best of it', Dr Khoury explained. 'You have to secure your family and your children, and I think this is the goal of every human being. And I think that so far we have done a good job'.

Dr Khoury's involvement with Canada nevertheless extends far beyond the matter of citizenship. In collaboration with the Canadian embassy, in spring 2004 he founded a Jordanian-Canadian Business Association (JOCABA), of which he is president and which absorbs much of his time. A key aim is to promote trade and investment between the two countries. In December, for example, a speaker would be coming from Ottawa to explain the Canadian Investment Development Agency's (CIDA's) grant programme for investment projects in Jordan. A second objective was to encourage social and cultural links. Recently, he said, the Association had organised a concert by Diana Karazon, 'the Jordanian superstar', at which she had sung her 'Song of Peace', urging the peoples of the world to live together in harmony. The concert's proceeds had been donated to the King Hussain Cancer Foundation. Another concert, by leading Canadian opera singer Julie Nesrallah, was planned for December. Its proceeds would go to the University Scholarship Fund, which provides grants to Jordanian university students from poorer families. A third aim of JOCABA was to encourage tourist exchanges between Jordan and Canada, while a fourth was to assist Canadian businesses seeking involvement in Iraq, in particular by facilitating contacts with Iraqi businessmen. 'Trade between Jordan and Iraq is growing rapidly, and I believe that it is vital to both countries, and especially to Jordan', said Dr Khoury. Promoting Jordanian-Iraqi and Canadian-Iraqi partnerships 'would benefit all parties'. In view of the persistent violence there, was he not pessimistic about Iraq? 'I can't say that I'm pessimistic', he replied. 'What has happened has happened, and we all must look to a future in which the present difficulties have been overcome. Then, the Iraqi people will start a new life. Hopefully, they will elect a new government and, hopefully, then they will be able to reconstruct their country. If we Jordanians can help, and I think we can for various geographical, historical, social and cultural reasons, it will be of benefit to everyone'. JOCABA is not the only trade association linked to the Khoury family. Ramsey is president of the

Jordanian-Scandinavian Business Club, which had been co-founded by his father, George, and the latter is president of the Jordanian-Korean Business Association.

Dr Khoury's Canadian dimension also manifests itself in the realm of sports. As well as being a keen swimmer, he is on the board of the Jordan Tennis Association and each Saturday plays against John Holmes, the Canadian ambassador. Sometimes, they play as partners in doubles matches, in which a regular opponent is the British ambassador, Christopher Prentice. 'We beat him last time', smiled Dr Khoury.

Dr Khoury's week

The week preceding our meeting had been the first working week after the Eid al-Adha holiday marking the end of Ramadan, the Muslim month of fasting, and it had not been unusual, said Dr Khoury. His first engagement after the holiday had been a meeting with his partner in the Najat Pharma–Iraq company, who had been passing through Amman *en route* from Baghdad to Germany, where he was to attend a training course. The following day, a Thursday, he had worked on a presentation for a leading international pharmaceutical company, returning home at 7.30 pm. He lives in the Khoury Residence Complex in the Shmeisani district of Amman, which occupies a 0.2 hectare plot and comprises two adjacent villas, one built in 1974 and the other in 1980. In the evening he watched a DVD version of the newly-released thriller movie *Man on Fire*, starring Denzel Washington. It is the story of how a tough, ex-CIA agent hired to protect the 9-year-old daughter of a Mexican industrialist wreaks vengeance against her kidnappers. Friday is a day-off in Jordan and in the morning Dr Khoury went swimming for an hour. Much of the rest of the day was spent working on another presentation, again for a pharmaceutical company. On the Saturday morning he attended a parents' day for his daughter Tamara's age group at the Baccalaureate School before having lunch with his father and two business guests. At 7.30 in the evening he drove to the airport in his 1999 silver BMW to meet his wife, Lina, and son, Kais, who were returning from a trip to Toronto. Dr Khoury and Lina went on to visit relatives on her side of the family to express their condolences on a recent death.

On Sunday morning Dr Khoury presided at a JOCABA board meeting, convened to discuss the association's programme for December. The board then attended a lunch at the Four Seasons Hotel for the Canadian embassy's commercial attaché and a Canadian government official responsible for advising on commercial policies towards Jordan, Iraq, Syria and Lebanon. In the evening Dr Khoury attended a dinner lecture for 400 doctors at the Radisson SAS hotel. It had been arranged by G. M. Khoury Drug Store and Bayer to mark the launch of Levitra, a new treatment for erectile dysfunction in men. 'It's better than its rivals, Viagra and Cialis', said Dr Khoury. 'It works much quicker than Viagra'. Had I not read somewhere that Cialis lasted for 48 hours? Wasn't that an advantage? He shrugged his shoulders. 'Who wants to have that for 48 hours?' he smiled. On the Monday morning he attended the opening of 'Meet the Buyers', the second of a series of conferences organised by a British company to introduce foreign businessmen to their Iraqi counterparts. Later, Dr Khoury gave a three-hour presentation on Mass Pharma, one of the group's two specialist Iraq-focused companies, to a team from a major pharmaceutical company. In the evening came the second phase of the Levitra launch, a dinner lecture for 450 pharmacists, again at the Radisson SAS. The two Levitra functions had been 'great, successful evenings, certainly the most enjoyable events of my week', he said. The following morning he and Lina attended a parents' day for his son, Kais's age group at the Baccalaureate School. At both this and the earlier parents' day for Tamara, the teachers had spoken highly of his children's progress. 'I left both events a proud father', said Dr Khoury. After our meeting on the Wednesday, he would preside at another JOCABA board meeting, and in the evening he and Lina had a dinner engagement with friends.

Liberalisation

Dr Khoury shares none of the scepticism of poorer Jordanians about the kingdom's economic liberalisation programme. 'Since King Abdullah took over the country's leadership, the economy has developed very positively', he insisted, adding that his group had benefited significantly from the improved business environment. 'The king is working as the country's CEO, promoting it very well', he continued. 'Many links between our business community and foreign businesses are being forged because of Jordan's reputation and His Majesty's efforts to attract business to this country'. He cautioned that the changes should be seen in their proper context: 'One must compare apples with apples'. Jordan should be compared with its Arab neighbours, 'and then you can see where we are', he said. 'Today, Jordan's stock market is booming and the banks here are highly profitable', he continued. 'From a banking point of view, Jordan is becoming the Switzerland of the Arabs. I see non-Jordanians depositing in Jordanian banks, including many whom we didn't see before, including Syrians and Iraqis. Why? Because of a feeling of banking security. Where does an economy begin? It begins with security, a good infrastructure and a bank. We've made a great start. In addition, I see big investors that have benefited from investment in Jordan. Last year, for example, the Canadians bought into our potash industry. The French invested in telecoms. I see that exports to the US from the Qualifying Industrial Zones (see p. 75) jumped from $300 million to $600 million, and are still growing. I see that every Jordanian has at least three computers in his house because of the king's initiative to liberate taxes on IT equipment. Whether they're children or adults, they all use computers and go on the internet. Industry has been helped by lower tariffs on imported raw materials. Hotels have been helped by the lifting of the sales tax on room charges, so they are now fully-booked'. Investors came to Jordan 'either to invest in the kingdom itself or to invest in Jordan as the gateway to Iraq', noted Dr Khoury, expressing confidence that while Jordan could not challenge Dubai as a regional magnet for foreign investment, it had 'the potential to be second to Dubai'.

I put it to him that while the economic liberalisation had certainly benefited the business community, it had so far failed to raise the living standards of most Jordanians, for large numbers of whom the daily realities were poverty and unemployment. 'It will', he replied with conviction. 'You have to give it time'. Noting that for the first time in several years his group would be raising the salaries of almost all its employees in 2005, by between five and ten per cent, he insisted: 'It's filtering down to Jordanians as a whole. Slowly but surely the incomes of average Jordanians will grow'. New CEOs of companies needed time to effect change, he said. 'If Jordan is viewed as a company, the king is its new CEO, and he, too, needs time'.

Notes

1   Interview with author, Amman, 24 November 2004.
2   William Dalrymple, *From the Holy Mountain* (London: Flamingo, 1998), p. 154.

CHAPTER 7

Abd al-Fatah al-Bustani – Dentist

'YOU NEED YOUR TEETH: for chewing food; for appearance; for good speech habits; for better health', declares the English language handout advertising Dr Abd al-Fatah al-Bustani's private dental practice in the Jabal Amman district of the Jordanian capital. It is illustrated with a large photo of a smiling model with dark hair and perfect teeth set in a sensuous mouth, and by a smaller photo of Dr Al-Bustani, also smiling, posing in smart suit, white shirt and patterned tie before a wall hung with professional awards. The flier – which is also available in Arabic and can be viewed on his website at www.dralbustani.an4i.com – goes on to exhort patients to brush their gums and teeth after eating; to 'eat fruits (mainly apples) instead of sticky sweets for a between-meals snack'; to stop smoking as it 'irritates your gum tissues and may lead to oral cancer'; and to visit the dentist twice a year as 'he can prevent trouble before it starts'.

Dr Al-Bustani, eminent dentist, sportsman, aficionado of the arts and culture and *habitué* of the diplomatic circuit, is a pillar of Amman's professional upper middle class. While the wealth and influence of the highest echelons of Jordanian society are beyond his world, so too is the daily, grinding struggle to make ends meet that is the lot of most Jordanians. In the manner of professionals the world over, Dr Al-Bustani lives very comfortably. But material security is far from being his sole focus. His agenda outside his professional commitments is wide-ranging and intensive, requiring unusual energy, organisation and dedication. Just listening to his story was exhausting! 'How do you manage to balance it all?' I asked him. 'Well, I enjoy people', he replied with a self-effacing smile. 'I communicate easily with people'.[1]

Dr Al-Bustani lives with his family in a delightful and cleverly designed house he built in 1985 near the Tariq bin Ziyad Mosque, not far from Amman's Seventh Circle. Finely located on the corner of Tayyeb Street and Al-Ithar Street, the house is of concrete faced with warm, mottled honey limestone quarried near the southern town of Ma'an. From the gate, red-tiled steps lead up to a small terrace bedecked with pot plants and shaded by vines. At this, its main level, the house is divided into two apartments, one at the front where Abd al-Fatah lives with his wife, Maysa'a, and daughter Laila. His eldest son, Hisham, occupies the rear apartment with his wife. A second son, Nizar, who is single, lives in an apartment below, and a third, Marwan, also single, occupies a basement apartment. In upper middle-class Amman, too, families stay close.

Precision

Born in Amman in 1937, Dr Al-Bustani is of medium build and clean-shaven with a high forehead and thinning black hair. He is dressed casually but smartly in dark slacks and a blue shirt, a pair of spectacles dangling on a cord around his neck. He is fit and slim – as might be expected of someone who takes his sports seriously – and he speaks and moves with controlled precision. This is a man who likes order, in his life and in his home. To illustrate his professional, cultural and sporting achievements he produces photographs, certificates and examples of his academic and other writings, all meticulously organised. The same attention to detail pervades his home. The main living space is organised into two areas, each with upholstered sofas, armchairs and coffee tables. One, more formal, is where guests are received. The other is more for everyday family use. In a corner of the guest area stands a large wooden dining table draped with a gold-and white-striped cloth, the white bands embroidered with gold designs. The tablecloth is itself covered by a protective transparent plastic sheet. Striking modernist oil paintings bedeck the walls. 'Painting is one of my hobbies', explains Dr Al-Bustani. In his dental practice, some three kilo-metres away, on a busy highway almost opposite the Intercontinental Hotel, he maintains a small art gallery. The paintings displayed in his home are 'mainly from south-east Asia', he explains. 'This one is from Bali in Indonesia. That one is from Manila in the Philippines. That one is from Hong Kong; the other two here from Manila. These are original oil paintings by a well-known artist, a lady named Aimee Lopez'.

Both Dr Al-Bustani's parents were from Damascus. His father, Subhi, was an activist in the Arab nationalist movement of the early 20th century, for which he incurred the wrath of the Ottoman authorities. He fled to Amman in 1916, when he was twenty years old and worked as a merchant near the Hussaini Mosque in the town centre. 'Hassan Dyranieh, my grandfather on my mother's side, who was also originally from Damascus, was in the same business, and they became partners. That's how my father met Zainab, his future wife and my mother', explained Dr Al-Bustani. He has one sister and three brothers. Of the latter, the youngest is a mechanical engineer who lives in Germany. Another is an accountant in Amman and the third an engineer, also in Amman. Dr Al-Bustani's eldest son, Hisham, 28, is also a dentist, who has practices in the city centre and in the Baqa'a Palestinian refugee camp north of the city. His second son, Nizar, aged 27, is a banker while the third, Marwan, 23, is presently studying for his Master's degree in business administration in Sydney. His 18-year-old daughter, Laila, is in the second year of her studies for an accountancy degree at Jordan University. Maysa'a, a Syrian from the Qasar district of Damascus, is Dr Al-Bustani's second wife. His first and the mother of his children was Amal, a Palestinian from Bethlehem in the West Bank, whom he married in 1974 and divorced in 1985.

The family is not deeply religious although by background it is Sunni. 'We never thought about whether or not we should be Sunni', laughs Dr Al-Bustani. 'We don't have a choice in such things. It's there. It's a given'.

His son Hisham is prominent in Jordan's secular opposition and has been arrested several times for his involvement in campaigns against the normalisation of relations with Israel and in support of the Palestinian *intifada* (see p. 61). Hisham, who qualified as a dentist at the Jordan University of Science and Technology in the northern town of Irbid, is a traditional pan-Arab nationalist who decries the region's British- and French-imposed division into separate states after the First World War. 'We think of ourselves as one Arab nation, one Arab people', he insists.[2] As for Israel, 'it is there on the map but we don't accept it being there'. Before opening his own surgery in the Baqa'a camp, he worked there with the respected charity Médecins du Monde, providing free treatment to some of Jordan's poorest inhabitants. His Baqa'a surgery is spartan, and its walls carry one large and several smaller posters of Che Guevara. Dr Al-Bustani, although not an actively political animal, is untroubled by all this. 'I am proud of Hisham', he declared. 'To start with, he's a fine dentist and sportsman. He plays tennis and squash and he's particularly good at swimming'. Although Dr Al-Bustani said that he largely agreed with his son's political opinions, he added: 'I don't always endorse the way he expresses them. Sometimes he can be a bit aggressive'. Hisham 'could present his case in a quieter manner, but that's our only disagreement in this area'. Laila also readily declares her pride in her brother: 'I always encourage him. He may sometimes be in some sort of danger but someone has to stand there. It happens to be my brother'.

In addition to the family home, Dr Al-Bustani owns a 56-dunam (1 dunam = 1,000 square metres) farm at Iraq al-Amir, a village nestling in a picturesque narrow limestone-walled valley 18 kilometres west of Amman. Planted with figs, olives and vines and watered by a winding stream wreathed in bushes and trees, the plot is far more a hobby and investment than a commercial enterprise. 'I bought it mainly because I love the land and nature', he explained. In summer, it is the scene of barbecues for family and friends. Throughout the year Dr Al-Bustani visits it regularly to absorb its bucolic charm – and to ensure that local farmers he employs to tend his crops are not slacking! An added attraction of the farm is that it is just three kilometres from Qasr al-Abd, a striking white limestone palace dating from the third century BC and partially restored by a French archaeological team some 25 years ago. 'Often in summer, around sunset, I walk from the palace to the farm, sometimes with friends, enjoying the cool', said Dr Al-Bustani. 'Sometimes in the early morning, soon after sunrise, I do the walk alone'.

A sparkling career

Dr Al-Bustani's career history sparkles. He received his first degree from Damascus University in 1960. In 1962–64 he pursued post-graduate studies at London University's Institute of Dental Surgery and at the prestigious Royal College of Surgeons. He then returned to Jordan and opened his first practice, in central Amman. In 1968 he went to Pittsburgh for further training, returning in 1970 to open his present practice. Since 1967 he has been a Member of the British Association of Oral and Periodontal Surgeons and since 1980 a Fellow of the US International College of Dentistry. Saturdays to Thursdays he works from 9.00 am until 2.00 pm and from 4.00 until 7.00 in the evening, with two afternoons off each week. His practice is extremely well-equipped. 'Usually, I renew my equipment every six to eight years', he explained. 'Just eight months ago I installed a new set of equipment. It's from Germany: first class, the best in the profession'. Dr Al-Bustani has built up an impressive clientele that includes many diplomats: 'I'm the dentist for half the foreign embassies here'. In addition to his more routine work, he regularly conducts oral surgery at three private hospitals in Amman. He now passes some of his work to his son, Hisham, who, he said, 'will take over the practice eventually'. He stressed, however, that he has 'no plans to retire for the moment', explaining: 'I'm enjoying the profession very much and I'm committed to a good number of institutions, embassies and families who rely on my practice. I'd like to continue as long as I remain in good health'.

The treatment of gum disease is an important element of his work. 'Generally, Jordanians have better teeth than people in north Europe because we have more sun here and Vitamin D from the sun has great importance for the calcification of bone and teeth', commented Dr Al-Bustani. 'Unfortunately, we have worse gums here. This is firstly because of lack of proper care. In north Europe much better dental care is available under national health services. Secondly, there's greater ignorance here about gum disease. You see the same problem in countries like India, Pakistan or Egypt. Many people in Jordan don't know that one can have gum disease'.

Treatment, however, is only one aspect of Dr Al-Bustani's professional life. He is a longstanding member of the Jordan Dental Association's Scientific Committee and since 1977 he has been the National Secretary for Jordan at the London-based International Dental Federation – 'the equivalent in dentistry to the World Health Organisation'. He often addresses conferences both in Jordan and abroad and has published numerous specialist articles. His conference papers, some co-authored with his son, Hisham, have covered such subjects as 'The Link between Periodontal Disease and Cardiovascular Patients', 'Oral Surgery for Aged Patients', 'Surgical Extraction of Impacted Third Molars' (i.e. wisdom teeth) and 'Teeth, Health and Appearance'.

Sports and culture

Dr Al-Bustani's talents and passions extend way beyond dentistry. 'All my life I've been very active in sports and I'm very proud of my sporting achievements', he declared. At high school and university he played basketball. When he was in England in the 1960s he took up squash, a game he still plays. On returning to Jordan he began playing tennis and was a founder member of the Jordan Tennis Federation. He served for many years on the Federation's board, six of them with responsibility for public relations. Later, he helped found the Jordan Veterans Tennis Association, whose members must be aged above 40. Also in the 1960s Dr Al-Bustani learned to water-ski at Aqaba on the Red Sea, receiving tuition from King Hussain's personal coach, Simon Khouri. He also took up wind-surfing and scuba-diving.

'In 1966 I was asked by several dignitaries here to join with them to found the Royal Riding Club [based at Marka, near the older of Amman's two airports], the first in this country for amateurs', he relates, noting that he had ridden while in England and also during holidays in France and Hungary. 'My record jump was 1.3 metres', noted Dr Al-Bustani. 'I stopped after that'. He is nevertheless still a member of the club, and of the British Show Jumping Association. He has lectured on Arabian horses to the Jordanian-Korean Friendship Society, to the Amman Rotary Club (of which he is also a founder member) and to the Home and Garden Club, 'a ladies' gathering that meets at the Marriott Hotel'. Proudly, he displays a magazine article he wrote about Arabian horses, entitled 'The Noble Breed' and illustrated with striking colour photos. He points to a beautiful full-page photo of two Arabian horses, explaining: 'I took the pictures in 1977 at the Royal Stables at Hummar [in north-western Amman]. I won a prize for this photo. The two horses are without reins. It's not easy to photograph two horses together, standing still as if they were posing for you!'

Archaeology is another interest. Dr Al-Bustani is an executive committee member of the Friends of Archaeology (FoA), an association founded in 1958 that seeks to enhance awareness of Jordan's heritage and whose honorary president is Queen Rania. 'We have one or two lectures each month and make field trips to different parts of Jordan and sometimes to neighbouring countries', he explained, adding: 'My children used to join me in these activities when they were younger although now they are very much independent'. The FoA's next lecture, by Dr Bilal Khreisat of the Hashemite University, would be on Islamic India, he noted. Dr Al-Bustani is responsible for the group's media relations and edits its monthly newsletter *Ancient Jordan*. The October 2003 issue includes articles entitled 'Cultural Life in Jordan', 'The Maya', 'Discover Egyptian Civilization...Land of Mystery' and 'Indian Civilization'. The

FoA's brochure declares the association's future plan to include 'building a national coalition of NGOs working for protection of cultural and natural heritage' and 'working with other relevant parties to develop a national parks management and protection system in Jordan'.

Travel – in the course of his work and for pleasure - has been one of Dr Al-Bustani's lifelong passions. He is particularly keen on Club Méditerrané because of the sports facilities it offers. 'My first trip with Club Med was in 1966 and since then I've been on more than twenty trips with them, to Tunisia, Morocco, Italy, Greece, Mexico, Thailand and Indonesia', he recounted. 'If you like to do sports during your vacation, it's ideal. Practically every sport you can think of is available: water sports, wind surfing, water-skiing. They have all the gear, the coaching. And they are good for all ages, for families with children, for single people. They are worldwide now, from Bali in the east to Cancun in Mexico in the west'. A favourite is the Club Med resort at Pompadour, near the central French town of Limoges, which has excellent horse-riding facilities and which Dr Al-Bustani has visited three times. Once, at a Club Med resort in Agadir on Morocco's Atlantic coast, he had met the renowned Egyptian actor Omar Sharif. Dr Al-Bustani's work commitments prevent him from taking too many extended trips but he does take frequent short holidays of a few days' duration. 'I can't afford to stay away from my practice for too long', he explained. 'Anything longer than one week away can cause problems, especially for patients who are already in hospital'. Some ten days previously he had returned from a five-day trip to the Egyptian Red Sea resort of Sharm ash-Shaikh, to which there are direct charter flights from Amman. 'We stayed at the Hyatt Regency Hotel and had a tennis tournament with an Egyptian team: the Jordan Veterans Tennis Association against the Egyptians', said Dr Al-Bustani. 'For three of the five days we played solid tennis. It was very nice'.

Interspersed with his working life and his cultural and sporting activities, Dr Al-Bustani leads a full social life. At his level of society, no less than others, the extended family is a key arena for socialising. 'Our basic family group numbers about twenty, including cousins and nephews', he explained. 'We visit each other quite often. Some of the family is in Zarqa, for example, and we go there to visit them and they come to visit us in Amman. Also we have relatives in Damascus and we go back and forth to see them. Family ties are still strong in Jordan and we like to encourage this as we consider it to be part of our culture'. By Jordanian standards, however, his family group is relatively small: 'There are much bigger families. Some of them extend to entire tribes!'

In addition to family visits, Dr Al-Bustani regularly attends diplomatic receptions, reflecting the important place of embassies amongst his clientele. Sometimes he is joined for these events by his wife and daughter. 'In one day, 2 October this year, we had the German National Day and the Korean National Day', he remarked and, flourishing a small wad of reception invitations, he declared: 'This, for Taiwan, will be on 9 October, followed by the Spanish on the 12th. I'm the dentist for all these embassies – for the German, the Korean, the Spanish'.

A nice week

'It was busy, as usual', responded Dr Al-Bustani when asked how he had spent the previous week. At work, it had been 'normal', and he had performed surgery twice in hospitals and twice on out-patients at his practice. 'One of the hospital cases was not very common', he said. 'It was a cystic lesion in the lower jaw. The operation, at the Amman Surgical Hospital, required a general anaesthetic'. In one of the out-patient cases he had performed wisdom teeth surgery and in the other periodontal, or gum, surgery. 'We do gum surgery in order not to lose the teeth', he explained. 'In the past, in the 1950s and 1960s, gum surgery was not well-established and most people with gum disease would lose their teeth. Nowadays we can save the majority of cases by surgery'.

Also in connection with his professional life, Dr Al-Bustani had been asked to prepare an article on periodontal changes during pregnancy. 'It's for *Ash-Sharqiat* ('Eastern Women'), a Jordanian monthly women's maga-zine', he explained. 'The chief editor is one of my patients and she asked me to write this article – and I must finish it in the next three or four days'. He added that he would 'also be touching on dental care for pregnant women in this article, because a lot of periodontal or gum changes occur in pregnancy, as well as in diabetic and leukaemic patients. These are three systemic factors that can affect gum health, besides the local factor of bacteria'. He noted that the most recent survey had shown that 22 per cent of Jordanians aged above 40 were diabetic, 'about the same as in Europe'.

Dr Al-Bustani had played twice in a tennis tournament organised by the Spanish embassy at the Dunes Club on the Airport Road some 15 minutes from west Amman. Opened in 1998 by King Abdullah's younger brother, Prince Faisal, this elite private club, with a built-up area of 13,500 square metres and 65,000 square metres of landscaped gardens, offers an impressive range of sports and leisure facilities to those who can afford them. 'The tournament is known as the Spanish Cup', continued Dr Al-Bustani. 'I won the first match and lost the second, so I'm out now'.

One evening after the tennis he and his daughter Laila had had dinner with two Japanese friends with whom he plays tennis. 'We ate outdoors at the Kalha Restaurant on Abdoun Circle (see p. 21), he said. 'It's one of the nicest spots in Amman'. On another evening he had attended, with his wife and daughter, a classical music concert organised by the Austrian embassy and staged at the King Hussain Cultural Centre in central Amman's Ra's al-Ain district. 'There were four musicians: a pianist and clarinet, trombone and trumpet players', he recounted. 'It was a good concert and it was followed by a reception arranged by the embassy. I was invited because I'm their dentist. I often get invited to such events'.

During the week Dr Al-Bustani had also attended a one-and-a-half-hour meeting of the Friends of Archaeology Executive Committee, held to discuss the group's programme for November 2003.

In the same week, the Israelis had bombed an alleged terrorist training camp near Damascus (see p. 101), while in Iraq attacks on the US-led occupation forces were continuing. Had these been topics of conversation during the week? 'Of course', responded Dr Al-Bustani. 'Of course we were concerned with this Israeli aggression, as was everyone in Jordan'. Violence in Iraq had become 'an everyday event' and he and his family kept up to date via the television news. A favourite is the Al-Jazeera satellite channel's *Hasad al-Yawm* ('Today's Harvest') daily 11.00 p.m. news programme. 'It's not just us', said Dr Al-Bustani. 'Most of my friends watch *Hasad al-Yawm* if they are at home at that time'.

The day before our interview he had paid one of his regular trips to his farm at Iraq al-Amir. 'I was there at 6.00 in the morning', he recounted. 'I stayed a couple of hours and it was cool and pleasant. I'd ordered a field to be ploughed a few days before and I wanted to check if it had been done, and how well. In fact, it was not very OK. They had missed the field's edges on both sides. They have to do it again. They have to repeat it, otherwise they won't get their money. This is the way to do it. Don't give the money until the work is done'.

En passant, Dr Al-Bustani noted that he can speak Arabic with several different accents. 'When I go to the farm at Iraq al-Amir and talk with the farmers, I speak with a *bedu* accent. Often, when my wife or daughter or someone else accompanies me they are surprised how good my *bedu* accent is', he laughed. 'When I talk in the house I use a partly Syrian accent – *lahja shamiya* – because my wife is Syrian. With my patients I use *fussha* – standard Arabic close to the language of the Islamic holy book, the *Qur'an,* which is used for official business, in the academic world and in the Arabic media.

During the week, Dr Al-Bustani had received good news from his son Marwan, who had travelled to Australia two months earlier to pursue his Master's degree. Two months before that he had been in the United States to sit the examination to become a certified public accountant. 'It was very pleasant news. He passed with distinction and sent me a copy of the certificate. That was very, very, very good news for him, and I'm delighted at his achievement', enthused Dr Al-Bustani.

What, if anything, had he been looking forward to in the immediate future? 'I'm having another holiday in two weeks' time, most likely to Damascus and Lebanon', he replied. 'Damascus for my wife, so that she can see her family, and Beirut perhaps to do some water skiing and other water sports. If I go to Beirut my wife will stay with her family in Damascus'. Would his daughter Laila be going too? 'It's up to her. If she wants to come, I'll take her. If not, she'll stay here'.

In short, it had been a good week. 'This week, really, I had no problems. In fact, the opposite', he said. 'I have a very happy family. My wife and children are very pleasant. In my family I have no problems. My patients too are all very nice, very pleasant. It was a very nice week'.

Notes

1   Interviews with Dr Abd al-Fatah Al-Bustani were conducted in Amman on 7 October 2003 and 10 October 2003.
2   Interview with author, Baqa'a camp, 21 July 2003.

CHAPTER 8

Abu Muhammad – Taxi Driver

'IN JORDAN, LIFE is very difficult', declares Ali Muhammad Abdul Fatah
Atwan, known as Abu Muhammad. 'If you don't work long hours, you
cannot make enough to live'. For him, the kingdom's economic reform
programme means nothing. 'We can't see anything positive. We see only
headaches: higher taxes and rising prices'.[1] A taxi driver for fourteen years,
he was brought up in the West Bank town of Hebron, where his father
was a *fellah*, or peasant farmer, and has lived in Amman for 25 years. He
feels both Palestinian and Jordanian. 'The body is Jordanian but the soul is
Palestinian', he smiled.

Abu Muhammad lives with his wife, Hanan, and six of his eleven
children in a first-floor apartment in a modest three-storey building that
hugs a hillside in the Qawasmeh district of south-east Amman, adjacent to
the Wahda Palestinian refugee camp near the King Abdullah Stadium. In
a front yard stands his wife's silver 1997 Daewoo Lanus saloon.
Dominating the small garden to the left of the building is a large
miramanda plant, whose leaves add poignancy to the taste of the boiled
tea so beloved in Jordan. Across the valley, the yellow-brown slopes,
broken by limestone outcrops, are dotted with simple concrete and
breeze-block dwellings with dust-stained whitewashed walls. The
plaintiff cry of the *muezzin* calling the faithful to prayer rises above the
noise of traffic on the narrow, winding road on which Abu Muhammad's
house stands. The road has no official name but it's known as Umm
Nuwara Street after the district on Amman's eastern edge to which it
leads. Abu Muhammad's apartment, which he owns, has been his home
for sixteen years. The biggest room by far is the reception salon whose
décor and furnishings are *à la mode* for the region but in Europe might be

described as kitsch. Richly upholstered imitation Louis XV chairs and sofas with ornate legs and bedecked with embroidered loose cushions line the room, interspersed with coffee tables, one low, rectangular and wooden, another taller, circular and glass-topped, with an ornate metal frame. Arrangements of brightly coloured plastic flowers shock the eye. During my interviews, Hanan and her step-daughters serve freshly-pressed lemon juice, small glass bowls of translucent pink *ruman*, or pomegranate, seeds and grapes from Syria, pink-and-green and deliciously sweet.

With his lean, almost slight, figure and sparkling eyes, Abu Muhammad looks younger than his fifty years even though his hair and full beard, both close-cropped, are grey. A nervous energy enhances the air of youthfulness. The relentless grind of working days that often start before dawn and end after midnight has crushed neither his optimism nor his spirit. A devout Sunni Muslim far removed from the extremes of Bin Laden and his ilk, Abu Muhammad is a gentle man who confronts the often harsh circumstances of his life with dignity and forbearance. Work and family, the twin foci of his life, leave little time for leisure. 'I love tennis and jogging, and I'd love to travel, but I don't have time for that', he sighed.

Tragedy

Hanan, aged 38, who works in the foreign department of the Islamic Bank, is Abu Muhammad's second wife. His first, Kawkab, by whom he had his first nine children, died of a stroke in 2000, aged 40 – a tragedy from which one senses that Abu Muhammad has never fully recovered. Both marriages were arranged. Kawkab's father, also from Hebron, was a soldier in the Jordanian army. With the 1967 defeat and Israeli occupation of the West Bank, he and his family came to Amman as refugees. In 1976 Abu Muhammad's parents travelled to Amman to ask for her hand 'without her or me even knowing about it', he recalls. 'My parents brought my wife to Palestine without me even knowing her, and we were married in Palestine. I'd never seen her before'. This, he explained, 'was normal 25 years ago. We wouldn't express an opinion about it. It happens still, but very rarely. Nowadays, your parents do help you out but you have to see your prospective spouse yourself. I've arranged the marriages of three of my daughters, but they went to assess their husbands beforehand'. If his daughters had declined to marry the chosen men, Abu Muhammad would not have forced the issue. 'I would have given my advice but I would not have ignored their views', he said. 'In our class of society, girls usually rely on their parents for such a decision. They don't take the decision by themselves'.

Kawkab missed her parents, and in 1979 Abu Muhammad with his wife and two children moved to Amman, where he worked on construction sites making the wooden formwork for concreting. To help make ends meet, he took up taxi-driving as a second job. 'I used to work for eight hours on construction sites and afterwards I'd work with the taxi until midnight, sometimes until one or two in the morning', he recalls. 'I was always exhausted'. Taxi drivers are regulated by the police's traffic department and require a special driving licence obtained after passing an exam. Having qualified, Abu Muhammad gave up his construction work. 'After Kawkab's death, I had to re-marry in order to have someone to help me with the kids', he explained. 'My present wife, Hanan, was the neighbour of a friend from the taxi company. He suggested that I go and see her. So I took my mother-in-law, and she made the decision for me. I didn't have even a single question. I had to obey my mother-in-law'. This, he said, was customary in such circumstances. For her part, Hanan says that she had 'a real choice' about whether to marry Abu Muhammad.

By Hanan, Abu Muhammad has a son and daughter, Bara'a ('Innocence'), aged only four months, and Bashar, two-and-a-half years. Abdullah (10), Hibba (11), Aya (14) and Bushra (15) are all still at school. The three girls attend public schools but Abdullah goes to a private school. 'We felt that he was particularly affected by his mother's death and needed special attention', explained Abu Muhammad. Ahmad, aged 21, has a law degree from the University of Jordan in Amman and has yet to find regular work. Amal, 23, who qualified as a teacher, is married to a dentist and lives in the Libyan capital of Tripoli. Suhair, 24, also a teacher, is married with two children and lives in Amman. Muhammad, 26, who has a Master's degree, is single and works in Saudi Arabia. Sawsan, 27 and married with children, lives in Amman.

Abu Muhammad rents his yellow 2003 Toyota Corolla taxi for $635 per month. 'I have to pay this to the taxi company whether I make $1 or $1,500', he noted ruefully. His trade is highly dependant on the tourist industry, which in turn is heavily affected by regional instability. 'Tourism is the basic factor. If it improves, my income improves, and *vice versa*. And it's not just tourists from outside the region. When they opened the border with Palestine [following Jordan's 1994 peace treaty with Israel], I had so many Palestinian customers, especially those going to the airport [Amman's Queen Alia International Airport]'. Now, times are hard. 'With Iraq and Palestine, the borders are closed, and the Europeans are fearful of the war in Iraq and stay away', he said. 'First came the war over Kuwait and then the second *intifada*. And now, with Iraq, George Bush and Tony Blair have completely ruined everything. I have a big family and I want to send my children to university. Water bills are high and so are electricity and telephone bills. We have to work double hours just to make ends meet'.

Tourism

Tourism has always been one of Jordan's biggest foreign exchange earners although the loss in 1967 of the West Bank, with its important religious and cultural sites of East Jerusalem and Bethlehem, was a severe blow. Until the 1980s, Jordan's tourist industry relied heavily on short visits by tourists based in Israel. Although Israelis and Jordanians were unable to visit each other's country freely, third-party tourists could cross the border without difficulty. During the late 1980s, however, the kingdom started to promote itself in earnest as a destination in its own right, with advertising campaigns highlighting in particular the spectacular ruined Roman city of Jerash in the north, the incomparable Nabatean city of Petra in the south, with its buildings carved from solid rock, the dramatic desert landscape of Wadi Rum, (see p. 10) and the delightful Red Sea resort of Aqaba, with its beaches and coral reefs. The government encouraged both the local private sector and brand-name international hotel chains to invest in tourist facilities. In 1992–2001 the number of hotels of all categories in Jordan increased from 241 with 16,315 beds to 472 with 37,385 beds.[2] Marriott hotels opened in Amman and by the Dead Sea, a Four Seasons in Amman, Mövenpicks in Aqaba, at Petra and by the Dead Sea and the SAS Radisson in Aqaba. Arrivals from Europe increased from 192,000 in 1994 to 327,000 in 2000. Those from America rose from 70,000 to 126,000 in the same period.[3] By 1995 Europeans were staying an average of 4.49 nights in Jordan, compared with an average for all visitors of 3.75 nights.[4]

Then came the second *intifada* and, a year later, the 11 September 2001 attacks in New York and Washington. European arrivals fell by 37 per cent in 2001, to 207,000, and American arrivals by 68 per cent, to 75,000. 'First there was a slowdown because of the *intifada*. But after 11 September, everything went', said Peter Hoesli, Mövenpick's manager in Aqaba, who formerly ran the two Mövenpick hotels at Petra. 'The cancellations were absolutely amazing. I've never seen anything like it'.[5] Omar Almetwaly, 40, proprietor of Aqaba-based Jordan Sinai Hotels & Tours, confirmed the severity of the slump. 'A lot of travel businesses closed and a lot of people lost their jobs', he said, noting: 'In international leisure tourism, we don't have any alternative. If there are no clients, there's no business. It's not like a supermarket where if bread sales are down maybe tomato sales are up'. Almetwaly, a business administration graduate from the University of Texas in Arlington, runs his company with his American wife, Jennifer. He returned to his native town in 1991 after eleven years in Dallas, where he worked for Ford and ran his own mobile phones business. Speaking shortly before the March 2003 invasion of Iraq, he added that uncertainty during the protracted run-up to hostilities had prevented any recovery during 2002. 'Nobody's investing or doing any new business because no-one knows what tomorrow will bring, if it's going to be full-scale war, if chemical weapons will be used'.[6]

In 2002, for the first time in years, the number of hotels actually declined, to 462, with 37,289 beds.[7] Of the luxury hotels, the worst hit by the crisis were Mövenpick's two hotels at Petra, which depended particularly heavily on leisure visitors from abroad. In 2002 they were effectively merged into a single business. At one, the Nabatean Castle, the bar, indoor swimming pool and conference rooms were kept open but the guest rooms and restaurant were closed and visitors were transferred to the main Mövenpick Petra Hotel. In the good times Mövenpick had employed about 1,500 people in Jordan. By mid-2003 the figure had fallen to under 1,000.[8] Hotels in Amman and Aqaba and at the Dead Sea were luckier because their trade was more varied. International leisure tourism may have slumped but they could still benefit from business and conference tourism and from functions for Jordanians.

It had been hoped that the 1994 Israeli-Jordanian peace treaty would trigger a sustained tourism boom. Indeed, the industry was seen as an important means of cementing the peace. It would be 'the critical first arena across which regional linkages would be formed and economic cooperation would begin'.[9] At a press conference with his Israeli counterpart in August 1994, shortly before the treaty was signed, Jordan's tourism minister declared: 'Tourism is a peace industry...[It] flourishes always within a peaceful environment that is based on stability and security. And we believe that all parties in the region...will benefit greatly once peace is achieved'.[10] In 1995 over 100,000 Israelis visited Jordan. With the subsequent cooling of Israeli-Jordanian relations and the outbreak of the *intifada*, however, the trade dropped away – although it was no great economic loss. The Israelis tended to stay only a very short time in the kingdom. 'Israeli tourism was day-trip. At best it was overnight', said Akel Biltaji, who at the time of the interview was Chief Commissioner of the Aqaba Special Economic Zone Authority which is charged with revitalising the Red Sea port city and its region. 'It wasn't what I'd call a critical mass for a takeoff of tourism'.[11]

Abu Muhammad, from his perspective at the sharp end of the tourist trade, agrees: 'The Israeli tourists didn't benefit the country at all. They rented buses to take them around and they didn't buy anything. They didn't spend money here'.

A week of work

'My week was neither good nor bad', declared Abu Muhammad. 'Like all my weeks, it was a week full of work'. On the Tuesday he drove a Saudi to the border with Saudi Arabia. 'He had been visiting Jordan and wanted to return home but couldn't find a seat on any planes or buses', he related. 'So he took my car to the border and managed to find a taxi there to take him on to Medina. I started at 6.30 in the morning and the round trip took four hours'. On returning to Amman, Abu Muhammad went to the *souq*, or market, in the nearby Wahda camp to buy groceries and then went home for lunch. Later, he took some customers to the airport. 'When I returned home I learned that my cousin, Salim, was arriving from Hebron for eye surgery', he said. 'With Hanan and Bashar, I went to greet him but he was out visiting another family so we came back'.

The following morning Abu Muhammad prayed at the local Hamzah Mosque from 5.30 until 6.00 before returning home to dress his son and take him to the school bus. After driving some customers from a hotel to the airport, he received a telephone call from his daughter Suhair's husband, Yousef, saying that he would shortly be arriving in Amman after completing an *umra'a* pilgrimage to Mecca. Unlike the main *hajj* pilgrimage, which takes place annually on a set date, *umra*, which involves fewer rites than the *hajj*, can be performed at any time. Abu Muhammad went to the bus station in the Abdali district to greet Yousef and then drove him to his home. There followed an uneventful afternoon in which Abu Muhammad plied his trade in Amman before returning home for dinner with his family. Later, he went to his son-in-law's house to invite him for dinner, as is customary when someone returns from *umra*. 'The custom is to make the invitation in person, with one's wife', explained Abu Muhammad. 'One can't do it just by telephone'. He had arranged to meet Hanan at Yousef's home but she wasn't there. 'I called home and they told me she'd gone to hospital. At dinner she'd complained of a fever and it had worsened'. Before being able to attend to his wife, however, Abu Muhammad had to take two Irish people to the airport. Returning home at about 8.30, he called the hospital and was told that Hanan had been diagnosed as having a chest infection and was on a glucose drip. Her sister was with her and she told him to stay home and rest and that they would call him when Hanan was ready to return home. 'I waited for the call, and I was so tired that I slept', said Abu Muhammad. 'After one and half hours Hanan's sister brought her home'.

On the Thursday he took a Japanese visitor on a tour embracing Jerash and Ajloun in the north, the Dead Sea, Madaba and Mount Nebo, where Moses is said to be buried. It was on Mount Nebo, on the eastern edge of the Jordan Valley, that God allegedly showed Moses the Holy Land after the Jews' forty years in the wilderness, declaring: 'This is the land which I sware unto Abraham, unto Isaac, and unto Jacob, saying, I will give it unto thy seed'.[12] His intervention is often used by some Zionists and many fundamentalist Christians to justify the distinctly ungodly dispossession of the Palestinians. 'We started the trip at 6.30 and it took about ten hours', said Abu Muhammad, noting that in Ajloun he'd bought some apples, pomegranates and grapes as they are cheaper and fresher there than in Amman. In the evening, he visited Salim, the cousin who had arrived two days before for eye surgery. 'The surgeon wanted to charge $2,115 for the operation', said Abu Muhammad. 'Salim asked me if I could find a way to have the price reduced. So I went to a doctor I know to ask him to intercede with the first doctor. He did, and the price was reduced by $420. It was all a matter of *wasta*.'

Abu Muhammad then returned home, where he received a troubling telephone call from his daughter, Sawsan, who lives in Hebron, and from his son, Muhammad, who had been stranded there while on a visit from

Saudi Arabia. 'He told me that he was in despair and begged me to do my best to help him. We were all very upset by this and couldn't sleep until late', recalled Abu Muhammad. The crisis involving his son illustrates the casual humiliations that Israel inflicts on the Palestinians. Muhammad, who holds a Jordanian passport, had been working in a hospital in Saudi Arabia for a year. In September 2003 he had travelled to Hebron with the aim of finding a wife. When he tried to return to Jordan, however, the Israeli authorities at the King Hussain bridge over the Jordan river, the main crossing-point between the West Bank and the kingdom, had refused to allow him to cross. No explanation was offered, but apparently his name had been on a list of 'suspects'. He was told only: 'Speak to our colleagues in Hebron'. Muhammad had returned to Hebron, where the Israeli authorities had told him that it had all been a mistake and that he was free to depart. An Israeli officer had assured him that his name would be removed from the blacklist. Muhammad had travelled back to the bridge, but once more had been refused permission to exit. On returning once more to Hebron, he had been assured a second time that there was nothing to stop him travelling and that his name was no longer on the blacklist. A third attempt to cross into Jordan had been no more successful than the first two – prompting the anguished telephone call to Abu Muhammad. The tangle was sorted out only several weeks later, when Muhammad, who had feared that he would lose his job because of his enforced absence, was finally able to return to Saudi Arabia. Never had he been accused of anything, but Abu Muhammad suspects that his son had fallen victim to the 'war on terrorism'. He is Palestinian; had once studied in Pakistan, where Usama Bin Laden's Al-Qa'ida organisation has adherents; and he had links to Saudi Arabia, where Bin Laden also has a following. In Israeli eyes, Abu Muhammad believes, all this would be enough to make his son a suspected 'Islamist extremist'.

On the Friday – the Muslim day of rest - Abu Muhammad started work at 8.00 a.m. by taking a fare to the airport, and then worked until noon in Amman. From 12.40 until 1.15 he attended Friday prayers at the Hamzah Mosque and then went home for a one-hour siesta. In mid-afternoon Abu Muhammad's daughter, Suhair, and her husband came for a meal to mark his return from the *umra* pilgrimage. Afterwards, Suhair stayed while her husband went to visit his sister Amneh, who in a fall had suffered a wound requiring eight stitches in her head. Abu Muhammad meanwhile visited his cousin, Salim, who had not yet had his eye operation, staying with him until 10.30. The demands of work then intervened once again. Abu Muhammad took a Dutch customer to the airport, arriving there at 11.30. Half an hour later he was hired by an Iraqi who had just landed from the Netherlands and wanted to go to the city centre. 'I returned home at 1.30 in the morning', said Abu Muhammad. 'Everyone was asleep'.

On the Saturday Abu Muhammad woke at 5.15, went to the mosque to pray until 6.00 and then returned home to sleep for an hour. Starting at 7.00, he worked 'as a normal taxi' for an hour before taking a German visitor to the Dead Sea and back, a round trip of 100 kilometres. 'Before returning home, I telephoned to ask if anything was needed', said Abu Muhammad. 'Hanan told me that Muhammad, my son who's now in Hebron, needed some spring clothes as clothing in Palestine is expensive. I then collected my daughter, Suhair, from her home and drove her and Hanan to the Wahda *souq* to try to find some clothes for Muhammad'. He then worked in Amman until 10.30. 'At home, the telephone rang', continued Abu Muhammad. 'It was my brother in Hebron, with the news that his wife had given birth to a boy. We were very happy and went out to buy some sweets. The children clapped and sang'.

In the week preceding my second interview with Abu Muhammad, Israel had bombed an alleged Palestinian guerrilla training camp near Damascus (see p. 101) and mounted a three-day raid on the Rafah refugee camp in the Gaza Strip in which eight Palestinians had been killed and many more wounded. 'People were very upset over both events', commented Abu Muhammad who, like many – perhaps most – people in the region, follows politics closely. Despite the kingdom's relative liberalism, however, he – like most Jordanians (see p. 241) – is reluctant to criticise Jordan's authorities publicly. 'If you ask me if I love Tony Blair or George Bush, or if I love Saddam, I could tell you', he said. 'But I wouldn't give you my opinion about the [Jordanian] government'. He has no illusions about the nature of Saddam Hussein and his regime but he considers the invasion of Iraq to have been a foolhardy venture that has deeply destabilised the region. Washington's stock in the Middle East had already been low because of its longstanding support for an aggressive Israel. For Abu Muhammad, the US operation in Iraq had been merely another example of Washington's drive to dominate the Arab world and its resources. He is, however, genuinely baffled at Blair's enthusiastic involvement. 'The British know this region. They were here for years. How could they have got involved in something so stupid?' he asked.

Notes

1   Interviews with Abu Muhammad were conducted in Amman on 6 October 2003 and 12 October 2003.

2   *Hashemite Kingdom of Jordan Statistical Yearbook 2002.*

3   'Tackling the downturn', in Andrew Jeffreys (ed.), *Emerging Jordan 2003* (London: The Oxford Business Group, 2003), p. 124.

4   Matthew Gray, 'Development strategies and the political economy of tourism in contemporary Jordan', in George Joffé (ed.), *Jordan in Transition 1990-2000* (London: Hurst & Company, 2002), p.322.

5   Interview with author, Aqaba, 1 March 2003.

6   Interview with author, Aqaba, 28 February 2003.

7   *Hashemite Kingdom of Jordan Statistical Yearbook 2002.*

8   Interview with Edgar Solenthaler, Mövenpick's Jordan Regional Manager, Dead Sea, 18 July 2003.

9   Waleed Hazbun, 'Mapping the landscape of the "New Middle East": the politics of tourism development and the peace process in Jordan', in George Joffé (ed.), *Jordan in Transition 1990–2000* (London: Hurst & Company, 2002), p.330.

10 *BBC Summary of World Broadcasts,* 19 August 1994.

11 Interview with author, Aqaba, 5 March 2003.

12 Deuteronomy 34:1, *The Bible*, Authorized Version (The British & Foreign Bible Society: London, 1954).

CHAPTER 9

Awad ash-Shubaiki – Farmer

IF WE'RE NOT *bedu*, who is?' asked Awad ash-Shubaiki, adjusting his red-and-white-checked *keffiya* and casting an eye on the sheep and goats penned nearby, huddling under their ramshackle, corrugated iron-roofed sunshade. 'The Shubaiki *a'ila* [extended family] is part of the Salaita *ashira* [tribe or, more correctly, clan], which has about 1,200 members. Originally, the Salaita came here from Arabia, hundreds of years ago. We've always been in this area. We're very proud of being *bedu*'.[1] His father, Falah, and brother, Eid, sitting cross-legged on elongated rectangular cushions on the floor of the family's summer tent, or *bait ash-sha'r*, nodded in agreement. Outside, under a clear blue sky, dust-devils meandered across the undulating limestone plateau, the remains of last spring's vegetation parched yellow and brown after the long summer.

Thick-set, with a full black beard and skin tanned dark by the sun and wind, Awad, aged 37, is reserved to the point of shyness. Before answering my questions he often consulted his father and brother, like Awad wearing *keffiyas* and grey, full-length *thawbs*. Sometimes it was they, rather than he, who responded. *Bedu* live communally, with little privacy. My interviews with Awad were as much discussions with his family as with him. As we spoke, his small son, Ghaith, aged one-and-a-half, repeatedly peeped out from behind a corner of the *saha*, the cloth wall with a pink flower design that divides the tent's reception area from its kitchen section, which is the domain of the women and small children. Overcoming his timidity, Ghaith, waving a long stick, occasionally gambolled playfully up to his father, uncle and grandfather to accept their kisses and cuddles. For refreshment, thick, sweet *bedu* tea was served, the small glasses being refilled as soon as they were emptied. 'The British love tea!' exclaimed Eid. 'But your tea is different'.

The Shubaiki family lives close to the hamlet of Ar-Rama. Not far away is the village of Umm ar-Rasas, famed for the ruins of a Byzantine church, which include a striking mosaic portraying plans of ancient Syrian and Egyptian cities. The site also boasts a 15-metre-high tower used by meditating hermits after the fashion of the time. Umm ar-Rasas lies some 30 kilometres south-east of the mainly Christian town of Madaba, itself 45 kilometres south-west of Amman. Not far west of Madaba, the Arabian plateau plunges down to the hot and humid depths of the Jordan Valley. Most of the Salaita are farmers, raising sheep and goats, cultivating wheat to the extent that the uncertain winter rains allow, and tending small olive groves. Some are civil servants and soldiers. The Shubaikis own 1,500 dunums (150 hectares), divided between three different plots. Between them, the fifteen members of the immediate extended family own some 1,800 sheep and 100 goats. The family's olive grove, fenced off on the side of a small valley near the tent, has 300 trees.

Awad married Nada, now aged 39, in 1985. 'Her father and my father are cousins', he explained. 'She's a Shubaiki as well'. Already they have nine children. The three sons are Muhammad, aged 13, Ali, 11, and the irrepressible Ghaith. The daughters are Abir, aged 17, Ghada, 15, Hanouf, 9, Ikhlas, 7, Wala, 5 and Wafa, 4. 'I'm planning on having more', declared Awad. His brother Eid, aged 40, married two years ago and has a baby daughter, Taif ('Rainbow'). Incongruously in this setting, Eid speaks English, having spent a year in Denver, Colorado, in the early 1980s. 'I went to study English, and I wanted to study engineering', explained Eid. 'But it wasn't feasible financially'. Awad's other brother, Ali, aged 22, is 'not married and is looking for a wife'. His six sisters, Fadhiyah, Khadra, Hamda, Fatima, Shima and Tammam, are all married. 'None of them works', said Awad. 'They live in various places, for example one in Qatrana [east of Karak], one in Madaba and one here in Ar-Rama'. In keeping with *bedu* custom, his father, Falah, 67, is the family's respected patriarch who controls the finances and in whose name its land is registered. He is married to Jamlah, 55, and Eid disclosed with a smile that his father was 'looking for another wife'.

Tents

'This is our summer tent', explained Awad. 'The winter tent, which is now packed away, is of black goat hair'. The summer tent, made of sacking, is about 25 metres long and 5 metres wide, with roughly finished wooden poles. Within, the side-walls are lined with brightly flowered drapes. Leather bridles with brass buckles are hung around the tent as decorations while a green plastic vine coils round the centre pole. The carpets, bought in Saudi Arabia in the late nineteenth century, are patterned in orange and red. Cushions, each about two metres long, are positioned around three sides of the reception area, each bearing smaller ones for support when reclining. In pride of place at the centre is a fireplace, an alloy tray for charcoal standing on short legs and containing an array of brass tea and coffee pots. During my visits, the fire was unlit. Tea was brought in from the adjacent kitchen area, which boasts a cooker fuelled by bottled gas. The family also has a modest two-storey house, a flat-roofed structure with concrete-rendered breeze-block walls sited a few hundred metres away across a small valley beyond the olive grove. 'Usually, I'm here in the tent', said Awad. 'I don't like to sleep in the house because here I'm near the animals. The children who attend school, six of them, live and sleep in the house. Those who are too young for school stay in the tent. Such arrangements are normal amongst those who raise sheep in this region'. The children attend the local state school in Ar-Rama, which caters for children aged six to eighteen. The fees are $5.64 per year. 'We value education highly', commented Awad's brother, Eid. 'But, financially, we're not able to pursue it beyond secondary school'.

After the rains have greened the desert fringes, the Shubaiki family migrates with its sheep to its traditional winter pastures some 45 kilometres east of Qatrana and about 80 kilometres from Ar-Rama. 'Only the children who are at school stay here. The others come with us to the desert near Qatrana', explained Awad. The family has a battered, black four-wheel-drive Nissan Patrol, a Volvo tractor, two water-tanker trucks and a truck for carrying animal feed and transporting the sheep between the winter and summer pastures. At Ar-Rama, the sheep are fed chaff from the wheat harvest, supplemented by a local plant, *udu*, which must first be dried and which was traditionally also used to make soap. 'In the desert, they eat wheat that we plant there for them, and sometimes we bring them fodder by truck', said Awad. The Shubaikis also own four camels and a horse. Ali and Muhammad ride the horse for fun', he smiled. 'We keep the camels just because we like them. If we run out of petrol we have to use the camels!'

The family's wheat crop varies dramatically according to the rains. 'Drought means that we get a good crop only every four or five years', said

Awad. 'In a good year we harvest 100 tonnes. In a bad year, sometimes it's zero. This year [2003] it's zero. When there's a harvest, the wheat is sold to merchants or to the national agricultural marketing company, at a fixed price of $85 per tonne. The sheep are sold at a market in Sahab, near Amman. 'The price depends on supply and demand,' he explained. 'Presently, prices are falling. Now they're about $85–$113, depending on the sheep's weight'. Increasing imports of sheep from Sudan and Syria, which are cheaper, is undermining demand for local animals. 'It's not just us. It's affecting the whole country', commented Awad. In the season, from March to June, the sheep produce 150–300 kilos of milk daily, which is sold for $0.68 per kilo to a private dairy near Karak, 60 kilometres to the south, Awad or his brother driving there and back each day. The olives are picked by hand in November. 'We eat some of them ourselves and take the rest to a press in Madaba, from which we get ten or fifteen containers of oil', said Awad.

'Usually, we end up in debt', said Awad. 'We manage to live, but very basically. If there are good prices, then we break even. If it's very, very good, farmers can make an annual profit of maybe $1,400–$2,800. The whole country is in debt!' Are their debts with the banks? 'We don't deal with banks', he replied. 'Only God provides us with money. Usually, the people we sell to will make advance payments'. Although farmers could borrow using land as collateral they do so only as a last resort. 'Many people got into difficulties because of the very high interest rates', he said.

'The low rainfall and the lack of water' are the two critical problems facing the family, Awad continued. 'Water is pumped only on Fridays, and then only for 12 hours, and the pressure is insufficient for it to reach the second floor of the house. And in Amman they change the water in their swimming pools every day!' He added: 'The government did drill a well but it's 40 kilometres away and the water is only for the sheep'. Water can be drawn from it only by those holding sheep cards from the Agriculture Ministry and water coupons from the Jordan Water Authority, both of which are free. 'Each day, those with sheep cards can receive 12 cubic metres of water without charge', noted Awad.

Water crisis

The water situation in Ar-Rama reflects a much wider crisis in Jordan. Of the kingdom's total area of 88,778 square kilometres, all but a tiny fraction is arid desert. Only 2,386 square kilometres – 2.7 per cent – is cultivated, and of this only 713 square kilometres is irrigated, much of it in the Jordan valley.[2] About 92 per cent of what rainfall does reach the country is lost to evaporation. Surface run-off accounts for about 3 per cent while about 5 per cent percolates to subterranean aquifers, which have been severely depleted by over-pumping.[3] The situation is critical and rationing has become routine. As in Ar-Rama, water is pumped through the Amman system only one day per week. Throughout the country, many households and farmers depend on water brought by tanker-trucks. Jordan was 'under the absolute water poverty line' with supplies averaging only 160 cubic metres per year (cm/y) per capita, Water and Irrigation Minister Dr Hazem al-Nasser told a media workshop on water in Amman in April 2004.[4] Even if all the planned new water supply schemes are implemented, they will be insufficient to overcome a mounting water deficit. In 2000 Jordan's water demand was running at 1,297 million cm/y. It is forecast to rise to 1,443 million cm/y by 2005 and 1,746 million cm/y by 2020. Supply capacity is expected to rise to 1,102 million cm/y by 2005, leaving a deficit of 341 million cm/y. By 2020 the deficit is expected to reach 455 million cm/y.[5] The government plans direct investment in the water sector of $5 billion in 2002–11, of which $2 billion had been spent by 2004. Budgetary constraints mean that the private sector has been assigned a key role in the water development programme – a strategy that fits well with the kingdom's wider liberalisation and privatisation programme. Already in 1999 the management services activities of the Jordan Water Authority (JWA) were transferred to LEMA, a joint venture of France's Suez Lyonnaise des Eaux and Jordan's Montgomery Watson-Arabtech Jardaneh.

The biggest project in hand is a $600-million scheme to pipe 100 million cm/y of underground water from the Disi area near the Saudi border to water-starved Amman, 320 kilometres to the north. The project, which will double the capital's water supplies, has been dogged by funding wrangles. Early this decade, when plans for Disi were being finalised, Libya informally agreed to grant $180 million plus half the large-diameter concrete pipes required. The project was high on the agenda during an October 2000 visit to Jordan by Libyan leader Muammar Qadhafi, his first to the kingdom for 17 years. Shortly after, however, a Dubai newspaper published an unflattering article about Qadhafi's daughter, who at the time was studying in Amman. According to a well-placed Jordanian official, an angry Qadhafi responded by withdrawing his support for Disi.[6] It was then resolved to proceed on a build-operate-transfer (BOT) basis, under which the contractor would build and then operate the project for forty years before transferring it to the government, which was to provide $200 million towards the construction costs. Bids from two consortia were opened in December 2003, and in February 2004 a group led by the Saudi Oger company was selected to start detailed negotiations. Eight months later, however, it was reported that the talks had stalled and that the government would instead implement the scheme on a conventional contractual basis.[7]

The contract for Jordan's first water sector BOT scheme, the $169-million Khirbet as-Samra waste-water treatment plant in Zarqa, near Amman, was signed in December 2003. Serving the 2.5 million inhabitants of Greater Amman – half Jordan's population – it will have a daily capacity of 268,000 cubic metres and will supply treated effluent for use in agriculture. The 25-year operating mandate is held by the Samra Plant Consortium (SPC), linking the Morganti Group and Infilco Degrémont, both of the United States. The water and irrigation ministry is providing finance of $14 million while $78 million has been granted by the US Agency for International Development (USAID) and the balance is being borrowed from a group of banks. The scheme, seen as a model for future Jordanian infrastructure projects, is scheduled for commissioning in 2006. Amman's water supply crisis will also be eased by a project to convey water from the Wadi Ma'in spring, on the Dead Sea, to a reservoir at Nabouq, near the city's Queen Alia International Airport. The $125-million contract to design, build and operate the scheme was won in September 2003 by a joint venture between the Morganti Group and Infilco Degrémont. It will comprise a 55-million cubic metres per day treatment plant near the Dead Sea and a 40-kilometre pipeline. USAID has granted $98 million for the scheme while the government is providing the balance.

Building dams to garner the kingdom's scarce water resources is a crucial element in Jordan's water programme. The biggest presently under way is the $119-million Wahda ('Unity') dam on the Yarmouk river that forms part of Jordan's frontier with Syria. The dam had been long mooted but was delayed by funding constraints and political frictions between Syria, Israel and Jordan. The 116-metre-high dam will store up to 110 million cubic metres of water. 30 million cm/y will be used for irrigation in the Jordan Valley while 50 million cm/y will be conveyed to Amman.

The main construction contract was won by Turkey's Ozaltin company in April 2003 and work started in June that year. The consultant is Harza Engineering of the United States.

By far the most ambitious scheme under consideration is a 180-kilometre canal to bring 1.8 billion cm/y from the Red Sea to the Dead Sea. A desalination plant would produce 850 million cm/y, to be shared by Jordan, Israel and Palestine, while the 410-metre altitude drop would be utilised to generate hydroelectricity. The Dead Sea has been contracting steadily for decades because of the diversion of its source waters for irrigation and other uses. About 1 billion cm/y of the canal's throughput would be discharged directly into the sea in order to restore its level. A World Bank-funded feasibility study for the estimated $3.8-billion scheme was completed in 1996 by Harza Engineering and in September 2003 Water and Irrigation Minister Hazem al-Nasser disclosed that consultations had started with Israel and the Palestine National Authority that has autonomous powers in the West Bank.[8] Speaking in June 2004, he said that Jordan was seeking World Bank funding for an estimated $10-million detailed feasibility study on the so-called Red-Dead Canal.[9]

Promises

As yet, none of this cuts much ice in Ar-Rama. 'Every year they promise improvements, but nothing actually happens', said Awad. The Shubaiki family feels that neither the government nor parliament takes much notice of farmers' problems. 'Parliament does nothing', says Awad. 'MPs are there only for the position and the money, and they only take note of influential members of tribes, such as the shaikhs. Before elections, MPs will go in their fast Mercedes cars into the desert to get the votes, but afterwards they don't care. They forget about us'. Ar-Rama lies in the *Badia Wasat* ('Central Desert') constituency. In the June 2003 general election the family voted for Dr Samih Hamad, a former interior minister, who failed to win a seat. 'We voted for him because he's a genuine *bedu* who is not afraid of the government', declared Awad. 'Not a single official asks after us', he continued. 'Neither the government nor our municipality is concerned about us. No-one bothers to visit us to ask what problems we might have'. But the family's disdain for officialdom does not extend to the monarchy. 'We love the Royal Family without limit', declared Awad. 'If you manage to reach them and tell them your problems, they help you a lot. But the problem is the people in the middle, between you and them. The problem is the officials, from the highest to the lowest. They aren't concerned about us, they don't know us or our problems'. When officials do visit the area, 'they always meet with the shaikhs. They don't know that the shaikhs do nothing'. The *bedu* remember with respect John Bagot Glubb – Glubb Pasha – the British commander of the Arab Legion until 1956 (see p. 29). 'He visited the *bedu* and liked them', said Awad's father, Falah. 'That's the problem today: the government never visits the *bedu*'.

The family has a television and follows the news on the Al-Jazeera channel, although Awad stressed: 'If we have work to do, we forget about everything else. If we have immediate [family or work] problems, we ignore the news'. They nevertheless hold strong views on the two major regional conflicts, in Palestine and Iraq. 'It's always wrong to have wars, and especially against the Arabs. We really hate Blair and Bush [because of their invasion of Iraq]. Many people are in despair after the war', he said, asking: 'If they thought that Saddam Hussain was bad, why did they hit the people? Why did they attack the country and not the ruler?' The family had followed the news from Iraq 'very closely' at the height of the crisis in spring 2003 but had since 'lost interest' because 'the soap opera is finished'. Awad described the situation in Palestine as 'very painful', asserting that the Israelis were 'attacking children and demolishing homes'. Bush, Blair and Israel's Prime Minister Ariel Sharon all had 'the same policies', he insisted. A week before, Israel had bombed Syria, causing outrage in the region. 'Now we're going to watch the Syrian soap opera, which has just started', joked Awad.

The family is Sunni Muslim but perhaps more by tradition than practice. Did they attend the local mosque, about one kilometre distant? '*Wallahi* ('By God'), it's a bit far away', said Awad. 'We know all the rules of Islam but we don't follow them all'. For him, being a Muslim meant 'to be honest, to believe in God and the afterlife; the most important thing is honesty'. The family vehemently rejects religious extremism. Fundamentalists 'do bad things', said Awad, citing as an example the murder in Amman in 2002 of Lawrence Foley, a US aid agency official (see p. 51). 'We don't like what these people are doing. We're not close to them in any way. Good Muslims don't do such things. They don't attack innocent people like Foley'.

Awad's week

In my second meeting with them, the Shubaikis outlined how they had spent the intervening week. It had been dominated by the annual migration to the winter pastures east of Qatrana. 'Although it's getting colder, the desert is still mostly barren', said Awad, 'but we did find a good place'. On the Sunday they had gone to the sheep market at Sahab, near Amman, and sold 13 animals for an average price of $85 each. The following day, using the proceeds of the sale, they drove down to Qatrana to buy eight tonnes of barley fodder. 'The rest of the day I just watched over the sheep here', said Awad. 'It was boring and tiring'. Later in the week they started transferring the sheep to the winter quarters. 'We started moving them with the truck on the Friday', he said. 'All the sheep except the young ones are already there and my brother Ali is looking after them right now'. Before they acquired their truck, the Shubaikis migrated on foot. 'We used to walk with the sheep, covering 10 or fifteen kilometres each day', recalled Awad. It was a delicate time of year for the sheep, he noted: 'They rarely fall sick but at this time of year some can suffer from lung illnesses caused by the dust and the change in the weather. Also, each year in November/December some of the sheep abort their lambs. It can be a big problem although so far this year we've had only one abortion, just before the move, and the mother survived'. Also on Friday, Awad and his father travelled to Amman to visit Awad's great uncle, who had suffered a heart attack and was recovering from an operation at the Hussain Medical Centre. The great uncle, who lives some fifteen kilometres from Ar-Rama, was 'getting on fine', said Awad. The following day Awad returned to Amman to buy fodder troughs and he, his father and brother Eid then spent the rest of the day with Ali and the sheep near Qatrana.

An unexpected problem during the week had been a demand for unpaid vehicle licence fees. 'We didn't pay the licence fees for the past three years because we understood that we were exempted', explained Awad. 'During the winter, Prince Ghazi visited the *bedu* and the *bedu* asked that their vehicles be exempted from licencing fees, and he responded positively. We saw a television report about this'. At the time, Prince Ghazi bin Muhammad, King Abdullah's cousin, was the king's adviser on tribal affairs although the position is now held by another cousin, Sharif Fawwaz Abdullah. 'A small car costs $280 per year, and we have three trucks and one car', said Awad. 'The demand was for $7,200. We replied that we simply didn't have the money'.

To mark my second visit, the Shubaikis prepared a delicious *mansaf*: a traditional *bedu* meal of rice and mutton dripping with sour milk, or *jameed*, eaten by hand from a large communal dish, with the sheep's head placed on top. The sheep had been specially slaughtered that day. A *mansaf* is more than just a meal. It is a manifestation of the generosity and hospitality that are highly valued in this culture. *Mansafs* are prepared for significant events such as weddings, funerals and rapprochements after disputes, cementing communal ties. 'You never eat the sheep's head or the eyes', noted Awad although, intriguingly, his father added, slightly mischievously: 'The eyes are tasty'.

The Shubaikis live as their forefathers have done since time immemorial, skilfully exploiting a marginal natural environment whose resources would otherwise go to waste. But times are changing. 'Living in a tent is very difficult, very tough', said Awad. 'Those with education go to the city and find a job in the public sector. In the city, life is easier. We've always lived like this, but education is changing our way of life. Only God knows what the future holds'.

Notes

1   Interviews with Awad ash-Shubaiki and his family were conducted in Ar-Rama on 6 October 2003 and 12 October 2003.
2   *Hashemite Kingdom of Jordan Statistical Yearbook 2003* (Amman: Department of Statistics).
3   www.mwi.gov.jo
4   Sahar Aloul, 'Water pumping increased to 46 hours per week this summer', *Jordan Times*, 19 April 2004.
5   *Middle East Economic Digest,* Vol. 48, No. 26, 25 June–1 July 2004, p. 5.
6   Interview with author, Amman, 29 June 2004. The interviewee requested anonymity.
7   *Middle East Economic Digest*, Vol. 48, No. 43, 22–28 October 2004, p. 23.
8   'Consultations on Red-Dead Canal feasibility study begin', *Jordan Times*, 7 September 2003.
9   *Middle East Economic Digest,* Vol. 48, No. 23, 4–10 June 2004, p. 18.

CHAPTER 10

Anisa Salim – Refugee

'I HAVE A COMPLAINT to make against the British government!' declared Anisa Salim, as the rickety train clattered slowly towards Mafraq across the dusty plateau north of Amman, the children laughing and dancing in the carriage. Her father-in-law had fought with the British army during the Second World War and had been killed during the battle of El Alamein in Egypt in 1943. 'They never found his body', she said. Her mother-in-law had received a monthly war widow's pension until her death in 1983. 'I went with my husband to the British Embassy in 1996 and explained that my husband was ill and unemployed', she said. 'We told them, "His father used to work for you in the army, so my husband deserves some assistance". They refused to help. They said that because his mother had died, the matter was finished. What could I do but accept that? I wanted to call the BBC so that my story could be heard in the UK'.[1]

I had arranged to interview the president of Aal Al-Bayt University, near the northern town of Mafraq, and had decided to travel there on the old Hejaz Railway – principal target of Lawrence's guerrilla campaign during the First World War. It was a bright, sunny July morning. At Amman station, which the Turks built solidly of limestone with a gabled roof at a time when Amman was just a village, a high-spirited crowd of women and children were milling on the platform. A motley collection of historic passenger and freight wagons stood in the sidings. More, plus Ottoman-era steam locomotives, were under repair in the nearby engineering sheds. Occasionally, modern diesel engines, painted bright orange or yellow, eased gingerly past the throng, their bells clanging to clear excited children off the tracks. Thrice daily, freight trains run from Amman to Damascus. Twice a week, on Mondays and Tuesdays, passenger trains operate, stopping at Zarqa and Mafraq before crossing into Syria and halting at Dera'a. There, they connect with another train destined for the Syrian capital. A one-way ticket costs $3.50. The trains run at only 25–35 kilometres per hour and take about six hours to cover the 222 kilometres between the Jordanian and Syrian capitals – but most of the passengers go by train for the sheer fun of it. In summer, during the school holidays, each train carries 100–200 passengers, compared with only 15-20 in winter.

Our train, hauled by an orange Caterpillar diesel engine, departs with a shudder at 8.15, sounding its hooter almost triumphantly. The children clap in excitement and some of the young girls ululate. The dilapidated wooden carriages are two-tone, cream above brown, with curved roofs. At each end are observation platforms with iron lattice-work gates. Within, the walls and ceilings are thinly veneered in nut-brown wood. Benches, their dark blue plastic upholstering in places torn and split, run the length of each wall. Ventilation comes from small sliding windows, eighteen per carriage. The passengers in my carriage, all women and children, comprise several family groups. All but one of the women, including Anisa, are in *hijab* – conservative Islamic garb of headscarf and long gown. Several of the older girls take care of babies. One group spreads a duvet on the worn reddish-pink lino floor, on which the children sit. A boy, perhaps ten years old, photographs them. Everyone chats and laughs excitedly. As we trundle towards Zarqa at about 15 kilometres per hour, along the bed of a winding, limestone-walled valley with irrigated fields and occasional eucalyptus trees, a cassette-player is turned on and blares rhythmic Arabic music. Two girls, Tufla and Fatat, both young teenagers, perform belly dances, swaying their hips while the onlookers clap in time and shout encouragement. We pass a flock of sheep. Dogs run alongside barking. Dust wafts in through the open windows. We enter a tunnel and the carriage is thrust into darkness, prompting the children to shriek with delight.

Anisa, wearing a cream headscarf and a body-length grey *thawb*, or gown, is plump with large brown eyes, full eyebrows and a round, tanned face; she looks younger than her 44 years. She is sitting opposite me and makes contact by offering me coffee from a vacuum flask. 'Write about our difficult life here!', she requests earnestly. At Zarqa station, another quaint Ottoman structure with gabled roof and a circular stone water tower, more passengers board, filling my carriage to capacity. North of Zarqa, the train picks up speed to about 45 kilometres per hour, swaying sometimes alarmingly as it traverses the undulating, arid plateau. The next stop is Samra, its small blockhouse of a station built of black basalt. We eventually reach Mafraq at 10.30, having covered the 61 kilometres from Amman at an average speed of 27 kilometres per hour. Most of the passengers alight here. They will enjoy a picnic in gardens beside the station before returning to Amman, exhausted, on an evening train.

The narrow-gauge Hejaz Railway, stretching 1,320 kilometres from Damascus to Medina, was completed in 1908. Lawrence's campaign badly damaged the line and attempts at refurbishment have been sporadic. The Amman–Damascus section is the only part that still functions although a refurbished section of its track north and south of Ma'an, between Al-Hasa and Batn al-Ghul, was incorporated in a new railway, opened in 1972, linking phosphate mines near Al-Hasa to the port at Aqaba. There are plans to upgrade the line between Amman and Damascus, and for a new line between Amman and its Queen Alia International Airport which would use refurbished historic carriages, including restaurant cars. The problem is funding. 'We are talking about hundreds of millions of dollars', said Abul Feilat Abdul Razzaq, director-general of Hejaz Jordan Railways. 'For a state like Jordan, it's not easy to invest in railways. The country has many more urgent needs'.[2] Also mooted is a project to bring tourists from Aqaba to Lawrence and Faisal's old base in Wadi Rum, via a new spur from the Aqaba–Al-Hasa phosphates railway. 'We're going to bring all the old Turkish-era steam engines down there', enthused King Abdullah. 'The tourists will be "attacked" by the local Sha'alan tribe, and then whisked away for lunch in Wadi Rum'.[3]

Jabal Hussain

Anisa Jamal al-Hajj Salim lives in the Jabal Hussain refugee camp in central Amman. 'Camp' is a misnomer. It started as a tented camp in 1948 but, as in other Palestinian camps in the region, the tents were replaced by modest concrete-framed breeze-block dwellings. At first, they were single-storey but many were later extended to have two or even three storeys. The camp now forms an integral part of the city and is indistinguishable from the adjacent quarters. Through its centre runs Ain Jalut Street, a busy thoroughfare lined with shops and workshops, dividing the camp into upper and lower districts. In all, the camp has one hundred streets, each identified by a number. Anisa's modest house in the upper part of the camp is divided into ground and first-floor apartments. She lives on the first floor, which is reached from the street by an outside concrete stairway. The walls of her tile-floored living room are two-tone, a white layer above cream. It is lined on three sides by ornate wooden settees, upholstered in black with elaborately embroidered silver leaf patterns. In one corner, the settees converge on a wooden shelving unit displaying framed photos of her children. In the centre of the room, within easy reach of the settees, a low coffee table carries two glass ashtrays and an arrangement of pink, red and white imitation roses. A black-and-white photo of Anisa's late father hangs above one of the settees. Adjacent is a photo, also black-and-white, of her husband, also deceased, in the camouflage uniform of the Syrian-backed Palestinian guerrilla group *As-Sa'iqa* ('Thunderbolt'). A small wooden table, set against the fourth wall, bears three arrangements of imitation flowers, each set in a wicker basket, and a teddy bear wearing a hat and clutching a round wicker basket between his outstretched arms. Above hangs a wooden clock with a short pendulum.

Anisa's family originates from the ancient port of Akka (Acre), across the bay from Haifa in what is now northern Israel. With the Arab defeat in the 1947–48 war, when Zionist forces ethnically cleansed Akka of its Palestinians, part of her family took refuge in the southern Lebanese port town of Sidon. Her parents, however, went initially to Syria before moving first to the Jabal Hussain camp and then, in 1954, to the northern Jordanian town of Irbid. Her father died in 1962 and the following year she went with her mother and two sisters to live with her mother's parents in Sidon. Her mother remarried and in 1967 they moved to Beirut to live with her stepfather, also a Palestinian from Akka. They lived in the city-centre, not in a refugee camp, and until she was 17 Anisa attended a school run by the UN Relief and Works Agency for Palestine refugees (UNRWA). In 1975 she married Hassan Muhammad Jabarkanji, a Palestinian whose family came from Jaffa. 'He had a Turkish name', she explained. 'One of his forebears ran a munitions store in Jaffa for the Ottoman army'. It was an arranged marriage. 'It was during the civil war in Lebanon and everyone wanted to marry off their daughters', she said. 'He was visiting from Kuwait, where he lived and worked, and he was well off. I didn't marry him because I loved him. It was arranged by my family. But I lived with him my whole life and I was happy. He was a good man'. They had six children, all boys: Adib, now 27, Jamal (25), Usama (23), Muhammad (19), Badr (14) and Abdulrahman (9). The four younger sons live with their mother in the second floor apartment. Usama is unemployed and still single. Muhammad works in a factory producing office furniture. Badr and Abdulrahman (nicknamed Abboud) are both at school. Although her marriage was arranged, Anisa is not against marriages based on love. 'My son Jamal announced that he wanted to marry his cousin – the daughter of his father's brother – because he loved her', she related. Adib wanted to marry her sister's daughter, not from love but because he considered her a suitable bride. 'I didn't object in either case', said Anis. Until recently, Adib, a mechanic, lived with his wife, Neveen, in the ground floor apartment of Anisa's house. He has just found work in Umm al-Qaiwan, one of the United Arab Emirates, and Neveen will join him there soon. Jamal, also a mechanic, lives nearby with his wife Suhair.

Kuwait

After marrying, Anisa joined her husband in Kuwait, where he worked as a driver for a construction company. Palestinian leader Yasser Arafat's support for Saddam Hussain during the 1990–91 Kuwait crisis caused a backlash against Palestinians in the Gulf state. After the Iraqi defeat, they were expelled *en masse*. The majority, numbering up to 400,000 and Anisa amongst them, held Jordanian passports (see p. 35). Like other foreigners, Palestinians in Kuwait were denied Kuwaiti nationality and often complained of discrimination. She nevertheless has fond memories of Kuwait. 'I lived there for 16 years', she said. 'It was very pleasant. It was calm. We lived a quiet life and no-one caused us any problems. The Kuwaitis are nice people. We weren't close to them during the occupation, but I'm talking about when I was there. I was happy'. Palestinians in Jordan face a degree of discrimination, albeit often subtle (see p. 25), but Anisa has been unaffected. 'We don't face discrimination here', she insisted. 'Everything is normal'.

In July 1990 – just weeks before the Iraqi invasion – Anisa travelled to Jordan to visit her relatives, notably her brother-in-law, who lives in the Jabal Hussain camp, and her two sisters, Nuha, now aged 40, who is married and lives in Irbid, and Wahiba, 50, who is also married and lives in Amman's Marka district. 'Because of the war, we had to stay here', she explained. 'The situation in Kuwait was unsettled and dangerous and my husband's parents urged us to move here and register the children in schools here. As soon as they opened the border, in October 1990, during the occupation, I returned to Kuwait to collect our belongings. My husband joined me in Amman early in 1991, just three days before the fighting started'. For the first three years they lived in the Tababour district, moving to Jabal Hussain in 1994 in order to be near her husband's brother at a time when her husband was gravely ill (see below). They bought the house – then just single-storey – using $13,000 that her husband received from the United Nations fund established to compensate victims of Iraq's aggression against Kuwait. In 1998 they added the second floor. 'We paid $11,000 for the house and it's now worth $25,000', said Anisa, adding: 'I never lived in a camp in Lebanon and I never wanted to live in a camp here. But I had to come here because of my relatives'. Was it unusual in Jabal Hussain for residents to own their properties? 'We are very normal', Anisa replied. 'Most people here own their houses'. The compensation payment was also used to pay for the marriages of her sons Adib and Jamal. 'We gave $1,400 to the father of Adib's wife, in Irbid', said Anisa. In the case of Jamal's wife, the *mahr* was in kind: 'We met all her wedding costs, mainly her jewellery and clothes'. Shortly after returning from Kuwait, her husband fell seriously ill. 'He had two heart attacks, both in 1991', related Anisa. 'Until his death in December 2000 he was in and out of hospital. He had difficulty breathing and he couldn't work'. The family's finances were stretched to the limit. 'My two eldest sons, then aged 14 and 16, had to leave school to earn money', she said. 'They worked as mechanics'. Her voice trembling, she sighed: 'My husband's death was a great loss. We were very close, and he and the children were also close. He was the head of the household and I had small children. Since then I've had to carry all the responsibility. There are no daughters and I have to do all the work in the house and pay all the bills'. Had she entered any new relationships with men since her husband's death? 'No. My sons are my life', she replied.

As a child in Lebanon Anisa had worked in a textiles factory. After her husband's death, she borrowed $7,800 from Jordan's Industrial Development Bank and bought a computerised weaving machine, hoping that she might boost the family's finances by making and selling clothes. 'It didn't work out', she said ruefully. 'Eventually I sold the machine for $350'. She then started making small wicker baskets and boxes, painted and decorated with imitation flowers and brightly coloured ribbons, which she sells as gifts and ornaments. By way of example, she pointed to the flower arrangements and teddy bear on the table below the clock. As a gift, she kindly presented me with another *ensemble*, created with Christmas in mind: a heart-shaped wicker box sporting red ribbons and a plastic gold bell. 'Now I do this for a living. People know about my work and come round when they want to buy one', she explained. 'I sell them for $13 each. In addition, she receives money from her sons. As UNRWA-registered refugees, Anisa and her family are eligible in principle for assistance from the agency but its rules mean that no help is actually forthcoming. Aid is available only to families without a bread-winner and in which the eldest son is under eighteen years old. Widows qualify for assistance only if their eldest sons aged over eighteen are married. 'Two years before my son was eighteen we presented all the relevant papers to UNRWA and we received aid for two years', explained Anisa. 'They used to give us flour, sugar and rice and $10 per person every three months. As a widow, I'm entitled to help but I have two unmarried sons aged over eighteen so I can't receive aid until they're married'. The problem is that by the time they marry, her two youngest sons will be eighteen. In respect of each of these latter, however, Anisa receives $32 per month in alms from a local religious charity, Al-Aboura. While Adib and his wife occupy the ground floor apartment, one room is rented for $70 per month to a couple with two children. In recent months, however, the tenants had failed to pay, forcing her to resort to legal action. The family spends more than it earns and Anisa meets the shortfall through personal loans from relatives. 'I do everything through loans, so I'm always in debt', she said, 'but somehow we manage'.

Struggle

Anisa's week, centred on her family and the endless struggle to make ends meet, had been typical, she said. On the Monday she had visited her niece, Haneen, at the Hussain Medical Centre in west Amman. 'She's only 14 and has cancer in her lymph glands', she sighed. 'She's been there for two months now'. She is full of praise for the Centre, declaring: 'It's like hospitals abroad, because the king himself oversees it'. After visiting her niece, Anisa joined neighbours and relatives in the street to drink tea, chat and enjoy the coolness. 'It's been very hot and we have no verandas or balconies, so I go downstairs and sit with my in-laws', she said. 'All the houses are joined together and the people here all know each other. We talked about everything! What we'd done, where we'd been. We talked about ourselves'. The day before, 5 October 2003, the Israelis had bombed an alleged Palestinian training camp near Damascus. Elsewhere in the region during the week, the *intifada* had continued in Palestine and the insurgency in Iraq had intensified. For Anisa, however, daily chores and worries leave little space for wider concerns. 'I only notice the really important things, and I get upset only when something really big happens', she explained, adding: 'I watch television very little'.

The next morning she went to the Qasr al-Adl (Palace of Justice; see p. 191) to obtain an order against her downstairs tenant. After non-compliance with three such orders, which are issued on application, without a hearing before a judge, a litigant can obtain judgment against a debtor. 'I obtained the first one in July but he didn't pay', said Anisa. 'He's in work. It's just because he's a bad man. The rent is $70 per month and it includes the water and electricity. He owes $500. But his wife is very nice and she's embarrassed by the situation. Because of her, I'm reluctant to make problems'.

From the Palace of Justice, Anisa went to the ministry of labour, near the parliament building in the Abdali district. 'I heard a rumour that they were distributing money as further compensation for the Kuwait crisis', she explained. 'But in fact nothing of the sort was happening'. In the early afternoon she met officials from the Al-Aboura charity, which subsidises her two sons. 'They told me that my boys had to attend meetings there on Fridays', she related. 'But I knew they didn't want to because they already attend the Mukhayim al-Hussain ('Hussain Camp') youth club on Fridays. So the Al-Aboura meeting upset me'. She returned home to prepare lunch for her sons and then walked in the camp and the adjacent Nujha district looking for some imitation roses to decorate her wicker creations. 'I found some, and then visited my neighbour to show them to her. She suggested that we go and visit another neighbour who was ill', continued Anisa. 'Afterwards, I returned home and told my sons about the Al-Aboura situation. They were very upset'. While speaking with them she suffered chest pains. 'I don't think it's a heart problem', she said. 'Maybe it was just the muscles in that area'. During the day, two bills arrived, for the electricity and the telephone, sapping her morale. 'Where am I going to find the money to pay them?' she asked. At about 10.30 she made dinner for the children before retiring to bed at midnight. 'Normally I get up at around 6.00 in the morning and go to bed at midnight or 12.30', she added. 'Usually I don't sleep during the day'. On the Wednesday she woke at 6.30 and prayed. 'Then I called my son who lives in Umm al-Qaiwan to congratulate him as it was his 27th birthday', she said. At 11.00 her son, Jamal, visited. 'He told me that he had a pain in his neck and had gone to the doctor about it', she related. 'The doctor said it was probably the result of the strong wind that had been blowing, and he gave him some powerful medicine. I rubbed some cream on his neck'. After he had left, Anisa worked on her boxes, recalling: 'I didn't stop until late in the evening. I made two and painted and then decorated two others'. She went to bed at 12.30.

Mahshi

After waking at 6.30 the next morning, Anisa made breakfast, washed the dishes and cleaned and tidied the house. She then went to the local market to buy vegetables with which to make *mahshi* – baked aubergines and squashes stuffed with rice. While the meal was cooking she washed clothes. 'I do this in two tubs', she noted. 'I don't have an automatic washing machine'. She then worked on her wicker baskets until her 4-year-old grandson visited. 'He said he had a toothache', recounted Anisa. 'My sons and grandsons all come to me with their aches and pains! I just tell them to go to the doctor'. She sat outside the house chatting with her relatives – including her son, Jamal, and his family – until 12.30. Before going to bed, she surfed the internet for half an hour. 'I bought the computer for the children', she noted. 'I don't have satellite television but I'm fascinated by the computer'.

On Friday – the Muslim day of rest – Anisa woke at 5.30 and prayed. 'For the first time in ages I then went back to bed and slept until 9.00', she recalled. Refreshed, she went to the market to buy minced beef to make *kufta* (deep-fried meat balls seasoned with chopped parsley). While the *kufta* was in the oven she made two more basket *ensembles*. 'In the evening, I went down and sat with the neighbours', she said. On the Saturday she woke again at 5.30, sent her son Abdulrahman to school, visited the post office to collect mail and went on to Abdulrahman's school to inform his teachers about the worrying situation with the Al-Aboura charity. Her son Badr attends the local UNRWA school. Abdulrahman had studied there for three years but had then moved to a private school, whose costs are met by Al-Aboura. 'I changed the school because he was not doing so well', explained Anisa. Together with her son, Jamal's, wife, Suhair, she then paid a visit to Suhair's sister, Hind, who lives in the nearby Marka district. Afterwards, Anisa and Suhair went to the Raghadan bus terminal in the old centre of Amman. 'Suhair wanted to buy some clothing for Jamal and there are stalls at the bus station that sell things cheaply', she explained. 'I bought some trousers and a shirt for $8.50 for my son Muhammad, but Suhair couldn't find anything suitable for her husband'. After accompanying Suhair to her house, Anisa went home to help Abdulrahman with his homework, buying more decorative materials for her basket-work *en route*. I met Anisa the following morning. That day, a Saturday, she planned to visit her mother, who lives with Anisa's sister, Wahiba, in Amman. From there, she would go to the Hussain Medical Centre to pay another visit to her niece, Haneen.

By any measure, Anisa's life has not been easy. She has suffered the upheaval of moves from Jordan to Lebanon, to Kuwait and back to Jordan. Her husband, the family's sole breadwinner, died after a long and incapacitating illness. She is the head of a family in a part of the world where that role is normally reserved for men. The gnawing worry of financial insecurity pervades, but this resourceful woman has neither yielded to despair nor allowed her spirit to be poisoned by bitterness. If Israelis or Britons wish to know the suffering they caused in 1948, respectively by stealing Palestine from its rightful owners and by allowing the theft, they need look no further than Anisa Salim – and even her situation is far better than that of many other Palestinians. 'I've worked and struggled all my life, ever since I was a small child', concluded Anisa. 'As long as I live, it will continue like that. I just have to keep going'.

Notes

1   Interviews with Anisa Salim were conducted on the Hejaz Railway on 24 July 2003 and in Amman on 6 October 2003 and 12 October 2003.
2   Interview with author, Amman, 24 February 2003.
3   Interview with author, Amman, 29 June 2004.

PART III

Institutions

CHAPTER 11

The 'Stratified Elite': The Royal Family and the Royal Court

THERE'S NO MISTAKING the location of Al-Maqar ('The Headquarters') - the complex of palaces and Royal Court offices within a 40-hectare compound on Jabal al-Hussain, near the old Hejaz Railway station and the Roman amphitheatre in central Amman. By its main entrance stands a 126-metre high flagpole sporting a 60-metre by 30-metre Jordanian flag. Erected in 2003, it is plainly visible from any high point in the kingdom's capital. Most cities grow concentrically, from a historic heart, their various districts differentiated by the contrasting architectural styles and street patterns of different eras. Amman's history was unique. In early 1948, before the flood of Palestinian refugees, it had only 50,000 people. By October 1950 there were 120,000. Amman sprawls across its hills and valleys, its monotony and blandness hindering the visitor from creating his personal mental map of the town. The flag is a welcome landmark. But there is a problem. In high winds, it flaps so violently that it disturbs nearby residents. 'In very windy weather we bring it down because there were complaints that it made quite a bit of noise', said Samir ar-Rifa'i, minister of the Royal Court.[1]

After arriving in Amman in March 1921, Prince Abdullah lived initially in a modest, Ottoman-style house opposite the amphitheatre. In 1923 work started on his Raghadan Palace on the edge of a plateau, Jabal Tahtour ('Pile of Rocks Mountain', later renamed Jabal al-Hussain), overlooking the old town. Chosen by the prince, the name derives from the verb *raghuda*, meaning 'to be or become pleasant, comfortable or easy'. Built of honey-coloured stone from the southern town of Ma'an – Abdullah's first base in Transjordan – and with coloured glass windows resembling those of the Al-Aqsa Mosque in Jerusalem, Raghadan, 'modest but dignified',[2] was completed in 1927. Two smaller palaces were built in the compound in the 1930s: Al-Ma'wa ('The Sanctuary'); and Al-Qasr as-Saghir ('The Small Palace'). In 1950 work started on the much larger Basman Palace, which was intended as a guesthouse for visiting dignitaries but also contained offices for the Court and a private wing for King Abdullah. In the early 1950s Basman became the main residence of King Hussain but in the mid-1970s he moved to the Hashimiya Palace, in the Hummar district of north-west Amman, and Basman became an office complex for the Court. The compound also includes the Nadwa ('Council') Palace, which was built as the residence of King Abdullah's second son, Nayef, and where King Hussain and Queen Noor lived for some time before moving to their final home, the Bab as-Salam Palace (see p. 85). Today it functions as a guest palace. Another feature is the Royal Cemetery, where King Abdullah I, King Talal and King Hussain were laid to rest, along with other family members, tribal leaders and several prime ministers.

The Royal Court, or Diwan al-Malaki, is 'the necessary political and administrative link between His Majesty the King and the Central Government, the Armed Forces and the Security Forces', explains King Abdullah's website[3]. 'It also provides a vital link between the King and the Jordanian people'. Minister Ar-Rifa'i, a 38-year-old from Amman who attended high school in the United States, studied as an undergraduate at Harvard and holds an M. Phil. from Cambridge, confirmed that his job was 'to liaise between the Court, His Majesty and the government'.[4] In Jordan's largely tribal society, individuals seek assistance or redress through direct, personal appeals to their shaikhs. The king functions as a paramount shaikh and is expected to be accessible to his subjects, with the Royal Court as the interface. 'It's a place that Jordanians consider their home', explained Ar-Rifa'i, scion of one of the kingdom's leading political families, both of his grandfathers and his father having served as prime ministers. 'In Arabic, we say it's the *Bait al-Urdunyeen* ('Home of the Jordanians'). Its doors are open to all Jordanians. People who have any grievance with any institution and feel that it cannot be resolved directly come to His Majesty, who is considered the father of Jordanians. They come for his intervention'. Were there many such approaches? 'Thousands!' exclaimed Ar-Rifa'i. 'We get the personal, the personal support, people criticising a minister, an institution, an NGO, a person who has some ideas he believes should be implemented. Many people come to the gates [in person]. Many send letters. And the follow-up is serious. We pride ourselves that every letter is answered – positively or negatively, because some of the requests are totally unrealistic!'

The Court, which had a government-sourced budget of $32.2 million in 2002,[5] is 'populated by a stratified elite including members of the extended Hashemite dynasty itself, notable families and tribal leaders', observed Milton-Edwards and Hinchcliffe.[6] Ar-Rifa'i, as the Minister – which is not a government position – holds the highest office in the Court's administrative structure. The Chief Chamberlain, Prince Ra'ad bin Zeid, the son of the first King Abdullah's youngest brother, Zeid, and the Private Chamberlain, Prince Ali bin Nayef, King Hussain's cousin, are responsible for the royal family's private affairs. The Keeper of the Privy Purse, Munir ad-Durra, is the king's chief financial officer. A battery of advisers, each with his own office, assists in the development of policy initiatives. Those with specific areas of responsibility comprise the Director of the General Intelligence Department, General Sa'ad Khair, who is Adviser on Security Issues and Rapporteur of the National Security Council, an advisory body on security matters with offices in the Royal Court; Shaikh Izzedin al-Khattab al-Tamimi, Adviser for Islamic Affairs; Fawwaz Zaben Abdullah, Adviser on Tribal Affairs; Issam Rawabdeh, Adviser for Legal Affairs; Sima Bahous, Media Adviser; Ali Fazza, Press Adviser; the king's Personal Envoy and Private Adviser, Prince Ghazi bin Muhammad, the monarch's cousin; and the king's Special Adviser, Yousef ad-Dalabeeh. Four other advisers do not have specific portfolios: Akel Biltaji (see p. 128), Yousef al-Malkawi, Tahseen Shurdum and Farouq Qasrawi.

The secretary-general, Yousef al-Esawi, oversees a series of specialist departments, each with units responsible for particular aspects of their department's work. A protocol division, headed by Al-Sharif Muhammad al-Luheimaq, supervises the king's daily work programme, ranging from audiences to state occasions and trips abroad. A finance division is headed by Rosy Boulad, a policy co-ordination division (formed in June 2004) by Abdullah Woriekat, an economic and development division by Muhammad ar-Rawashdah and a communications and information division by Sima Bahous. Rania Atallah is chief of staff at Queen Rania's office. In all, the Court has an operational staff of some 300 plus the same number of support personnel such as gardeners and cleaners. 'It's our job to ensure that His Majesty's programmes reflect the themes that he wants to pursue', said Ar-Rifa'i. 'We meet regularly to discuss his daily and monthly pro-grammes, his trip programmes and post-event programmes'.[7] While the Royal Court as a whole is 'His Majesty's office', explained Ar-Rifa'i, 'all the members of the royal family function under the Court's umbrella'. The leading royals all have offices in the Court although most are modest. The exceptions are those of the two most important royals after the monarch, Queen Rania and, until November 2004 (see p. 166), Prince Hamzah, which have their own specialised departments.

Until November 2003, when King Abdullah abolished the position, the chief of the Royal Court was the *Diwan's* most powerful official and the third-ranking official in the kingdom, after the king and prime minister. The post was 'the traditional training ground for future prime ministers'.[8] Indeed, chiefs of the court often wielded 'more political clout than the prime minister'.[9] The king's official web site explains blandly that the post was abolished 'in line with His Majesty's vision of modernization and development'. An inevitable result, however, was to stamp Abdullah's authority over the Court even more firmly. 'As in all Courts, power and influence vary with the individual standing of the senior courtiers at any one time', note Milton-Edwards and Hinchcliffe,[10] adding that this was especially so with the chief of the Royal Court, his influence depending 'almost entirely on the degree of his personal rapport with the King'. It appears that a new 'training ground for prime ministers' may now be the post of Royal Court minister. Faisal al-Fayez, who had been Royal Court Minister since March 2003 and before that the Court's chief of protocol, was appointed premier in October 2003.

Within weeks of succeeding to the throne in February 1999, Abdullah made important personnel changes at the Court, replacing officials deemed close to the now ex-Crown Prince Hassan with longstanding loyalists of his father. Abdelkarim al-Kabariti, who had been prime minister in 1996–97, was appointed as chief of the Court in place of Jawad Anani. Abdullah Touqan was named as scientific adviser and assistant to Prince Talal, the NSC's office director. Samir ar-Rifa'i became the court's secretary-general. Adnan Abu Odeh, who had been chief of the royal court in the early 1990s and subsequently a political adviser to King Hussain, was re-appointed as political adviser, while Nabil Ammari, Planning Minister in the outgoing government of Fayez Tarawneh, became economic adviser.

The real government?

The king is the undisputed centre of power in Jordan and, regardless of its official role as an advisory body and a link between the monarch and the government, the Royal Court has sometimes acted as a quasi-government. 'Historically, [the Royal Court] has played a more important role in government than its official position might indicate', observed Milton-Edwards and Hinchcliffe. 'The Royal Court is much more than an "errand boy" between ruler and ruled'.[11] The reality is that Jordanian governments have relatively little power. Their key role is to implement policy initiatives that come from the king, advised and assisted by the Royal Court. 'It is this small group of individuals [in the Court] that advises the King and allows him the opportunity to sound out particular strategies or programmes before the fait accompli of policy is presented to the Jordanian people, via the Council of Ministers and Parliament, for rubber stamping', Milton-Edwards and Hinchcliffe noted. 'It is, therefore, this small group along with their King who have some responsibility for both the successes and failures of Jordanian policy'.[12] Relations between governments and the Court have sometimes been uneasy, and even tense, as they have jockeyed for influence. This was particularly so under King Hussain, whose rule was highly personalised and whose closest courtiers carried far more sway with him than some prime ministers. That said, the Court's overall influence with Hussain waned in the final decade of his reign. 'As [he] grew in political stature and authority the importance of individuals within the Royal Court declined', Milton-Edwards and Hinchcliffe wrote. 'By the 1990s they were on the whole courtiers rather than influential advisers'.[13] The king became increasingly impatient with those who did not share his views and, fearful of being rebuffed, even his oldest and most trusted advisers kept a prudent distance. By the early 1990s Hussain's advisers were 'little more than sycophantic courtiers reminiscent of the court of King Henry VIII rather than a twentieth century monarchy'.[14]

At the outset of Abdullah's reign, it appeared that little had changed. His first Royal Court chief, Abdelkarim al-Kabariti, was widely thought to be much more influential than his first prime minister, Abdur Rauf ar-Rawabdah, and the two were often at loggerheads. Reporting Al-Kabariti's replacement in January 2000 by Fayez Tarawneh, the *Jordan Times* commented that it had come 'after months of rivalry' between Al-Kabariti and Ar-Rawabdah and was expected 'to ring in a new era of harmony as Tarawneh is said to enjoy excellent working relations with Rawabdeh'.[15] But Abdullah has done more than just juggle the cast. As well as abolishing the Court's traditional highest post, he has reformed its structures and systematised its procedures. While this has been in line with his declared commitment to institution-building, it has also had the effect of limiting the Court's potential as an independent power centre. Speaking of his schedule of audiences, he disclosed: 'At the beginning, there was no structure. So, most of the week was taken up having people complain. I had to get a system in that cut down the time you have to tell your problems. Now, there's a system'.[16] He nevertheless spends 'close to 60–70 per cent' of an average week on audiences. He commented that people 'feel that their problems or grievances can only be solved by the king, which was great in my father's time, when it was a patriarchal society. Today [we're moving] more towards institution-building. The reason they come to me is because institutions are not yet strong enough'.

Samir ar-Rifa'i agreed that the Court in the past had sometimes acted as a parallel government but he stressed that King Abdullah strongly opposed any such duplication of responsibilities. 'His Majesty doesn't believe in parallel systems and he was unhappy when the Royal Court played that role', he said. 'His Majesty believes that each area needs to be covered by the entity in charge of it'.[17] The Court develops and formalises the king's initiatives, he explained. 'Those that need to go to the government are sent to the government. Those that don't need the government's involvement are undertaken on a private basis by the Royal Court. We don't micro-manage what the government does. This is the Court that His Majesty wants'. The Royal Court nevertheless continues to involve itself directly in some initiatives that might more obviously fall within the government's purview. It is playing a key role, for example, in King Abdullah's project to combat unemployment through training programmes run by the armed forces and private sector, which does not involve the government (see Chapter 4).

Quite apart from its formal functions, the Diwan acts as an important means of bolstering the monarchy's legitimacy by disseminating its policies throughout society. Writing of King Hussain's reign, Milton-Edwards and Hinchcliffe noted: 'With a small population, limited territory and notions of national identity constructed around the theme of tribe, family and clan, the officials of the Diwan were able to represent the monarch's policy directly back to their localised spheres of power and use this in turn to keep the King in touch with the "grassroots"'.[18] This aspect of the Court's role continues under King Abdullah. 'One of my jobs is to see members of society, political groups and so on', explained Ar-Rifa'i. 'They sit down and talk extremely openly and honestly and critically. They feel able to do this, and they want His Majesty to hear what they have to say'.[19]

Another, more prosaic, function of the Royal Court has been to act as a repository for 'senior politicians (or fringe members of the Hashemite family) whose political shelf life [has] expired and who [can] enjoy a well deserved semi-retirement in an important sounding position but with no real authority'.[20]

King Abdullah

King Abdullah, no less than his forebears, stands at the very heart of the Jordanian state. Articles 28–40 of the Constitution affirm that the monarch appoints the prime minister, the members and speaker of parliament's upper house, judges and other senior military and civil service officials; that he ratifies and promulgates laws, commands the armed forces, declares war, concludes peace and ratifies treaties; that he convenes and opens parliamentary sessions and may adjourn them; that he may dissolve the legislature, and orders and may postpone elections; and that his decisions may be overruled only by a two-thirds majority of a joint session of the two houses of parliament. Article 30 stipulates: 'The King is the Head of State and is immune from any liability and responsibility'. With such powers at their kings' disposal, it is fortunate indeed for Jordanians that none of their monarchs have been cruel or vicious dictators.

Born in Amman on 30 January 1962, Abdullah is the eldest son of King Hussain and his British second wife, Antoinette (Toni) Gardiner, who converted to Islam and took the name Muna al-Hussain. Princess Muna was the daughter of Lieutenant-Colonel Walker Gardiner of the British Royal Engineers, who was advising the Jordanian government on water conservation. 'Toni was a vivacious outdoors girl with simple tastes and no intellectual pretensions', observed King Hussain's biographer, Roland Dallas. 'She was pretty, charming and the same height as the king. Like Hussain, she enjoyed riding, swimming, dancing and parties'. When introduced to King Hussain, at a fancy-dress party in 1961, she commented: 'You look pretty scruffy, your majesty!'[21] The marriage ended in divorce in 1972, the same year that Hussain met and fell deeply in love with Alia Toukan, a member of a prominent Salt family with strong Palestinian ties, who became his third wife.

Abdullah's primary education started at Amman's Islamic Educational College and continued at St Edmund's School in Hindhead, in the southern English county of Surrey. From there he went on to Eaglebrook School and Deerfield Academy, both in Deerfield, Massachusetts.[22] The king has particularly fond memories of his three years at Deerfield, from grades 10 to 12, describing them as 'my happiest time'.[23] Having completed his secondary education he returned to the United Kingdom in 1980 to attend the Royal Military Academy at Sandhurst, gaining a commission as a second lieutenant the following year. He was then appointed as a reconnaissance troop leader in the 13th/18th Battalion of the British army's Royal Hussars, seeing service both in England and the then West Germany. 'My term in the British Army was wonderful', King Abdullah told me, adding that he was particularly appreciative of his sergeant, a down-to-earth northerner. 'He didn't give a hoot who I was', he recalled. 'I think I was very lucky to have a sergeant that put me in the right direction'.[24] Twenty years later, in 2003, Queen Elizabeth invited him to become colonel-in-chief of the Light Dragoons, formed from a 1992 amalgamation of the 13th/18th Royal Hussars with the 15th/19th King's Royal Hussars. Abdullah rounded off his period in England in 1982 with a year's course in Middle Eastern affairs at Oxford University's Pembroke College.

Returning to Jordan, Abdullah served with the armoured branch of the armed forces, winning promotion to first lieutenant and then captain and in 1985 attending the Armoured Officers Advanced Course at the US Army's Fort Knox Armor School in Kentucky. In 1986–87 he served with the air force's Helicopter Anti-Tank Wing, gaining his wings and becoming a qualified Cobra helicopter attack pilot. The king's bland official curriculum vitae records that in 1987–88 he took a one-year course at Georgetown University's School of Foreign Service in Washington but it does not say why. 'The unhappiest time of my life was probably in the late 1980s', he said. 'It happens to most career officers when they reach the rank of captain or major. Was I going to put up with all the nonsense that bureaucracies and armies have, where you feel you're not making an impact?'[25] In addition, he was being harassed by senior officers who apparently feared him as a potential threat to their influence with King Hussain. 'There were people around my father who were making life extremely difficult for me', he recalled. 'Through the army, they were making life miserable for my soldiers by holding inspections of my particular company more than any other in the army. I think there were senior generals that thought I was an upcoming threat. I was so fed up with the problems I was facing. As a result, I went to the US for a year because I wanted to make a decision whether or not I was going to stick it out in the armed forces'.

Stick it out he did, relating: 'When I came back, a member of the family asked: "Are you going to give those guys the satisfaction?" I'll never forget that statement, and I resolved to persist'. He was promoted to major in 1990 and during that year returned to England to attend the Royal Staff College at Camberley in Surrey. In the build-up to the 1990–91 Kuwait crisis, he was astonished to receive call-up papers from the British army, issued in error. 'I had to call them to say, "you know, guys, I'm now a major in the Jordanian army, and I'm maybe not the right person to lead a squadron or whatever into Iraq"', he laughed.[26] But the harassment continued. 'On battalion testing there were senior generals coming to say, "look, the attack tomorrow is going to come from the right". And then another would come six hours later and say, "actually, it'll come from the left"', recalled King Abdullah. 'They could see that one day I might make it to chief of staff. Also, corruption was a major problem in the army, and they didn't like me [reporting this] to His Majesty [King Hussain]'.

Abdullah may have informed his father of the corruption but he did not ask Hussain to shield him from the harassment. 'If a member of my family asked my father for help, he'd step in', said the king. 'But then he would write you off in his books, as it were. He'd pamper you and give you the easy way out. I never asked, so he never did this, and I think that's one of the reasons why my father and I had a special relationship'. Years later, six months before he died, Hussain expressed feelings of guilt that he had not intervened. King Abdullah recalled: 'He said to me, "listen, I've been very hard and I think as a father I've let you down because I know what you went through and I never stepped in to help you". And I said to my father: "I remember those days. There were times I was very angry with you because I felt you knew what was going on and you did nothing"'. With hindsight, however, Abdullah has no regrets. 'If I hadn't had that rough time, I don't think I'd be the type of person I am today', he said. 'But the late 1980s was a time when I was frustrated with the system and with the people around my father. I almost threw in the towel and gave up on my career with the armed forces, which would have been a major mistake'.

The year 1991 was spent as the Armoured Corps' representative in the office of the inspector-general of Jordan's armed forces. Having returned to field duties, he was promoted to colonel in 1993 and in the same year became deputy commander of Jordan's Special Forces. In 1994 he was appointed their commander, with the rank of brigadier, and in 1996 supervised the reorganisation of the Special Forces and other elite units into a Special Operations Command under his leadership. He attained the rank of major-general in 1998.

Abdullah was proclaimed crown prince on his birth and remained so until 1 April 1965, when the title was transferred to King Hussain's younger brother, Hassan (see p. 168). On 24 January 1999, shortly before his death, Hussain reinstated Abdullah as crown prince, to Hassan's consternation. Hussain, who had been undergoing treatment for cancer at the Mayo Clinic in Rochester, Minnesota, returned to Jordan on 19 January 1999. 'The minute he stepped off the aircraft I knew, because he ignored me in the receiving line', related King Abdullah. 'He hugged and kissed everybody else. To me, he just said "hi" and walked off. I realised he didn't want to put any attention on me, so I realised that he'd made a decision. [After] two or three days he called me to the house and he said: "I'm going to make you crown prince"'.[27]

Within days, Hussain's condition deteriorated and he returned to Rochester. Abdullah was filled with apprehension. 'I'd just been made crown prince, but what if something were to happen to my father [i.e. if he was to die shortly]? That was very hard to deal with', he said. 'Not only was there the responsibility of being crown prince, but, I mean, you want your father to be around for ever, but also you want your father to be around so you can learn and ask questions. There I was in the number two position for what might have been a very short period of time, without the ability to [ask] my father, "What is your vision? What do you want me to do? I needed that learning curve, that apprenticeship that I suddenly realised might never happen'. At the same time, with the king on his deathbed, factions were jockeying for position. 'You had different groups manoeuvring', said Abdullah. 'I was suddenly thrown into the deep end, from being a soldier. Leading a military life was far easier because you knew who your enemies were'. He recalled that, just before his death, King Hussain had reminded him of 'the old adage "Keep your friends close, and your enemies even closer"'. It was, continued Abdullah, 'the darkest part of my life, because I was losing my father but I was [also] being thrown into a massive position of responsibility that I honestly didn't know if I was capable of [managing]. Time will tell if I succeed or not. But I think that the main driving force was that my father, in a very private discussion that we had, said: "Look, you're the hope that I have". And all the pundits in the first phase were saying, "Well, you know, this is an awful choice". One of my driving forces is to prove that my father's decision was the correct one'.

King Abdullah has one full brother, Faisal (born 11 October 1963), and two full twin sisters, Aisha and Zein (23 April 1968). From 2002 until his sudden and as yet unexplained appointment as a special adviser to his brother in September 2004, Faisal was commander of Jordan's air force. He has often acted as regent when the king has been abroad, a role he continued to perform after his change of post in 2004. The king also has a half-sister, Alia (born 13 February 1956), from his father's first marriage, to Queen Dina, and three half-brothers and four half-sisters from King Hussain's marriages to Queens Alia and Noor (see p. 170). On 10 June 1993 King Abdullah married Queen Rania (see below). They have one son, Hussain, (born on 28 June 1994), and two daughters, Iman, (27 September 1996), and Salma (26 September 2000), and on 31 August 2004 – the Queen's birthday – it was announced that the couple were expecting another child.

Queen Rania

Queen Rania al-Abdullah, formerly Rania al-Yasin, is from a Palestinian-Jordanian family that was forced out of Kuwait during the 1990–91 Gulf crisis. Born in Kuwait in 1970, Rania completed her schooling there and in 1991 graduated with a business administration degree from the American University in Cairo. She then returned to Jordan to work first in banking and subsequently in information technology. Like Jordan's queens before her, and especially Noor, she has established an international reputation for good works. For King Abdullah, however, her Palestinian origins are perhaps her greatest political asset, underlining his determination to foster harmony between his potentially fractious Palestinian and East Bank subjects. Queen Rania's stunning good looks have done nothing to undermine her local and international appeal, although she and Abdullah's jet-set lifestyle and 'fondness for appearing in the pages of *Hello* magazine and other glossies'[28] have caused some grumbling, especially amongst the kingdom's austere Islamists and the significant section of the population that lives below the poverty line.

The range of Rania's charitable and other activities is astounding. They 'encompass issues of national concern, such as the environment, youth, human rights, tourism and culture, among others', says her official website.[29] 'She also has a special interest in several core issues: the development of income-generating projects and the advancement of best practices in the field of microfinance, the promotion of family safety and the protection of children from violence, the promotion of early childhood development and the incorporation of information technology into the educational system; and the promotion of tourism and the preservation of Jordan's heritage'. The queen heads three national councils, each acting as a steering group for concerned organisations: the National Team for Family Safety; the National Team for Early Childhood Development; and a national council to oversee initiatives related to UNESCO's designation of Amman as Arab Cultural Capital for 2002. She is also the president or honorary chairperson of 5 international and 13 Arab and Jordanian social, cultural and medical organisations.

Prince Hamzah

Prince Hamzah bin al-Hussain, born on 29 March 1980, was the first of King Hussain's four children from his marriage with his fourth and final wife, Queen Noor. After attending elementary school in Amman, he pursued his secondary studies at Harrow School in England and in January 1999 entered Sandhurst. King Abdullah appointed him crown prince on 7 February 1999, the same day as their father's death. Hamzah graduated from Sandhurst in December 1999 and, like his half-brother Abdullah, went on to specialise in the armoured branch of the armed forces, reaching the rank of captain in June 2001. His duties have included a tour with the joint Jordanian-United Arab Emirates contingent serving as part of the UN peacekeeping operation in ex-Yugoslavia. In September 2001 Hamzah interrupted his military career to pursue undergraduate studies at Harvard University in the United States. Since 1999 he has been President of the Aal al-Bait Foundation for Islamic Thought, a Jordan-based international charitable organisation founded to 'promote, propagate and preserve moderate, orthodox Islamic thought and intellectual heritage'.[30] In the same year he became honorary president of the Jordan Basketball Federation.

He is also president of the Royal Aerosports Club of Jordan and chairs the board of trustees of the Royal Car Museum, a spectacular facility on a hilltop in the centre of the newly-established Al-Hussain National Park in western Amman which houses his late father's magnificent fleet of classic and sports cars. Like his father before him and King Abdullah (see Chapter 4), Hamzah is an action-man, his website listing his personal interests as including 'piloting helicopters, shooting, parachuting, sky-diving, motorcycling and water sports, scuba-diving, taekwondo [a martial art originating in Korea] and fencing'.

Hamzah was King Hussain's favourite son and bears 'an uncanny, disconcerting resemblance to his father when he succeeded back in 1953'.[31] It appears that, all other things being equal, Hamzah might have become king rather than Abdullah. On his eighteenth birthday in 1997, King Hussain sent Hamzah an open letter expressing his view that the prince was destined for 'great achievements' and noting that he himself had been only 18 years old when he assumed the throne. It was 'the first real sign that a Hasan succession might be in trouble'[32] and it may also have reflected the influence of Hamzah's mother, Queen Noor, whose relations with Hassan's wife, Princess Sarvath, had long been fraught. King Hussain is said to have named Abdullah as crown prince on condition that Hamzah would be next in line for the throne. 'It seemed that Abdullah was the compromise candidate for a monarch who feared that rushing the succession to his favourite would be a step too far', noted Robins.[33] Without warning, however, on 28 November 2004, King Abdullah stripped Hamzah of his title as crown prince. In a letter to Hamzah, he explained only that he had taken the step 'in order to give you the freedom to work and undertake any mission or responsibility I entrust you'.[34] The king left the position of crown prince vacant, while affirming in his letter to Hamzah that he was giving the matter his 'sincere attention'. Article 28 of the Constitution stipulates that the throne should normally pass to the king's eldest son, but that the king 'may select one of his brothers as heir apparent'. A well-placed Royal Court official said that Abdullah had no immediate plans to name a successor to Hamzah, explaining: 'His Majesty wants all potential candidates to be able to interact freely in society, and to support him without the constraints involved in being crown prince'.[35]

On 29 August 2003 Prince Hamzah married Princess Noor bint Asem bin Nayef, then aged 21. Princess Noor is a great-granddaughter of King Abdullah I, her father being Prince Asem, a son of King Talal's brother, Prince Nayef. Her mother, Princess Firouzeh, née Vokhshouri, was Prince Asem's second wife. Princess Noor pursued her secondary school studies in Spain and, like her husband, is presently an undergraduate in the USA.

Prince Hassan

While his charismatic brother, Hussain, liked to jump from aircraft and ride fast motorbikes, Prince Hassan is bookish and shuns the limelight. Born in Amman on 20 March 1947, he studied at Harrow School and Oxford University's Christ Church College, gaining an honours degree in Oriental Studies. Unlike Hussain and other key Hashemite royals, he did not pursue a military career. Hassan was named crown prince in April 1965 and acted as his brother's closest political adviser. He heads a clutch of local organisations including the Royal Scientific Society, the Higher Council for Science and Technology and the Royal Institute for Inter-Faith Studies – the latter reflecting Hassan's commitment to harmonious co-existence between the religions.[36] Beyond Jordan, he heads or helps direct a series of institutions concerned with international affairs including the Club of Rome and the World Conference on Religion and Peace. The author of seven books, he is a prolific contributor to academic and current affairs journals. In 1968 he married Princess Sarvath, the daughter of a leading Pakistani diplomat. They have four children: Princesses Rahma, Sumaya and Badiya, and Prince Rashid.

Until today, it is uncertain exactly why King Hussain deposed his brother as crown prince. Possibly, he simply judged that Abdullah would make a better king and that his eldest son would be hampered by Hassan's continued presence as crown prince. Certainly Hussain had been unhappy with Hassan's performance as regent while the king had been undergoing treatment in the United States. A letter he wrote to Hassan on 25 January 1999 explaining his decision referred to 'meddling in the affairs of the army [designed] to settle scores' that had included 'retiring efficient officers whose ... bright records are beyond reproach', and to the 'transfer of efficient ambassadors without reason except the reason of age'. King Hussain also cited differences over a proposed family council that would 'ensure the unity of the Hashemite family' and give it 'a great role in naming the most suitable successor'. Hussain had wanted its immediate formation, but Hassan had demurred. His response to the proposal 'did not reflect [its] spirit', claimed the letter.[37] Beyond all this, Hassan's deposal may have been part of a manoeuvre by Hussain, encouraged by Noor, to place his favourite, Hamzah, in pole position for a future succession.

Initially, there were fears that Hassan might try to take the throne anyway. On 20 January 1999, after returning to Jordan for the last-but-one time, King Hussain gave an interview to CNN in which he hinted that he might change the succession. 'The repercussions were immediate', wrote Queen Noor. 'Hassan met late that night with officials from the government, the military and the intelligence services, all deeply concerned about what lay ahead'.[38] Noor also recorded that on 26 January – two days after Abdullah had been named crown prince – while Hussain, Abdullah, Rania and she were driving to the airport, the first stage of a journey back to Rochester for a final round of treatment, she had 'tried to calm [Rania's] intense anxiety and fears about Prince Hassan and others who might attempt to interfere with the succession'.[39] Prince Hassan vehemently denies that he ever harboured such ambitions, and certainly he took no concrete steps that might have justified Rania's fears. 'With the king's sentiments now out in public, the hangers-on quickly distanced themselves from Hasan', observed Robins. 'Apart from some of his old technocratic colleagues he was left quite alone, and was certainly ill-placed to make a stand. Wisely, he chose a demeanour of quiet dignity as a mask for his deep sense of loss'.[40]

Queen Noor

Although she retains a high profile internationally, Queen Noor has faded noticeably from the local limelight since her husband's death and is believed not to be close to King Abdullah. The American daughter of a former airline executive and head of the US Federal Aviation Administration, Lisa Halaby was born in 1951 and educated in the US, gaining an architecture degree from Princeton University in 1974. She first met King Hussain at Amman airport, where she was accompanying her father at a ceremony marking the delivery of the Jordanian national airline's first Boeing 747, and became his fourth wife on 15 June 1978, converting to Islam and taking the name Noor al-Hussain ('Light of Hussain'). In addition to Hamzah, the couple had one son, Hashim (born 10 June 1981) and two daughters, Iman (born 24 April 1983) and Raiyah (9 February 1986). Their family also included the two children of Hussain's previous marriage to Queen Alia, Princess Haya and Prince Ali, and Ms Abir Muheisan, whom Hussain and Alia had adopted as a baby in December 1973 after a Russian plane had crashed onto her family's home near Amman airport, killing her parents. In April 2004 Princess Haya, then nearing 30 years of age, married the Crown Prince and Defence Minister of Dubai, General Shaikh Muhammad bin Rashid al-Maktoum. In September that year Prince Ali, who heads a special force charged with guarding the monarch, married Reem al-Brahimi, a CNN reporter and daughter of the UN's envoy to Iraq, Lakhdar al-Brahimi.

Queen Noor has 'initiated, directed and sponsored projects and activities in Jordan...in the areas of education, culture, women's and children's welfare, human rights, conflict resolution, community development, environmental and architectural conservation, public architecture and urban planning', notes her website, www.noor.gov.jo. 'She is also actively involved with international and UN organisations that address global challenges in these fields'. Queen Noor is patron of, or adviser to, numerous local and international organisations, ranging from the Noor al-Hussain Foundation, which encourages community development, to the Landmine Survivors Network. At the time of writing, she was visiting conflict-ridden Colombia where she conferred with landmine victims and attended the demolition of mines stockpiled by the army.

The royal family's personal dedication to worthy causes is not in doubt, and surely bolsters their popularity at home. But their activities also constitute a powerful and sophisticated international advertisement for Jordan and its monarchy. The message is constant and clear: the Jordanian royals are caring and concerned. Quite apart from their role as the kingdom's political and social elite, they function as a highly efficient public relations machine. Some at the bottom of the pile may resent the family's glamour and wealth, but Jordan relies on international, especially Western, financial and other support, which in turn depends largely on the goodwill that good public relations fosters. Collectively, the family surely ranks amongst Jordan's biggest hard currency earners.

Notes

1 Interview with author, Amman, 29 June 2004.
2 Mary C. Wilson, *King Abdullah, Britain and the Making of Jordan* (Cambridge: Cambridge University Press, 1987), p. 94.
3 www.kingabdullah.jo.
4 Interview with author, Amman, 29 June 2004.
5 *Hashemite Kingdom of Jordan Statistical Yearbook 2003* (Amman: Department of Statistics).
6 Beverley Milton-Edwards and Peter Hinchcliffe, *Jordan: A Hashemite Legacy* (London: Routledge, 2001), p. 40.
7 Interview with author, Amman, 29 June 2004.
8 Philip Robins, *A History of Jordan* (Cambridge: Cambridge University Press, 2004), p. 155.
9 Beverley Milton-Edwards and Peter Hinchcliffe, *Jordan*, p. 91.
10 Ibid., p. 92.
11 Ibid., p. 91.
12 Ibid., p. 93.
13 Ibid., p. 41.
14 Ibid., p. 93.
15 Saad G. Hattar, 'Tarawneh renamed Royal Court chief after government service record', *Jordan Times*, 14–15 January 2000.
16 Interview with author, London, 5 October 2004.
17 Interview with author, Amman, 29 June 2004.
18 Beverley Milton-Edwards and Peter Hinchcliffe, *Jordan*, p. 41.
19 Interview with author, Amman, 29 June 2004.
20 Beverley Milton-Edwards and Peter Hinchcliffe, *Jordan*, p. 41.
21 Roland Dallas, *King Hussein: A Life on the Edge* (London: Profile Books, 1999), p. 90.
22 www.kingabdullah.jo.
23 Interview with author, London, 5 October 2004.
24 Ibid.
25 Ibid.
26 Ibid.
27 Ibid.
28 Philip Robins, *A History of Jordan*, p. 201.
29 www.queenrania.jo.
30 www.princehamzah.jo.
31 Philip Robins, *A History of Jordan*, pp. 165-6.
32 Ibid., p. 166.
33 Ibid.

34 'Letter to HRH Prince Hamzah, Freeing him from the Constraints of the Honorary Position of Crown Prince', 28 November 2004, www.mfa.gov.jo.
35 Email communication from senior Royal Court official, 5 December 2004.
36 www.princehassan.gov.jo.
37 Roland Dallas, *King Hussein*, pp. 282-3.
38 Queen Noor, *Leap of Faith: Memoirs of an Unexpected Life* (London: Phoenix, 2003), p. 433.
39 Ibid., p. 437.
40 Philip Robins, *A History of Jordan*, pp. 196-7.

CHAPTER 12

'*Strengthening the Moderate Majority*':
Parliament and Parties

PASTEL GREENS DOMINATE the decor of Jordan's dome-roofed lower house of parliament. The circular chamber, with five concentric stepped levels leading down to a central well, boasts a thick-piled, green carpet. On each level stand pale straw-coloured wooden desk units, each with space for two deputies. The high-backed seats are upholstered in green leather. The walls are clad with wood panels the same colour as the desks, divided by pastel green strips. Above, a visitors' gallery surrounds the chamber, its seats of green plastic. The chamber's focal point, on the second step up, is a mottled green marble dais wide enough to accommodate five officials. Above it, on the highest step is another massive marble dais, for the Speaker and his two deputies. Beyond that is a small stage, faced with the same green marble, on which stand two wooden lecterns. The wall behind is draped with a large curtain, again in pastel green. Hanging at its centre, overseeing the entire chamber, is the Hashemite coat-of-arms. At its top, a crown rests on a scarlet sash. Below, an eagle perches on a globe, its wings outspread and touching two fluttering national flags. Framed by the flags is a bronze shield with spears, swords, bows and arrow. Below the shield to the left are three ears of wheat. To the right is a palm frond. The official website of the late King Hussain explains that the shield 'represents the defence of truth and right in the world'.

It is 23 July 2003 and the first ordinary session of the parliament elected a month before, after a two-year suspension. The deputies stand in groups, congratulating each other and discussing tactics. Almost all are men. Most wear smart business suits although several sport traditional dress: body-length white, brown or black gowns, or *thawbs*, and white or red-and-white-checked *keffiyas*. They include Shaikh Barjas al-Hadid, wearing a brown, gold-trimmed *thawb* and white *keffiya* (see Chapter 5). Some mix the two styles, wearing suits and *keffiyas*. Most of the very few women deputies are in *hijab*, although one, Nariman ar-Rusan, from the northern town of Irbid, wears a smart suit and her head is uncovered. The Speaker, Sa'ad Hayel Srour, calls the deputies to order. The main business is the election of 14 permanent committees but another matter must first be dealt with. Article 80 of the Constitution stipulates that every deputy, before taking his seat, must take the following oath: 'I swear by Almighty God to be loyal to the king and to the country and to uphold the Constitution, serve the nation and duly perform the duties entrusted to me'. At an extraordinary session on 16 July, however, 31 of the new deputies had added their own phrases to the oath. Islamists had sworn to carry out their duties 'in obeying God and His Prophet'. Others had included patriotic slogans. Mamdouh Abbadi, a former mayor of Amman, for example, had vowed to preserve a democratic and civilised Jordan. In a reference to the Jordan First campaign (see p. 49), others had declared that they would work to keep 'Jordan First, always and forever'. The debate degenerates into a slanging match during which a bearded Islamist deputy harangues the chamber, prompting the Speaker to warn: 'If you go on and on, I'll simply close the subject'. Eventually, the 31 whose oaths had differed from the approved version raised their hands to indicate that they concurred with the correct text. It proved not to be the end of the matter. It was finally laid to rest in a closed session five days later when they re-swore their oaths while prefacing their pledges with their unauthorised phrases.

Marginal role

The grandeur of its building belies the marginal role parliament plays in Jordan's political life. The Constitution defines the kingdom as a 'parliamentary hereditary monarchy'. To date it has been more monarchical and hereditary than parliamentary. The Constitution permits the king to dissolve the bicameral parliament virtually at will. On those occasions when it has posed a challenge to the established order, it has simply been brushed aside. In the 1957 crisis King Hussain banned all political parties, and subsequent general elections were carefully managed by the regime. 'After 1957 the legislature and cabinet assumed a subordinate, emasculated and virtually advisory function', note Milton-Edwards and

Hinchcliffe[1], adding: 'The legislative functions of the lower house of Parliament were rarely utilised (other than to rubber stamp decisions from the monarch)...Franchise, limited rather than universal, became meaningless in a political environment where elected representatives had no real power to formulate policies within the kingdom'.[2]

Parliament, also known as the National Assembly, nevertheless does have some teeth. It comprises an upper house (the Senate or House of Notables) appointed by the king and an elected lower house (House of Representatives or Chamber of Deputies). Prime ministers must submit their cabinets to parliament for a vote of confidence. At any stage, the lower house can submit a motion of no confidence in a government or an individual minister; if passed by a majority, the cabinet or minister must resign. Lower house members are entitled to question the government on any public issue. Governments submit legislative proposals to the lower house for debate and approval by majority vote; bills are then passed to the Senate for debate and approval, again by majority vote. After approval there, a bill goes to the king, who may either grant his assent by royal decree or return it to the lower house with an explanation of his objections. The deputies then review and vote on an amended version. Bills rejected by the Senate are returned to the lower house for amendment. If the two houses cannot agree on a bill, the matter is settled by a two-thirds majority vote at a joint session of the two; likewise, the monarch's veto on legislation can be overruled by a two-thirds majority vote at a joint session of the two houses. If the government amends or enacts a law when parliament is not sitting, the law must be submitted for approval when parliament next convenes.

The Constitution stipulates that the number of senators cannot be more than half the number of deputies. Most recently, in November 2003, the number of senators was raised to 55, in line with the latest rise in the number of deputies. In 1947, a year after Jordan's nominal independence from the United Kingdom, a 21-member Legislative Council that had been formed in 1929 was reorganised into a parliament comprising a 20-seat elected lower house and a 10-seat appointed upper house. Their numbers were doubled in 1950 to take account of the West Bank's incorporation into the kingdom. In the 1950s and 1960s the number of lower house deputies was increased first to 50 and then to 60, and it was raised to 80 in time for the 1989 elections. An electoral law decreed in July 2001 raised the number again, to 104. Continuing a longstanding practice, of these, nine are reserved for Christians, nine for *bedu* and three for either Circassians or Chechens. In February 2003 King Abdullah decreed that six further seats should be reserved for women, bringing the total to 110. Since 1973, when women gained the vote, suffrage has been universal. Senators, comprising former prime ministers and ministers, tribal leaders, retired senior military officers, former diplomats and judges and the like, are appointed for four-year terms, with half retiring each two years. The 2003 Senate, which includes seven women, boasts four ex-prime ministers and 24 ex-ministers. Deputies are elected for four-year terms. Lower and upper house sessions are held simultaneously and parliament sits for only four months annually – an important reason for its limited role in the country's political life.

Traditionally, half the members of each house had come from each bank of the Jordan river. General elections had been held in April 1967 but in 1970, citing the continued Israeli occupation of the West Bank, King Hussain postponed elections due that year and decreed that serving deputies would remain in office. In 1974 the Arab summit in Rabat declared the PLO the sole representative of the Palestinian people, seriously undermining Jordan's claim to the West Bank. In response, Hussain dissolved the House of Representatives. Subsequently he announced that new elections would be staged in March 1976. Whether or not the West Bank would be included was a political hot potato with grave implications for Jordan's relations with the PLO and the Palestinians. As the date approached, the king opted for prudence. In February 1976 he recalled the old chamber, with its West Bank members, which convened long enough only to approve the indefinite suspension of new elections before adjourning. Two years later the king appointed a 60-member National Consultative Council (NCC), which had no West Bank members, to act as an interim quasi-parliament. The NCC, however, was a purely consultative body whose mandate did not extend beyond studying, debating and offering advice on bills drafted by the government (also appointed by the monarch) and advising the government on general policy issues when requested by the prime minister. In January 1984 Hussain dismissed the NCC and reconvened the long-adjourned National Assembly. Although appointing new members to the Senate, he recalled the same lower house that had been elected in 1967 and had last met, albeit briefly, in 1976. Seven vacant West Bank seats were filled by individuals elected by the existing parliament while eight East Bank members who had died since the 1967 elections were replaced in by-elections in March 1984. In 1987 the registration of Jordanians on the East Bank was started with a view to new elections in 1988 but at the end of the year the process was halted when the king decreed a two-year postponement of the poll. In July 1988 Jordan formally cut its ties with the West Bank. The king dissolved the House of Representatives and in October 1988 decreed an indefinite postponement of elections. Following the riots of April 1989, however (see p. 38), elections were scheduled for November of that year to a reorganised legislature with 80 deputies, all from the East Bank.

The 1989 elections, the first for more than 22 years and with a turnout of 70 per cent, were widely acknowledged to be free and fair. 'The campaign and polling day were the freest ever experienced in the country', observed Milton-Edwards and Hinchcliffe, 'although it should be noted that political parties were still prohibited, the press remained censored and human rights abuses continued to be reported by organisations like Amnesty International'.[3] Almost half the seats were won by oppositionists – in the sense of candidates not from the traditional East Bank establishment. Conservative Islamists emerged as the biggest single parliamentary bloc with the Ikhwan al-Muslimoun, or Muslim Brotherhood, winning 22 of the 80 seats and independent Islamists a further 10-14 seats, depending on the definition used. Leftists, pan-Arabists, liberals and reformers won between 10 and 15 seats. Loyalist traditionalists – urban and rural notables, *bedu* shaikhs and former senior officials – won 31 seats. The parliament, which sat from 1989 to 1993, was livelier by far than its rubber-stamp predecessors, hotly debating matters that had previously been taboo. As Bonn University's Renate Dieterich has observed, it 'dared to discuss topics as sensitive as corruption in the highest offices of state and was the most outspoken and critical Jordan has known'.[4]

One man, one vote

Although the 1989–93 parliament never fundamentally challenged the *status quo*, the regime was taking no chances. In 1993, shortly before the elections scheduled for November that year and after the previous parliament had been dissolved, the electoral law was amended by royal decree to prevent the opposition from building on its success. Previously, each voter in Jordan's multi-candidate constituencies had one vote per candidate and could cast as many of those votes as they desired (although they could not vote more than once for the same candidate). This meant that in addition to voting on the basis of tribal or local loyalties, they could also vote for 'ideological' candidates such as Islamists. The new, so-called 'one man, one vote' system permitted only a single vote. Given most Jordanians' strong allegiances to tribe and locality, the inevitable and intended result would be to favour traditional, loyalist candidates. The amendment had been designed 'to strengthen traditional forces, to perpetuate the influence of those traditionally loyal to the government', said Hani Hourani, of the Amman-based New Jordan Research Centre, an NGO that undertakes research on issues relating to civil society and democracy.[5]

It is not the only means by which the electoral system has been engineered to maintain the primacy of the traditional, East Bank elite. In 1989, following the disengagement from the West Bank, the kingdom's electoral districts were carefully redrawn in a way that profoundly favoured East Bankers at the expense of Jordanians of Palestinian origin. The East Bankers had demanded this, records historian Kamal Salibi, 'on the grounds that they were the original Jordanians who had always provided the country with its backbone'.[6] The 2001 electoral law increased the number of parliamentary seats from 80 to 104 and the number of constituencies from 21 to 45; but it did nothing to redress the underrepresentation of the major cities, where most Palestinian Jordanians reside. Amman and Zarqa, the kingdom's biggest cities, accounted for 54 per cent of the total population in 1999. Yet the 2001 electoral law allocated these two constituencies only 33 seats – 32 per cent of the lower house's total. The much smaller towns of Mafraq, Karak, Tafila and Ma'an, which act as centres for large rural areas that have traditionally shown strong support for the monarchy, have only 12 per cent of the population but 22 parliamentary seats, or 21 per cent of the total. Observed political analyst Francesca Sawalha: 'By increasing the number of seats across the Kingdom and maintaining more or less the same ratio of representation, the government appears to have sent a clear message that it would continue the policy of keeping Jordanians of Palestinian origin (more than half the population) under-represented'.[7] No wonder that the 2003 parliament included only 16 deputies and seven senators of Palestinian origin.

As well as being major concentrations of Palestinian Jordanians, the largest cities are home to a professional class that is generally far more interested in ideological and foreign policy issues than rural dwellers and has strongly opposed Jordan's stance on matters such as relations with Israel and the US-led invasion of Iraq. Perceptively, the International Crisis Group (ICG) has noted: 'Given the predominance of the Palestinian-origin population (including the large refugee camps) in urban centres, the regime is particularly concerned about a possible combination of the two, that the political radicalism of the cities would often take on a pronounced Palestinian and Islamist hue, accentuating the perceived urban-based opposition threat to the Kingdom's stability'.[8] In short, said the ICG, 'the government has chosen to depend on the conservative tribal nature of segments of society to act as a counterweight to the organised opposition. Not surprisingly, therefore, the government's reluctance to reform the electoral law – and the political system more generally – in a meaningful way produced elections in 1993, 1997 and 2003 that ushered in parliaments that were by and large tribal assemblies'.[9]

Only 26 oppositionists won seats in the 1993 election. The 1997 results were even more flawed because the Islamic Action Front (IAF – the party of the Muslim Brotherhood) and seven smaller parties boycotted the poll in protest at the 1993 electoral law amendment and at the wider erosion of liberties since the start of the decade. The election scheduled for November 2001 was postponed, first on the grounds that more time was needed for the drafting of a new electoral law and then because of the 'difficult regional situation' (see pp. 48–9). The election was eventually staged on 17 June 2003 and, like the earlier polls, was generally free and fair. This time, despite threats to boycott this poll too, the IAF participated but won only 17 seats. Five independent Islamists, who generally vote with the IAF, were also elected. Some 55 per cent of the seats were won by tribal and other conservative independents. Only 25 representatives of political parties gained seats and the traditional leftist and pan-Arab nationalist parties such as the Ba'ath and Communists failed to win any. None of the 54 women who stood for election won seats outright. Instead, the six who polled the highest numbers of votes (one of them, Hayat al-Museimi, an IAF candidate) took the six seats reserved for women. The turnout was 58.8 per cent – well down on the 1989 figure. The lowest turnout, at 44.6 per cent, was in Amman, where, the ICG noted, 'media interviews with people in the streets seemed to suggest pronounced disillusionment with the institution of parliament'.[10]

'Electoral engineering' has also featured at the level of Jordan's 99 municipalities. In 2002, while parliament was still suspended, the municipal elections law was amended to permit the government to appoint half the members of town councils and name the mayors. Previously, all had been elected, other than in the Greater Amman Municipality (GAM) where half had been appointed. In protest, the IAF boycotted local elections held on 26–27 July 2003, although it participated in the poll in the GAM, where the system had not changed. 'Citizens used to elect their candidates at a time when Jordan was under the British mandate', complained Shaikh Hamzah Mansour, head of the IAF. 'Now we are in the third millennium and the government still thinks that people are not qualified or equipped enough to elect all municipal council members'.[11] The turnout in the local elections was 58 per cent – about the same as for the general election staged the previous month.

The very basis of the Jordanian political system, in which policy-making is reserved for the king while his governments are mere executors of his decisions, precludes a fully-functioning democracy. But even within the limits imposed by that underlying reality, it is not only through gerrymandering and manipulation of the voting system that the regime corrodes the democratic process and parliament's authority. It weakens them further by resorting to unelected commissions, such as those for the National Charter and Jordan First (see Chapters 2 and 3), to formulate and issue major policy documents, and by maintaining its own direct, extra-parliamentary links to the opposition. Dieterich observes:

> Only a minor part of the formal political discussion is actually carried out in parliament, while the Jordanian regime uses different channels to communicate with the opposition. This is euphemistically called the 'national dialogue'. The king and his prime ministers, as well as other leading members of the cabinet, meet regularly with representatives of influential organisations, especially from the professional associations, the ranks of the Islamists and tribal circles. During these meetings the various factions make their demands and formulate their criticisms. They are as well an important opportunity for the regime to co-opt those who are willing to restrict or even abandon their criticism in exchange for influential and lucrative posts in government and administration'.[12]

Parties

Jordan has some 30 registered political parties but all bar one are small and most are ideologically hard to differentiate. The only organised, effective party with a national following is the IAF. Created in 1992 when parties were legalised, the Front, which has 23 branches across the country, is the political wing of the conservative Muslim Brotherhood (Ikhwan al-Muslimoun) although its members also include independent Islamists. The IAF advocates Islamist social reforms and vehemently opposes Jordan's peace treaty with Israel and acquiescence in the Western occupation of Iraq. But it is stoutly loyal to the monarchy: unsurprisingly as the Jordanian Ikhwan, the local branch of a fundamentalist Sunni movement established in Egypt in 1928, has been a staunch supporter of the regime since its formation in 1946 in the days of King Abdullah I. When King Hussain banned political parties in 1957, the Ikhwan was exempted on the grounds that it was not formally a party. When we met in his spartan office in a nondescript building near the Islamic Hospital in Amman's Abdali district, Abdul Majid al-Thnaibat, Superindendent-General of the Jordanian Ikhwan since 1994, stressed that the Brotherhood opposed violent change. 'We believe in democracy and the political process. We are against violence and use peaceful methods. We respect others' opinions', he declared, pointing out that the Brotherhood had participated in Jordanian elections since 1940.[13] Born in 1945 in the southern town of Karak and married with six children, Al-Thnaibat graduated from Damascus University in 1968 and then worked as a lawyer. He is diminutive and balding with a thin beard and an ill-fitting dark suit, a mild-mannered man who speaks quietly, choosing his words with care: hardly the Western stereotype of an Islamic fundamentalist.

Both the IAF and the Ikhwan decry the one man, one vote system, which is largely directed against them. 'The government doesn't believe in democracy', insisted Shaikh Hamzah Mansour, head of the IAF. 'A democratic government respects the results of elections. A democratic government gives the people the opportunity to choose their representatives. That's why the problems have arisen in this country. If the people were able to choose their real representatives, the result would be victory for the Islamists and oppositionists in general'.[14] Mansour, wearing a beige *thawb* and red and white-checked *keffiya*, works from a modest office in a two-storey, limestone-faced building in the Abdali district, near the trade and industry ministry. He is burly and affable with a ready smile and laughing eyes. Speaking in early 2003, he said that he believed the 2001 election had been postponed in order to blunt opposition to Jordan's pro-Western stance. 'This arose from pressures from outside Jordan', he averred. 'If they [the authorities] believed that an election would produce results pleasing to the US, UK and the Zionists, the elections would be held tomorrow'.

Al-Thnaibat and Mansour may indeed be democrats but that does not mean that an Islamist Jordan would be democratic, at least in the Western sense. I asked them whether an Islamist-ruled state would permit journalists to write articles declaring that God did not exist. 'Anyone who insults sacred things should go before the court', said Mansour. 'We cannot forgive a man who says bad things about the Prophet, peace be upon Him, or Jesus'.[15] The same line was taken by Al-Thnaibat: there would be 'complete freedom' under an Islamic system 'except the freedom to attack the highest authority', i.e. God.[16] I asked them whether, in a state they controlled, women would suffer discrimination and be forced into *hijab*. 'I believe that Islam gives women full rights', replied Mansour. Many Arab women, particularly educated women, would not agree, I responded. 'It's because they don't know Islam', he said. 'Even if they are Arab or Muslim, they don't know Islam. Schoolteachers don't teach Islam in a correct way'. Under an Islamic system, he insisted, women would be taught correctly. On women's dress codes, Al-Thnaibat explained: 'We would leave it for the lady's beliefs, by convincing her, without force'. Mansour, however, went further. If education and persuasion failed, sterner measures would be used. 'The Islamic system starts with education, before sanctions', he said. 'The sanctions come after education'. Nidal Abbadi, an Islamist deputy from Amman, has offered a further glimpse of how life might be in an Islamist Jordan. In a December 2003 speech in parliament he called for swift action against all forms of 'moral corruption and degradation'. The *Jordan Times* reported that he had demanded 'the closure of all nightclubs, unisex swimming pools and male-run hair salons for women, and called for a true implementation of Islamic doctrines'. He had 'urged the government to make Islamic dress for women mandatory, saying that modern fashions seen on Jordanian women today should be banned'. To underline his point, Abbadi declared: 'In our times women used to wear mini- and micro-jupes. Nowadays they are not even wearing the jupes' – a comment that had aroused 'roaring laughter in the house'.[17]

The leftist and nationalist parties, including two Ba'ath Parties (one leaning towards Syria, the other towards Saddam Hussain's now fallen Ba'athist regime in Iraq), the Nasserists and two Communist Parties, retain small followings but suffer the legacy of having been banned and repressed from 1957 until 1992. Perhaps more profoundly, their ideologies have been discredited, the Communists by the collapse of the Soviet Union and the nationalists by the Arab defeat in the 1967 war with Israel and by the cruelty and incompetence of nationalist regimes in Egypt, Syria and Iraq. 'All these old parties came into the light in 1992 but they remain small', said Bassam Hadidin, a centre-left Christian deputy from Zarqa who was imprisoned for five years in the 1980s for his political activities.[18] 'No-one trusts these old ideological parties', he added. 'Internally, they don't have a culture of democracy. I was one of them, but I've changed'. I met Hadidin, aged 53, a member of one of Jordan's biggest Christian tribes and formerly a journalist and researcher, in his smart, modern office in the parliament building. Of athletic build although slightly heavy, cleanshaven and tanned, with grey-white hair and arresting black eyebrows speckled with grey, he cuts a striking figure. He studied in Italy and his clothes echo the best of Italian fashion: checked shirt and khaki slacks, casual brown leather shoes and matching brown leather belt. He would not look out of place strolling down Rome's Via Condotti.

Other than the Islamists, there were only two 'ideological' parties in the 2003 parliament, continued Hadidin: his own Hizb al-Yasar ad-Dimuqrati (Democratic Leftist Party), which has only two deputies; and the Hizb al-Watani ad-Dustouri (National Constitutional Party), which has three. 'This party, founded by former Speaker Abdul Hadi Majali, call themselves centrists, but for me they are rightists', added Hadidin. 'They have a nationalist ideology'. The biggest non-Islamist parliamentary factions, however, are loose, almost ad hoc, groupings that essentially support the status quo, can barely be distinguished from each other ideologically and frequently splinter and merge. 'They are based above all on personal relations and common interests, and each is centred on a major figure, a big boss', explained Hadidin.

In late 2004, the various parliamentary factions coalesced into two main umbrella groups: a National Democratic Parliamentary Coalition (NDPC – At-Tajamu an-Niabi al-Watani ad-Dimuqrati); and a Reform and Change Coalition (RCC – At-Tajamu lil-Islah wa at-Taghrayir). The NDPC comprised:

- The National Parliamentary Action Front (Al-Jabhat al-Amal al-Barlamani al-Watani), headed by Abdul Hadi Majali, comprising 25 deputies;

- The 11-member National Front (Al-Jabhat al-Wataniya);

- The 4-member New Reformists Bloc (Al-Kutlat al-Islahyoun al-Judud);

- The 10-member National Democratic Alliance (At-Tajamu ad-Dimuqrati al-Watani);

- Most of the 12 members of the conservative Homeland Bloc (Al-Kutlat al-Watan).

The RCC linked the 15-member National Democratic Bloc (Al-Kutlat al-Wataniya al-Dimuqratiya), headed by former prime minister Abdul Rauf ar-Rawabdah; the IAF; and the other members of the Homeland Bloc. Eight of the 16 independents in the Chamber of Deputies are organised into an Alliance of Independent Deputies (At-Tajamu an-Nuwab al-Mustaqaleen). While some of this faction's members – like some of the non-organised independent MPs – have joined one or other of the two main parliamentary umbrella groups, the Alliance has not formally affiliated to either.

The imprecision of these non-ideological groupings' programmes can be gauged from the agenda of the Homeland for Reform Bloc (Al-Kutlat al-Watan lil-Islah) which was the outcome of a now defunct merger in late 2003 between the Homeland Bloc and the Reformists' Bloc (Al-Kutlat al-Islahyeen). Announcing the bloc's formation, Suleiman Obeidat, a senior member of the group, said that it would work for 'all that serves Jordan'. Another member, Jamal Dmour, declared: 'We will do our best to translate the Jordan First slogan and enforce the sense of belonging'.[19] Reporting the NDPC's formation, the national news agency, Petra, said that the group 'seeks to energize parliamentary performance based on the Constitution, work to maintain the national constants and reinforce co-operation between all blocs of the Lower House'.[20]

The reality, strikingly expressed by Quintan Wiktorowicz, is that 'political parties [in Jordan] hold little relevance for people, even in politics'.[21] In a public opinion survey conducted in 2000 by Jordan University's Centre for Strategic Studies (CSS), 98.6 per cent of respondents said that they had never joined a political party while 92.6 per cent stated that they had no intention of doing so in the future.[22] Another CSS poll, in 1995, revealed that only 43 per cent of Jordanians had even heard of the IAF and less than one quarter were aware of any other party. Fewer than 5 per cent were aware of some 13 smaller parties.[23] 'This level of awareness is certainly related to the novelty of political parties and their rapid proliferation since the political party law was enacted [in 1992]', commented Wiktorowicz, 'but it is also due to the fact that political parties, even the largest ones, have little impact in society'.[24] A CSS poll conducted in 2004 – nearly a decade later – showed that little had changed, with 84 per cent of respondents believing that none of the kingdom's political parties was qualified to form a government.[25]

Change

While studiously ignoring their own culpability, the authorities readily acknowledge the failings of parliament and parties and call for change – but very much on their own terms. 'Parliament is under fire at the moment. People are pretty fed up with them', said King Abdullah, insisting that he wants elections where 'you're actually electing someone on the basis of what he's capable of and not because he comes from this or that village or sector'.[26] His vision is for a development of ideological parties of the left, centre and right, along Western lines. 'How do you go from 30 parties to left, right and centre: to two or three or four parties?' he asked. 'I can't step in and create political parties. I can only encourage. And what I've done with the parliament is sat down with them and said: what does it mean for you to be a centrist? What does it mean on education? What does it mean on health? What does it mean on regional policy? That thinking has not yet come about. These are questions that until now they've not thought of. His hope is that at the next elections, scheduled for 2007, 'people will stand and say not, "I'm from the Bani Hassan or some other tribe", but "I'm actually here because this is what I believe on social security, on education, on health"'. Part of the problem was 'the dynamics of parliament', he continued. On the one hand was the Muslim Brotherhood, which was 'a very organised small bloc'. On the other were an 'Old Guard that I think are more in for their personal agendas as opposed to creating a political party'. He had said much the same in his speech opening the 2003 parliament: 'We believe that the presence of political parties, including those of the national opposition, is both vital and necessary for the modern state. We look forward to the day when nationalist opposition parties that are loyal to Jordan will be partners in making our national decisions. These political parties should have comprehensive, integrated national programmes and should be established and launched by the grassroots, not by individuals or groups that are brought together by transient interests. Thus, our political parties will be able to acquire credibility and the ability to bring about aspired-for change'.[27]

In line with the king's prescription, a ministry for political development was created in October 2003, the first such agency in the Arab and Islamic worlds. Muhammad Daoudia, its minister until October 2004, when he was ousted in a cabinet reshuffle and his portfolio was divided between a ministry of political affairs and civic society and a ministry of parliamentary affairs, declared his mission to be 'to encourage new, strong parties' by 'establishing a positive atmosphere for political development'.[28] Born in 1947, Daoudia is from the southern town of Tafila and is married to a Jordanian Palestinian from Lydda with whom he has five children. In the 1970s and 1980s, when he worked as a journalist and writer, he was a radical republican, but he went on to serve as a member of parliament, ambassador to Morocco, head of public relations at the Royal Court and minister for youth. 'The problem is that we have only one big party, and this isn't healthy for democracy', he explained. The Muslim Brotherhood was strong because, unlike other Jordanian parties, it had never been repressed. 'This party was alone for forty years and that's why it's so strong', he said. For decades, party membership had been illegal. 'People lost their jobs [because of this]. They were dismissed from university. They were put in jail', he continued. 'So there's an anti-party culture. Now, from the king down, we'll start to encourage people to join parties. We want to move from an anti-party culture to a participatory culture, from a silent majority to a participatory majority'. He readily agreed that 'talk is not enough'. Concrete measures were being considered. 'In student council elections at universities, for example, the students now vote for Islamists', said Daoudia. 'They only participate on the Islamist side. It's the old culture and the culture of fear of participating'. Possible counter-measures would be 'making participation in these elections obligatory' or 'granting several academic grades to those who vote, as an incentive'. But could it not be that the Islamists won elections simply because they genuinely commanded majority support? Was all this not simply an attempt by the establishment to counter the Islamists? Not at all, insisted the minister. If the end result was that Islamists gained even bigger majorities, or that Communists won elections, would the authorities be content? 'Yes, sure'. What would be the position of a party that advocated Jordan's transformation into a republic? 'A republican party would not be permitted under the Constitution'. Could a system that proscribed such parties be described as democratic? 'That is a question', replied Daoudia, while noting that parties that advocated violence, racism or religious or gender discrimination would also be illegal.

That the regime would be untroubled by even stronger electoral showings by the Islamists is certainly not the king's view. 'We'd like to strengthen political parties', said King Abdullah. 'But I'll have to be quite honest: I want to strengthen the right ones. I have a vision for the country and there are elements in our society that have a 180 degree difference [of view]. My personal view is that once the Muslim Brotherhood got into power there would be no democracy'.[29] He added: 'As you start to open up on political reforms, you want to strengthen the moderate majority, and that is more difficult than clashing with the extremist minority'. Asked what was his time frame for achieving his vision of a Jordan with fully-functioning, programme-based political parties, King Abdullah replied: 'It depends on how strong these parties become in the right way. I'll be honest: if I see that it's the Ikhwan that are in control, it's going to take a lot longer. [Theirs] is not the vision that I have for Jordan'.

The then information minister Muhammad Afash Idwan was equally scathing about the opposition. 'They [the Ikhwan] want freedom only when they want it, and only for themselves, but they don't want it for others', he said. 'This is the paradox of these kinds of so-called opposition parties. It's fine to have democracy as long as they benefit from it, but they don't want it for others'.[30] The pan-Arab opposition parties were no better. They were 'tied to states that have never been known for their democracy. They'll sing and dance for regimes that could never in fifty years come near our democracy in Jordan'. The 'so-called opposition' were highly vocal but were a tiny minority, he claimed. 'You're not talking about the opposition in a Western sense', continued Idwan. 'You're not talking about Democrats versus Republicans or Labour versus the Conservatives. You're talking about less than one per cent of the Jordanian population'.

The public's indifference towards parliament and parties and the marginal role of both in the kingdom's political life are also acknowledged by some senior parliamentarians, although their explanation is more convincing than the regime's. 'People understand that this [2003] parliament won't represent their real voice. It won't be any different than in the past', said Deputy Speaker Ali Abu as-Sukkar, an Islamist deputy from Zarqa.[31] A former secretary-general of the Engineers' Association and chairman of its Anti-Normalisation Committee, which worked to block the development of normal relations with Israel, As-Sukkar in 2001-2 was twice imprisoned because of the authorities' irritation at his Committee's activities. 'The main problems are the one man, one vote system and the question of constituency boundaries', he continued. 'At the same time, parties are very weak. There's no government support for them to play a real role in parliament'. As for the independent deputies, 'maybe there are factions whose leaders have visions on this or that subject, but mostly it's personal'. But weren't the authorities working for change? 'There are no practical moves', he replied.

Notes

1   Beverley Milton-Edwards and Peter Hinchcliffe, *Jordan: A Hashemite Legacy* (London: Routledge, 2001), p. 40.
2   Ibid., pp. 39-40.
3   Ibid., p. 60.
4   Renate Dieterich, 'The weakness of the ruled is the strength of the ruler: the role of the opposition in contemporary Jordan', in George Joffé (ed.), *Jordan in Transition 1990–2000* (London: Hurst & Company, 2002), p. 134.
5   Interview with author, Amman, 21 July 2003.
6   Kamal Salibi, *The Modern History of Jordan* (London: I B Tauris, 1998), p. 270.
7   International Crisis Group (ICG), *The Challenge of Political Reform: Jordanian Democratisation and Regional Instability* (Amman and Brussels: ICG, 8 October 2003), pp. 17–18.
8   Ibid., p. 17.
9   Ibid., p. 19.
10   Ibid., p. 18.
11   Alia Shukri Hamzeh and Khalid Dalal, '58% voters cast ballots in municipal elections', *Jordan Times*, 29 July 2003.
12   Renate Dieterich, 'The weakness of the ruled', p. 135.
13   Interview with author, Amman, 22 February 2003.
14   Interview with author, Amman, 22 February 2003.
15   Ibid.

16   Interview with author, Amman, 22 February 2003.
17   Alia Shukri Hamzeh and Sahar Aloul, 'Parliament deliberations continue for second day', *Jordan Times*, 22 December 2003.
18   Interview with author, Amman, 20 April 2004.
19   Dina al-Wakeel, 'Al Watan for Reform pledges "revised and powerful charter"', *Jordan Times*, 8 October 2003.
20   'New parliamentary coalition formed', Petra News Agency, 12 November 2004.
21   Quintan Wiktorowicz, 'Embedded authoritarianism: bureaucratic power and the limits to non-governmental organisations in Jordan', in George Joffé (ed.), *Jordan in Transition 1990–2000* (London: Hurst & Company, 2002), p. 119.
22   Ibid.
23   Ibid.
24   Ibid.
25   *Democracy in Jordan*, Public Opinion Poll Unit, Centre for Strategic Studies, University of Jordan, October 2004.
26   Interview with author, Amman, 29 June 2004.
27   www.kingabdullah.jo.
28   Interview with author, Amman, 20 April 2004.
29   Interview with author, Amman, 29 June 2004.
30   Interview with author, Amman, 24 February 2003.
31   Interview with author, Amman, 23 July 2003.

CHAPTER 13

'The Basis of Governance':
The Legal System

THE YOUNG MAN in loose white slacks, blue flip-flops and khaki sweat shirt with 'IC Boys' stencilled on the front shuffles into the courtroom, handcuffed, shackled at the ankles and escorted by two stocky guards from the Public Security Department, smartly turned out in navy-blue uniforms and bearing sub-machine guns. The young man is both agitated and distracted. After being locked into one of the two steel-barred cages on one side of the courtroom, he crouches, then rises, before crouching again. Accused of murdering a woman in the southern town of Karak, his defence is insanity. He had been brought to the court from the Fuheis special hospital in Amman. A grizzled old man in a blue prison uniform, *Markaz Islah wa Ta'heel Juweida* ('Juweida Correction and Rehabilitation Centre') stencilled in white on its back, stands quietly in the second steel cage. A year ago in Madaba he had argued with another man about who should be the first to take water from a storage tank. The argument had escalated into a fight in which the accused had struck his protagonist a blow to his head with a rock, killing him. Two women, handcuffed and in blue uniforms with *Markaz Islah wa Ta'heel Birain* ('Birain Correction and Rehabilitation Centre' – in Zarqa) sit in a corner of the rectangular courtroom, guarded by a smartly uniformed, headscarved female warder. The older of the two, from Amman's Qawasmeh district, is large and composed, the other, a Filipino, slight and distraught. They had given some medicine to a friend, who had then died. Their defence is that the friend had died not from poisoning but from a heart attack.

Amman's Higher Criminal Court in the central downtown district is located within a bland building on busy King Hussain Street. Nearby, the traffic roars across an ugly flyover. The courtroom is spacious and airy with light grey walls. Light floods in through large windows along the wall opposite the steel cages. The three judges, in black robes with three green flashes on the arms, sit at a raised wooden bench stretching from wall-to-wall across one end of the rectangular room. Above them hang colour posters of kings Hussain and Abdullah. High on the same wall an air conditioning unit gently hums while a three-bladed fan hangs motionless from the ceiling above. To the judges' left, also on the bench, sits a clerk before a computer. Desks for defence and prosecution lawyers, the latter identified by the three red flashes on their black gowns, stand before the judges and to their right. Along the opposite wall stand the steel cages. At the far end of the courtroom, opposite the bench, the main well of the court is filled with rows of chairs for non-violent defendants, friends and relatives of the accused and the public. Other than myself and my assistant, Riham, the only occupants are the two accused women and their escort.

The proceedings are subdued and dignified, but brisk. Today's decisions are all steps along longer judicial roads. The mentally disturbed youth is sent for assessment. The old man from Madaba's lawyer was unable to attend, and one of the judges is anyway new and wants more time to study the case, which is adjourned. The case of a family of nine, jointly accused of beating to death the wife of one of the sons, is also adjourned because the prison authorities had failed to bring them to court. So too is the case of four men accused of attempted murder, because the doctor who had examined the victim had failed to attend in court. Outside in the large central lobby, floored with slabs of pink marble and lined with chairs, perhaps 50 defendants and witnesses wait their turn. 'Higher Criminal Court' is engraved on a metre-square brass plaque attached to one wall. Opposite, across the marble floor, two massive pillars rise into the ceiling. Slight apprehension hangs in the air and conversation is hushed. Occasionally a black-gowned lawyer appears from a side corridor to consult with a client. A woman in white headscarf and black gown sits hunched in a chair, beside a man in grey trousers and a white shirt, a crutch resting beside him. Nearby sits a woman in a beige headscarf and wine-coloured gown. A group of four women in *hijab* sit together under the brass plaque, two wearing white headscarves, one a black headscarf and one a blue headscarf with a yellow pattern.

The slightly run-down building contrasts starkly with the gleaming white Qasr al-Adl ('Palace of Justice') across town in the Abdali district.

Officially opened by King Hussain in November 1996, the five-storey structure is arranged around a central atrium, floored with white limestone slabs inset with arabesque designs in pink marble. Above and surrounding the atrium, three successive storeys are marked by vaulted balconies while a final level is without balconies, the whole forming a vast cone. The atmosphere is a cross between a busy railway station and a cathedral. Lawyers talk strategy with their clients, the latter generally more smartly dressed than their counterparts in the Higher Criminal Court, reflecting the universal link between civil litigation and money. A young lawyer in a black gown with three yellow flashes on the sleeves stands alone, smoking a cigarette almost furtively. Incongruously in this modernist temple, a white-bearded old man in white *keffiya* and black *thawb*, bent double by his years, shuffles by with the aid of a wooden walking stick. Beyond, young women lawyers in black trouser-suits strut purposefully to and from the lifts, clutching thick files and leather brief-cases. The Palace contains no fewer than 76 courtrooms and is visited each day by some 7,000 people. One-hundred-and-ninety judges are based here – about one third of Jordan's total. In addition to Magistrate, First Instance and Appeal Courts, the Palace is home to Jordan's Court of Cassation and Higher Court of Justice. Offices on the fourth floor house the High Judicial Council (see p. 194). On the ground floor, surrounding the atrium, is the Department of Forensic Medicine. Nearby there's a post office and a branch of the Cairo-Amman Bank.

Courts

The Western and traditional dress styles of those thronging Amman's Higher Criminal Court and Palace of Justice are mirrored by the legal system's mix of European and Islamic *shari'a* traditions. During the nine-teenth century, when the territory was part of a reforming Ottoman empire, civil and criminal codes were introduced based on French law but modified to accommodate Islamic precepts. English common law was introduced into British-mandated Palestine but in Transjordan, where Britain did not rule directly, the older legal system persisted although with extensive amendments that strengthened its European aspects. In 1956 parliament adopted a new criminal code modelled on those in Syria and Lebanon, which in turn derived from the French system. Reflecting this background, there is no jury system and it is the judges who weigh evidence and pronounce verdicts as well as ruling on matters of law. The Constitution provides for three types of court: civil, religious and 'special'. Religious courts deal with personal status and family matters, including marriage, divorce inheritance and alimony, while the civil courts adjudicate routine criminal and civil cases. The religious courts include *shari'a* courts for Muslims and canon law courts respectively for Greek Orthodox, Roman Catholics and Anglicans, although these Christian courts apply *shari'a* law in inheritance matters in accordance with longstanding custom. A special court appointed by the Court of Cassation (see below) rules on disputes between different religious courts and between religious and civil courts. Jordan's civil (*nizamiya*) jurisdiction embraces a four-tiered hierarchy of courts. The 14 Magistrate (*sulh*) Courts hear lesser cases involving small claims and offences punishable by small fines or up to two years' imprisonment. More serious cases are heard by the seven Courts of First Instance (of which Amman's Higher Criminal Court is one), each with a panel of three judges for criminal matters and two judges for misdemeanours and civil matters. The First Instance Courts also hear appeals from the Magistrate Courts. Appeal courts, comprising a panel of three judges, hear appeals both from the First Instance Courts and from the religious courts. There are three Appeal Courts, in Amman, Irbid and Ma'an, respectively serving the central, northern and southern parts of the kingdom. Contested Appeal Court decisions are heard by the five-judge Court of Cassation, which is Jordan's supreme court. The civil court system also includes the Higher Court of Justice, which hears cases against governmental agencies, and specialised courts for cases in the areas of taxation and customs.

Parallel to the civil court system are a series of special courts. The State Security Court (see p. 197), comprising a panel of two military and one civilian judges, deals with cases involving sedition, armed insurrection, offences against the royal family, financial crimes affecting the national economy and weapons- and drug-trafficking. Military courts try cases involving all offences by armed forces personnel. A High Tribunal may try ministers and may interpret the Constitution on the request of the cabinet or either house of parliament. Its interpretations are binding. The Tribunal comprises the Speaker of the Senate, three Senate members who are elected by the Senate and five senior judges. At the behest of the prime minister, a Special Tribunal, whose decisions are also binding, may interpret the provisions of any law that the courts have not yet interpreted.

It comprises the presidents of the highest civil courts, two other senior judges, a senior administrative official appointed by the cabinet and a senior official appointed by the concerned minister. Neither the High Tribunal nor the Special Tribunal are standing bodies, both being convened only when required – in practice very rarely.

Judicial independence

The independence of the judiciary and the courts is enshrined in the Constitution. 'Judges are independent, and in the exercise of their judicial functions they are subject to no authority other than that of the law', declares Article 97. 'The courts shall be open to all and shall be free from any interference in their affairs', affirms Article 101. In the great majority of routine cases, the judiciary and courts are independent and citizens can expect fair trials, albeit that the process can sometimes be very lengthy, with frequent adjournments, reflecting the high level of demand in relation to resources and the persistence of outdated work methods, often including the recording of proceedings and the drafting of judgements in longhand. Where cases involve 'national security' or threaten the financial or other interests of powerful officials, however, the picture can be less rosy. The US State Department's *Country Reports on Human Rights Practices 2003 – Jordan* does not mince its words: 'The judiciary was not independent in practice and remained subject to pressure and outside interference'.[1] There's little of the systematic financial corruption and crude official interference that typify the legal systems in other Middle Eastern countries such as neighbouring Syria. In Jordan, it's much more subtle. Scope for abuse is offered by the system's structure. As a whole, it is funded and administered by the ministry of justice. Judges are appointed, assigned to jurisdictions and cases and evaluated by a theoretically independent High Judicial Council of 12 senior judges who in turn are appointed by the king. But the council is overseen day-to-day by the ministry, which has been accused of undermining its independence. A June 2001 law introduced measures to distance the ministry from the council but allegations of interference persist. 'In theory and in the Constitution, the Judicial Council is independent', said Farouq al-Kilani, himself a former council chairman. 'In practice, some people interfere'.[2]

The pressures focus on more delicate cases, especially in the State Security Court and the Higher Court of Justice, said Professor Muhammad

Hammouri, a former Dean of the University of Jordan's Law Faculty and a former minister of higher education and of culture and national heritage. Jordanian judges should not be compared to those in other countries in the region 'who wait to smell what the headmaster wants, and judge accordingly', he insisted, and 'they [the authorities] do not pick up the telephone and tell the court what to do'.[3] In politically sensitive cases, however, 'weak judges' tend to lean towards the government, calculating that this will best serve their career prospects. Promotion can be slow for judges who defy powerful interests. On occasion, judges have been transferred in order to influence the outcomes of particular cases. 'There were numerous allegations in previous years, and some this year [2003], that judges were "reassigned" temporarily to another court or judicial district to remove them from a particular proceeding', says the State Department report.[4]

The experiences of Farouq al-Kilani, one of the kingdom's most respected lawyers, are instructive. In 1998, when he was head of the Judicial Council and a Court of Cassation judge, he swam against the official tide in a matter involving what the US State Department called 'an influential member of society' whom the criminal court had found guilty of selling babies born out of wedlock to foreign adoptive parents.[5] An Appeal Court, whose panel of judges was allegedly carefully selected to favour the baby-trafficker, then reversed the decision of the lower court. 'The US authorities [who had taken a close interest in the case] called King Hussain and voiced their surprise', recalled Al-Kilani. 'The king asked me to come and see him, and he told me about the corruption and how he had been called by US officials'.[6] Having learned all this, Al-Kilani in February 1998 recommended that the three Appeal Court judges be retired but this was refused. The same month Al-Kilani was himself forcibly retired from the Court of Cassation, to which he had only recently been appointed. In January that year he had been a member of a Higher Court of Justice panel which, to the government's deep embarrassment, had ruled that May 1997 amendments to the Press Law were unconstitutional (see Chapter 14), and he strongly suspects that this had already put him in bad odour with the authorities. Today, the reception area of his private law firm is adorned with a large set of scales – the traditional symbol of justice – with one of its pans permanently weighed down with money.

The legal system's independence and integrity are also threatened by *wasta* (see p. 69), which is used to secure appointments and advancement and to influence legal rulings, and by the continuing importance of traditional tribal codes of conduct and dispute resolution. Al-Kilani cited the case of one Judicial Council head who had appointed no less than 40 judges who were members of his tribe.[7] A Transparency International report on Jordan noted 'the dominance of traditions that allow notables to go to judges pleading with them to change their minds or to issue the desired ruling'.[8] That the formal and traditional systems cannot necessarily co-exist harmoniously was dramatically underlined by the Ma'an crisis of 2002 (see Chapter 3). In its report on the episode, the International Crisis Group noted: 'The government and police often allowed Ma'anis to resolve local disputes according to local traditions and gave family elders custody of detained men instead of sending them to court or prison…This approach maintained security for decades but problems emerged in the 1990s when small armed groups began to interpret and enforce the law as they saw fit, using their own traditions and weapons and disregarding the state's laws, courts and police'.[9]

For diehard pan-Arabists, the very legitimacy of the legal system is open to question. Somewhat disconcertingly, for he is president of the 12,000-member Lawyers' Association, Hussain al-Mujalli pointed out that Article 1 of Jordan's Constitution asserts that 'the people of Jordan form a part of the Arab Nation', and that Article 24 affirms that 'the Nation is the source of all powers'. Therefore, he insisted, 'all the Arab countries are one nation, and that is the only legal state. No regional country [i.e. subdivision of the Arab world] is constitutional and neither is its legislature. All [Jordanian] laws are supposed to reflect the will of the *whole* nation, and any law that does not is not legal'.[10] It followed that in Jordan 'the law reflects neither the will of Jordanians nor the spirit of the Constitution'. Born in Jerash in 1937 and married with four children, Al-Mujalli cuts a striking figure with his grey suit, grey hair and grey-streaked moustache and eyebrows. He is a staunch Nasserist, and a black-and-white photo of the late Egyptian leader is displayed high on a wall of his office. Since 1985 he has been elected to five two-year terms as president of the association, membership of which is obligatory for Jordanian lawyers. Was it not difficult to reconcile his stance with his professional responsibilities? 'It's difficult', he replied, 'but I was elected by the lawyers, who know my position'. Subject to the caveat concerning the legitimacy of the kingdom and its law-making process, Al-Mujalli nevertheless concedes that the authorities do 'respect the law, relatively speaking, in comparison with other countries'.

State Security Court

The civil court system is not immune from abuse but, generally, it delivers justice. In contrast, State Security Court proceedings have done much to tarnish Jordan's claim to be a country that respects the rule of law. The court, which is the successor to the military tribunals of the martial law period and to which cases are brought by a special state security prosecutor, may have two military and one civilian judges although usually it has been staffed by military judges. Cases and trials are normally open to the public although some are open only to the press. Decisions may be appealed to the Court of Cassation, which can review both matters of fact and of law, and such appeals are mandatory where the death sentence has been imposed. Under a contentious temporary law issued in 2001, however, a former right of appeal for misdemeanours was abolished (see p. 202). Although the court's procedures are based on those of the criminal courts, there are fewer safeguards for defendants. Amnesty International asserts that the State Security Court 'does not provide the same guarantees of independence and impartiality provided by the ordinary courts'.[11]

In Jordan, said then information minister Muhammad Idwan, suspects 'are represented by lawyers and charged with crimes specified in the various laws. You don't just grab them and put them in prison'.[12] True, but not always entirely so. Often, State Security Court defendants are held in lengthy incommunicado pre-trial detention and there have been frequent allegations of the use of torture to extract confessions. Although the Court of Cassation has ruled confessions obtained under torture to be inadmissible and has quashed State Security Court verdicts as a result, independent observers insist that miscarriages of justice nevertheless occur. Amnesty International has highlighted the case of Jamal Darwish Fatayer, a Palestinian born in Iraq who was sentenced to death by the State Security Court on 17 December 2002 for his alleged role in the murder in Beirut in 1994 of a Jordanian diplomat, Na'ib Umran al-Ma'aytah.[13] His case was appealed to the Court of Cassation, which in April 2003 upheld the verdict and sentence. Fatayer had been arrested in Libya in October 2001 and deported to Jordan on 27 December 2001. He was held in incommunicado detention by the General Intelligence Department (GID) for about one month before being transferred to Juweida prison. He claimed that a confession he made was the result of torture by the GID, and that he was in Sudan at the time of the diplomat's murder. In

December 2002, Yasser Abu Shannar, another defendant in the same case, was executed. In his trial he had testified that he had never met Jamal Fatayer. On 26 August 2003, following Fatayer's execution, Amnesty International issued a press release asserting that his trial had fallen 'seriously short of international standards' and noting that Fatayer's 'claims that "confessions" had been extracted under torture were ignored by both the State Security Court and the Court of Cassation'.[14]

Criminal proceedings in the civil courts have sometimes been marred in the same way. An example was the case of Ali Taher Ali, an Iraqi who in January 2003 was sentenced to death by the Criminal Court after confessing to a murder. Although his trial was criticised by Amnesty International as 'apparently unfair', the Court of Cassation upheld the verdict and sentence.[15] A Jordanian, Ward Amin Abd al-Qader Abdullah, was found guilty with Ali, and was also sentenced to death. Declaring itself 'extremely concerned' at reports that Ali had been tortured while in police custody, Amnesty noted that it had 'frequently voiced its concerns over reports of the torture and ill-treatment in Jordan of detainees to extract "confessions"'. It also noted that the courts sometimes accepted such 'confessions' even though the Penal Code stipulated that a confession should be accepted as the sole evidence in a case only where it was voluntary, clear and consistent with the crime details.

Honour crimes

Jordan has signed and ratified a series of international treaties on human and other rights including the International Covenant on Civil and Political Rights, the International Covenant on Economic, Social and Cultural Rights, the International Convention on the Elimination of All Forms of Racial Discrimination and the Convention Against Torture and other Cruel, Inhuman or Degrading Treatment or Punishment. Its record on one of these treaties, the International Convention on the Elimination of All Forms of Discrimination against Women, however, remains deeply contentious. Jordan ratified the accord in 1992 but it has still not been published in the kingdom's *Official Gazette*, the step that makes legislation effective. A key point of conflict between the Convention and the kingdom's Penal Code is the latter's continued sanctioning of so-called 'honour crimes'. In Jordan, as in other parts of the region, a family's honour rests largely on the correct conduct of its female members in their dealings with men. In order to 'cleanse' a family's good name, women who have transgressed social norms are sometimes murdered by their male relatives. Although often portrayed as an Islamic phenomenon, in reality it is far more a matter of tradition. Nothing in Islam provides for such brutality. In Jordan, about 25 women fall victim to honour crimes each year, accounting for a large proportion of all murders in the kingdom. Articles 340 and 98 of the Penal Code effectively encourage the practice. Until its amendment in 2001, Article 340 exempted from any penalty a man who killed or wounded his wife or a female relative after discovering her in the act of committing adultery. A combination of local campaigning by human rights activists and international pressure spurred the authorities into action. In 1999 King Abdullah, whose wife, Rania, has been a leading campaigner against honour crimes, formed a special committee to review the legislation. This recommended the repeal of Article 340 and the proposal was presented to parliament in November 1999 and again in January 2000. On both occasions, however, it was approved by the appointed Senate but rejected by the elected Chamber of Deputies, dominated by conservative Islamists and traditionally-minded tribal and other notables. In 2001, while parliament was suspended, a temporary law was issued that amended Article 340, lifting its blanket exoneration for men who had perpetrated honour crimes but holding that they could plead the circumstances as a mitigating factor.

The amended article also applied to women who attacked their husbands (although not their male relatives) in similar circumstances – an empty gesture because honour crimes are almost exclusively directed against women. After the mid-2003 elections the temporary law amending Article 340 was twice presented to parliament for ratification, on each occasion again being approved by the Senate but rejected by the Chamber of Deputies. As at the end of 2004, the matter was still pending.

In practice, Article 340 has rarely been invoked, if only because it is rare for a woman to be discovered in flagrante. The usual defence in honour crime cases has been Article 98 of the Penal Code, which provides for reduced penalties for those who commit crimes 'in a fit of fury caused by an unlawful and dangerous act on the part of the victim'. In cases where the crime would normally be punishable by death, Article 98, whose language may appear gender-neutral but in practice is applied only to the benefit of men, provides for a minimum sentence of one year's imprisonment. For other felonies it is reduced to a prison term of between six months and two years. In addition, courts may halve the sentence where the victim's family waives its right to file a crime complaint. Human Rights Watch has observed: 'In murders for "honor", given the family's complicity in the crime, the family nearly always "waives" the right to file a complaint. Thus, "honor" killers may receive sentences of six months – and often do. If a killer has served that much time awaiting trial, the sentence may be commuted to time served and he may walk away a free man'.[16] The courts frequently accept defences under Article 98 for murders that, far from arising from 'a fit of fury', were plainly premeditated. They also accept a mere suspicion of sexual indiscretion as sufficient justification for the invocation of Article 98. One case in which it was applied in 2001 involved a man who had killed his sister after seeing a man leave her house. In 2002 it was deployed in the case of a man who had murdered his sister after she had talked to a man at a wedding party.

The Penal Code's provisions on honour crimes are not the only Jordanian laws that conflict with the Convention on the Elimination of All Forms of Discrimination against Women. Temporary laws issued in 2001 included several granting equality to women in matters such as nationality, passports and retirement, and an amended Personal Status Law which, as well as giving women the right to divorce their husbands in return for financial compensation, raised the legal age of marriage from 15 and 16 for girls and boys to 18 for both. Parliamentary resistance to these measures has been as strong as to the amended Article 340. Reporting the Chamber of Deputies' June 2004 refusal, for the second time, to approve the amended Personal Status Law, the *Jordan Times* said that opponents had argued that 'the amended law "encourages immorality, is against Islamic *shari'a* and disintegrates family values'. Suleiman Swiss, president of the Jordan Human Rights Society, was quoted as saying: 'Deputies are against these laws because they think if women secure more achievements, males in our society would lose their authority. Many are using religion as an excuse to resist these changes'.[17]

Reforms

From the start of his reign, King Abdullah has stressed the importance of judicial independence and the need for reforms to boost the legal system's efficiency. In his Letter of Designation to his first prime minister, Abdur Rauf ar-Rawabdah, on 4 March 1999, he called for new legislation 'to ensure the independence of the judiciary' and for measures aimed at 'improving the working conditions of the judges and promoting legislation that governs the judicial process in order to facilitate and speed up the process of securing the rights of all'.[18] There were few signs of tangible progress and in his Designation Letter to Ali Abu Ragheb in June 2000 the king called again for measures to 'protect [the judiciary's] independence and promote its efficiency and ability to expedite judicial procedures', including steps to improve judges' professional skills. He also stressed 'the importance of securing means of satisfaction and honourable living for all those working in this important sector', affirming that 'justice is the basis of governance'.[19] In August 2000 a Royal Commission on the Judiciary was established to prepare a judicial development programme. Its recommendations included doubling the number of judges, raising their salaries and sending them on training courses, computerising the court system, and building new court complexes in the kingdom's main towns. In early 2001 there were some 400 judges. By mid-2004 there were 600, of whom 19 were women, and further expansion is planned.[20] Strikingly absent from the reform programme, however, are plans for the establishment of a specialised Constitutional Court, a project that had been recommended both in the National Charter and the Jordan First Document. Although the civil courts have asserted a right to review the constitutionality of legislation, this right has not been confirmed and the position remains uncertain.

In letter and spirit?

In Jordan's official discourse, the rule of law is paramount. The quasi-constitutional National Charter of 1991 declares Jordan's 'adherence to the principle of the supremacy of the law'. The Jordan First Document of 2002 affirms: 'From the state, citizens expect justice, equality, the Rule of Law, transparency and accountability'. Both reaffirm the Constitution as the fundamental basis of the state. But while the Constitution sets out in detail the rights and responsibilities of citizens and state agencies, these are qualified as being 'subject to the law' (see Chapter 2). In effect, constitutional safeguards against an overweening state take second place to the law. Often, governments and politicians have paid more heed to the Constitution's letter than to its spirit, using the law to nullify constitutional freedoms and to shield the wealthy and powerful from accountability – in the process undermining the very rule of law to which the establishment habitually professes such fierce allegiance.

In 2001–03, when parliament was suspended, Ali Abu Ragheb's government issued some 220 temporary laws, many with grave consequences for civil liberties. They were promulgated on the basis of Article 94 of the Constitution, which permits laws to be issued while parliament is not sitting only in respect of matters 'which admit of no delay or which necessitate expenditures incapable of postponement'. Critics insist that there was no urgency that could have warranted Abu Ragheb's temporary laws, condemning them as a cynical and unconstitutional ploy by his government to further its agenda with a minimum of opposition and oversight. The International Crisis Group has observed that the temporary laws 'harmed the credibility of the legislative process'.[21] The Constitution requires that temporary laws be placed before parliament for approval, amendment or rejection as soon as it reconvenes. At the time of writing the parliament resulting from the June 2003 elections was still working its way through the long list of temporary laws.

In 2004 Muhammad Hammouri was amongst the lawyers acting for a group of 28 political figures who had lodged a Higher Court of Justice challenge to the legality of the 2003 elections on the basis that they had been staged under a temporary electoral law issued in July 2001. 'The government said that this temporary law had been issued according to the condition of necessity', he observed. 'How on earth can I understand that there was a necessity to abolish the permanent [electoral] law and issue a temporary law? I understand what necessity means: war, earthquake or something like that'.[22] On learning that a series of temporary laws was planned, Hammouri had written an article in the daily *Ad-Dustour* warning the prime minister that they would be unconstitutional. 'He didn't listen', said Hammouri. 'And after a person has killed the first victim and seen the blood, he doesn't care if he kills a lot of people. In other countries, issuing a law takes much work in specialised committees and much time. Here, in this period between 17 July 2001 [the day parliament was dissolved] and 16 June 2003 [the day before the elections], on average the cabinet met twice a week and issued one law per meeting'.

A readiness to sail close to the legal wind has also permeated the authorities' efforts to curb over-critical democracy and human rights activists. An example was the manner in which the Jordanian Society for Citizens' Rights (JSCR) was dissolved in September 2002. The pretext was that it had violated Law 33 of 1966, governing associations, by failing to submit financial and administrative reports to the interior ministry for 1999–2001. Dr Fawzi Samhouri, formerly the JSCR's Chairman, insists that Law 33 applies only to 'associations or unions' and not to 'societies'. There was 'nothing in this law or any other requiring us to submit annual reports to the ministry', he said, adding: 'Despite that, had they asked us for the reports we would have sent them'.[23] Under Law 33, the ministry is required to inform a society in writing of any transgressions, and the society then has one month to rectify the situation. If the society ignores the warning, the minister can dissolve its board pending the election of a new board within two months. Even though the ministry invoked Law 33 to justify its action against the JSCR, it failed to issue any written warning and, rather than dissolving the board, it closed down the entire society.

Although the fight against corruption is high on the official agenda, the wealthy and powerful have blatantly used legal loopholes to evade justice. A celebrated example was the failure of attempts to prosecute former ministers, including an ex-prime minister, in eight major corruption scandals in the late 1980s. The cases related to gold purchases from the Central Bank, housing construction in the Abu Nuseir district of Amman, the construction of Suwaqa prison, some 70 kilometres south of the capital, and commission-taking on other major projects. The Constitution stipulates that ministers accused of law-breaking must be tried by a specially constituted High Tribunal (see p. 193). Because the accused in the corruption cases were no longer in government, the cases against them were raised in the ordinary civil courts. This was challenged on the grounds that the High Tribunal should hear cases involving both serving and former ministers. After lengthy deliberations in parliament and by legal specialists, the challenge was upheld. The cases were excluded from the civil courts but, partly because of the time that had elapsed and partly because of an absence of political will, no steps were taken to convene a High Tribunal, requiring a two-thirds majority vote of the lower house. To impeach a serving minister had been difficult enough. The outcome of the eight corruption cases 'set a precedent against prosecuting former ministers as well'.[24]

In related vein, Milton-Edwards and Hinchcliffe (the latter a former British ambassador to Jordan) have observed: 'The super rich of suburban Amman live in ostentatious splendour, seemingly unscathed by financial stringency… Popular belief equates much of their wealth with unscrupulous and opportunist land speculation and corruption. From their ranks come most of the ruling clique, including some of the senior members of the [then] government who have large question marks against their personal integrity and whose past (all too public) misdemeanours have gone unpunished because of personal influence with the system of justice'.[25] The International Commission of Jurists (ICJ) has cited a case where 'a judge gave a reception to celebrate the verdict of innocence of a politician...He was given a promotion afterwards'.[26]

It would be going too far to assert that the Jordanian establishment cares nothing for the rule of law. But there is certainly a predilection on the part of some to push the law to its limits, and sometimes beyond, that seriously erodes wider public confidence in the legal system. Professor Hammouri believes that the establishment's sometimes cavalier attitude to the law stems fundamentally from the unaccountability of the political process. The overriding priority was to 'keep the monarch separate from everything negative: from wrongdoings by the government, by anyone. And, under the law, no-one can criticise the king. Full stop,' he said. 'The king selects a government. If he finds that they made a mess, he dismisses them and brings in another cabinet. But the former cabinet is never held liable for its actions'. As a result, politicians 'have no incentive to give a damn about ruling the country in a proper manner, according to the Constitution'.

Notes

1   US State Department, *Country Reports on Human Rights Practices 2003 – Jordan* (Washington DC: Bureau of Democracy, Human Rights and Labor, 25 February 2004).

2   Interview with author, Amman, 7 October 2003.

3   Interview with author, Amman, 18 April 2004.

4   US State Department, *Country Reports on Human Rights Practices 2003 – Jordan*.

5   US State Department, *Jordan Country Report on Human Rights Practices for 1998* (Washington DC: Bureau of Democracy, Human Rights and Labor, 26 February 1999).

6   Interview with author, Amman, 7 October 2003.

7   Ibid.

8   Basem Sakijha and Saeda Kilani, *National Integrity Systems: Country Study Report: Jordan 2001* (Berlin: Transparency International: 2001), p. 8.

9 International Crisis Group (ICG), *Red Alert in Jordan: Recurrent Unrest in Maan* (Amman and Brussels: ICG, 19 February 2003), p. 9.
10 Interview with author, Amman, 9 October 2003.
11 Amnesty International, *Jordan: An Absence of Safeguards* (London: Amnesty International, 1 November 1998), p. 9.
12 Interview with author, Amman, 24 February 2003.
13 Amnesty International, *Jordan: Jamal Darwish Fatayer*, 19 December 2002.
14 Amnesty International, *Halt the Death Penalty*, News Service No. 198, 26 August 2003.
15 Amnesty International, *Jordan: Ali Jabbar Taher Ali; Ward Amin Abd al-Qader Abdullah*, 11 July 2003.
16 Human Rights Watch, *Honoring the Killers: Justice Denied for 'Honor' Crimes in Jordan* (New York: Human Rights Watch, April 2004).
17 Rana Husseini, 'House rejection of khuloe law dismays human rights activists', *Jordan Times*, 29 June 2004.
18 www.kingabdullah.jo
19 Ibid.
20 Rami Abdelrahman, 'King reiterates support for judicial reform programme', *Jordan Times*, 25–6 June 2004.
21 International Crisis Group (ICG), *The Challenge of Political Reform: Jordanian Democratisation and Regional Instability* (Amman and Brussels: ICG, 8 October 2003), p. 7.
22 Interview with author, Amman, 18 April 2004.
23 Interview with author, Amman, 5 October 2003.
24 Basem Sakijha and Sa'eda Kilani, *National Integrity Systems*, p. 6.
25 Beverley Milton-Edwards and Peter Hinchcliffe, *Jordan: A Hashemite Legacy* (London: Routledge, 2001), p. 123.
26 International Commission of Jurists (ICJ), *Attacks on Justice 2000 – Jordan*, (Geneva: ICJ, 13 August, 2001), p. 3.

CHAPTER 14

'The Sky's the Limit': The Media

'I HAVE 40 YEARS' experience as a journalist, 30 years as a political writer, and they drag me off to prison in handcuffs like a common criminal!' complained Fahd al-Rimawi, editor-in-chief and proprietor of the weekly newspaper *Al-Majd*.[1] On arriving at Amman's Queen Alia international airport on 9 May 2004 after a trip to the United States, Al-Rimawi was questioned for several hours but not detained. The following day, however, he was arrested and taken to Juweida prison, on the southern edge of Amman, pending an appearance before the State Security Court for 'harming relations with a brotherly Arab country', a charge carrying a maximum penalty of five years' imprisonment. For good measure, his newspaper was suspended as of 10 May. Al-Rimawi's offence was to have published an editorial entitled 'Cowardice as Policy' in which he had accused the Saudi Arabian authorities of acting like 'lackeys of the United States'. While in the US, he had watched a television interview with the Saudi ambassador, Prince Bandar bin Sultan, about the revelation in *Washington Post* reporter Bob Woodward's book *Plan of Attack* that Prince Bandar had known of US plans to invade Iraq even before Secretary of State Colin Powell. Al-Rimawi's arrest prompted an outcry from international press freedom watchdogs such as Paris-based Reporters Sans Frontières. Following intervention by Prime Minister Faisal Fayez and mediation by Ibrahim Izzadine, president of the Higher Media Council (see p. 220), he was freed after 36 hours in detention, the charge against him was dropped and the ban on *Al-Majd* was lifted. In return, Al-Rimawi undertook to publish an article in the next issue of his paper explicitly praising relations between Jordan and Saudi Arabia.

It was the first of two clashes between *Al-Majd* and the authorities during 2004. On 19 September the State Security Court prosecutor banned the paper from going to press after Al-Rimawi had refused to remove from its forthcoming issue a front-page opinion piece about oil grants to Jordan from Gulf states and a news report on Israeli-Jordanian trade relations. It was allowed to publish its subsequent edition only after Al-Rimawi had agreed that it would not carry the offending articles. Al-Rimawi observed that the issue would be 'somewhat grey, not provocative'.[2]

Al-Rimawi is a Nasserist who left his home town of Ramallah in the West Bank in 1969 after coming under pressure from the Israeli occupiers because of his nationalist stance. A stockily built cigar-smoker with receding hair, white at the sides, he has an intense glare that some might find forbidding, accentuated by his grey-white eyebrows. Speaking in his slightly shabby office, above a shop selling songbirds in Amman's Dahiya district, Al-Rimawi recalled that *Al-Majd* had first been closed, for three months, in 1997 as the result of the financial provisions of a media law promulgated that year (see p. 215). In 1999 it had been closed for one week after reporting that Prince Hassan, on learning that he was to lose his title of Crown Prince, had presented his personal pistol to King Hussain, saying: 'If you doubt my loyalty, shoot me now'. On that occasion, he had been referred to the Court of First Instance. 'Two armed police officers came to take me to court', he said. 'I was treated in a very civil manner. I drank coffee with the police and was allowed to speak with my lawyer. I was only arrested for three hours'.[3] The case against him personally was abandoned. He filed a case against the government challenging his paper's closure, and the court found in his favour. Only one issue of *Al-Majd* was lost.

He fell foul of the authorities again in 2002. 'On 13 January – it was my 60th birthday – I was summoned to the State Security Court, where I was arrested by the General Intelligence Department (GID)', he related. 'I was transferred to Juweida where I was to have spent 15 days. There was an outcry, within Jordan and internationally, that forced the prime minister to order my release after four days'.[4] He was accused of 'writing and publishing false information and rumours that may harm the prestige and reputation of the state and slander the integrity and reputation of its members'.[5] The offending article had called on the government to resign in the light of an opinion survey by Jordan University's Centre for Strategic Studies that had shown it to enjoy the support of only 13 per cent of the public. 'Any government in such a position should resign', said Al-Rimawi. 'Instead, they put me in jail'.[6]

Unsavoury episodes

The recent history of Jordan's media is peppered with such unsavoury episodes. On 16 January 2003 three journalists from the weekly *Al-Hilal* were arrested and their publication was shut down after it had published an article speculating about the Prophet Muhammad's sexual potency after marrying Aisha, his favourite of 14 wives. Jordan's Islamic establishment was scandalised. 'The prophets were men of religion, not sex', protested former minister for religious affairs Brahim Zaid Kilani, a leading cleric with the Islamic Action Front (IAF).[7] On 21 January the IAF's committee of clerics issued a *fatwa*, or religious edict, affirming: 'Islamic *shari'a* [religious law] deems those who abase the Prophet, insult or slander him or his message as apostates and renegades who, according to the Holy *Qur'an*, will burn in hell for eternity'.[8] On 17 February the State Security Court ordered *Al-Hilal* to close for two months and convicted editor-in-chief, Nasser Qamash, managing editor, Roman Haddad, and writer Muhannad Mbaidin of defaming the Prophet; insulting the dignity of the state and individuals, leading to incitement; insulting divine religions; and publishing false information and rumour. Mbaidin was sentenced to six months in prison, Qamash to three months and Haddad to two months. Haddad and Qamash were allowed to pay fines in lieu of serving the remainder of their sentences and were freed on 18 February. Mbaidin served his full six months.

At 10.00 p.m. on 10 November 2002 police raided the home in Amman of Yasser Abu Hilala, a columnist for the daily *Ar-Ra'i*, detained him and seized a laptop computer and some of his files. Shortly before, Abu Hilala had sent information about the clashes then taking place in the southern town of Ma'an (see Chapter 3) to the headquarters in Qatar of the Arab satellite TV channel Al-Jazeera. The same night, plain-clothes police arrested Abu Hilala's cousin, Samir, at the offices of the daily *Al-Arab al-Yawm*. His arrest came minutes after Al-Jazeera had broadcast a telephone interview with him about the Ma'an crisis. Both were accused of disseminating 'false information', a crime punishable by up to six months imprisonment, but were released after 24 hours after a state security prosecutor ruled that there was no basis for the accusation against them.

On 14 August 2002 Ma'moun al-Roussan, editor-in-chief of the weekly journal *Al-Jazeera* (which is unconnected to the television channel of the same name), and Sakher Abu Anzeh, its publisher and chairman of its board, were arrested after the journal published an article and photo-montage lampooning the Qatari authorities. The offending article had raised questions about Qatar's relations with Israel while the montage had depicted Qatar's head of state, Hamad bin Khalifa al-Thani, as a female singer and his foreign minister, Hamad bin Jassem al-Thani, as a belly-dancer. Al-Roussan and Abu Anzeh were accused of 'harming relations with a foreign country', 'contempt toward a foreign head of state and his foreign minister' and 'disseminating false reports'.[9] Abu Anzeh was freed on bail on 15 August while Al-Roussan was released after a week in detention.

A week earlier, on 7 August 2002, the then Information Minister Muhammad Idwan revoked the Al-Jazeera TV station's licence to operate in Jordan and barred its staff from working in the kingdom after it had broadcast a talk show in which the monarchy had been severely criticised. The broadcast had 'surpassed all kinds of decency in its programmes by attacking the nation's leaders and nobilities', asserted Idwan. It had con-stituted 'pure defamation against Jordan and the royal family'.[10] On 11 August officials at Amman airport seized 29 video cassettes belonging to Al-Jazeera's sports correspondent, who was on his way to Qatar. The station's Amman bureau remained closed until March 2003.

'Reasonable' red lines

I asked Fahd al-Rimawi what was his assessment of the level of press freedom in Jordan. 'There is none', he replied.[11] That's surely an over-statement, but his underlying point holds good. The Jordanian media is certainly more free and therefore more diverse and lively than its counter-parts in many other regional states, but it is subject to severe legal con-straints as well as a range of potent informal pressures. 'Freedom is not absolute', the then Information Minister Muhammad Idwan, told me. 'If it's absolute, it becomes the rule of the jungle. All freedoms, including freedom of expression and the press, have red lines'. In Jordan, the main red lines are the royal family, religion and national security. These were 'red lines that everybody knows, everybody respects', he said, adding: 'We feel that our red lines are reasonable'.[12]

The same ambivalence permeates the 1991 National Charter and the 2002 Jordan First Document (see Chapter 3). The Charter declares that 'Jordan's information philosophy must be based on the principles of freedom, national responsibility, respect for the truth and regard for the values of the Arab and Islamic nation', and that 'freedom of thought and expression, and access to information, must be viewed as a right of every citizen, as well as of the press and other mass media'. It goes on to affirm, however, that while 'the state must guarantee free access to information', this should only be 'to the extent that it does not jeopardise national security or the national interest'. The media 'must have a formative role in shaping citizen attitudes of commitment to their country and nation and pride in their Arab and Islamic heritage' and must exercise this function 'in a manner that would…contribute to preserving social harmony and national unity'. The Jordan First Document affirms that 'the information model we want places Jordanian national interests in the forefront of its priorities', stressing that the media should exercise 'its monitoring role in *responsible freedom*' (my italics). King Abdullah's 'Media Vision', posted on his website, proclaims the importance of 'creating a modern free Jordanian media'.[13] It goes on, however, to assert that the media should operate in 'a climate of independence and *responsible freedom*' (my italics again) and that its practices should be 'based upon professionalism, excellence, creativity and *responsible freedom*'.

On media freedom, insists King Abdullah, 'the sky's the limit'.[14] But he adds that he draws a line where 'national interests' are at stake. In such cases, he said, 'I can't be very democratic'. Media reports likely to affect Jordan's foreign relations were one key area of concern, and certainly there have been numerous instances of adverse reporting souring relations between Middle Eastern states, sometimes with grave consequences for aid and trade. Equally intolerable were reports that destabilised Jordan by sowing discord between its communities, he said, citing as examples 'articles saying Jordanians of Palestinian origin are bad, or Christians are bad, or Muslims are this [or that]'. On all other domestic matters, there were no constraints. 'If you want to report on me, or you want to report on the government, or you want to report on crime or on corruption, then I think that's fine', said the king. Much of the authorities' heavy-handed treatment of the media had resulted from over-sensitive prime ministers, he averred. 'The problem in the past has come back to prime ministers who have taken it personally'. Before taking power, politicians were 'very thick-skinned'. But 'the minute they get into government it's "how dare he write about me?" Government leadership has to mature to be able to take the shots that the rest of us have been used to taking for quite a while'. The king contrasted the pique displayed by certain prime ministers with his own stance. 'Sima [Dr Sima Bahous, director of the Royal Court's communications and information division, who was present] sends me all sorts of things that people write about me. You don't see me taking people to court'.

Jordan's media

Jordan's biggest-selling daily newspaper, *Ar-Ra'i* ('Opinion') was established in 1971 and has a circulation of a little over 100,000. Although its publisher, the Jordan Press Foundation, is 62 per cent owned by the government via the Social Security Fund, the paper gained a reputation during the martial law era for pushing at the limits of what the authorities would tolerate. As a result it suffered much government interference and harassment, culminating in 1988 with the dissolution of its board and its replacement with government appointees. Although the sacked board was restored in 1989, the paper has continued to adopt a conservative line while giving space to independent commentators in its opinion pages.

In second place amongst the dailies, with a circulation of about 100,000, is *Ad-Dustour* ('The Constitution'), which was founded in 1967. 'The paper is characterised by its moderate approach, a middle-of-the-road approach', said editor-in-chief Nabil Sharif. 'We never really sided with any government. We tried to remain neutral and to have allegiance to the king and to the country without being considered this or that prime minister's newspaper'.[15] Another, and not necessarily conflicting, view comes from a 1997 report by the media freedom organisation Article 19. 'With the exception of its columnists, *Ad-Dustour* deviates very little from what it believes to be the official view', it said. 'Most of its coverage is concentrated on the Royal Family and government announcements and shows little sign of investigative reporting'.[16] Article 19 added, however, that the paper 'is now developing a new look, dedicating space to opposition views and giving special attention to the coverage of press freedom and human rights'.

Ad-Dustour was originally an independent publication, owned by Sharif's family, but, he said, 'over the years successive governments bought shares – sometimes through pressure, by twisting martial laws'.[17] Thirty-one per cent of the paper is held by the Social Security Fund. Maintaining editorial independence had not been easy, said Sharif. As at *Ar-Ra'i*, the government in 1988 sacked *Ad-Dustour*'s entire board and replaced it with appointees, although the step was overturned in 1989. 'The degree of freedom that we enjoy matches the extent of the government's stake', observed Sharif. Already a member of the Higher Media Council (see below), Sharif on the day I met him was appointed minister of information.

The privately-owned daily *Al-Arab al-Yawm* ('The Arabs Today') was launched in April 1997 and quickly established a reputation for its independent political line and investigative stance – traits that the establishment equally quickly found intolerable. The paper was subjected to a sustained campaign that included law suits from the government and the Jordan Press Association (JPA – see p. 218), regulatory action against its staff by the JPA, a suspension of advertising by government agencies and companies, a suspension of news reports from the state news agency, Petra, and the arrest and detention, albeit for only a day, of its publisher, Riad Hroub, on corruption charges which he angrily denounced as fabricated. The battle between *Al-Arab al-Yawm* and the authorities climaxed in early 2000 when Hroub, reeling from the financial consequences of the government's campaign, sold out to Al-Ahli Bank. Since then, the paper has toed the official line. August 2004 saw the launch of another independently owned Arabic daily, *Al-Ghad*, which has emulated *Al-Arab al-Yawm*'s former independence and has been well received by the public.

The sole English-language daily is the *Jordan Times*, which, like *Ar-Ra'i*, is owned by the government-controlled Jordan Press Foundation. The paper, which has a circulation of around 7,000, is respected for its professional standards and has carved out a niche for itself as a 'window' on Jordan for the international community. Perhaps because the authorities like to emphasise the relative freedom of the kingdom's media, the paper has had slightly more room for manoeuvre than the local Arabic language press. 'We always felt that our "red lines" were a bit further away, and we always, slowly, gradually, pushed them a bit', said the paper's chief editor, Jennifer Hamarneh.[18]

Jordan boasts a range of Arabic language weeklies, most dating from the early 1990s when the law was changed to permit private ownership of publications. Most notable are the Islamist *As-Sabeel*, the liberal independent *Al-Urdun* and *Al-Hadath*; the Arab nationalist *Al-Majd* and *Al-Wahda*; and the pro-government *Al-Hilal*. All these publications have small circulations and limited revenues. All have suffered greatly from governmental moves to curb their independence, including the imposition of highly restrictive capital requirements and bans on advertising from state agencies and companies – measures that forced the closure of many other weeklies (see p. 215). More commercially successful have been the tabloid weeklies *Shihan* and *Al-Wasit*, the latter carrying only advertisements. The sole English-language weekly is the *Star*, published by the same company that owns the Arabic daily *Ad-Dustour*.

The state-owned Jordan Radio and Television Corporation, established in 1962, broadcasts Arabic and English radio services and on three television channels, one concentrating on news, current affairs and light entertainment, the second on local and international sports and the third offering mostly foreign cartoons and movies. Syrian and Israeli channels can also be received without satellite dishes. Arabic satellite channels, and especially Qatar-based Al-Jazeera, enjoy wide audiences in Jordan, mainly because of the professionalism and reliability of their news and current affairs coverage. The internet has been available in Jordan since April 1996 and is increasingly popular. Official agencies, including the Royal Court and even the General Intelligence Department (GID), maintain sometimes informative and usually well-constructed web sites.

Legal constraints

The media's 'red lines' are explicitly embedded in Jordan's Constitution and laws but their precise locations have always been defined vaguely, allowing the authorities to interpret them widely. The Constitution purports to guarantee freedom of expression and publication but subordinates this to legal constraints. Article 15 affirms: 'The State shall guarantee freedom of opinion. Every Jordanian shall be free to express his opinion by speech, in writing, or by means of photographic representation and other forms of expression, *provided that such does not violate the law*' (my italics). It stipulates that 'freedom of the press and publications shall be ensured *within the limits of the law*' and that 'newspapers shall not be suspended from publication nor shall their permits be revoked *except in accordance with the provisions of the law*'.

In 1993, in tune with the liberal climate that prevailed following the kingdom's first free and fair general election in 1989, a new Press and Publications Law was promulgated which, while including provisions severely curtailing media freedom, was the most liberal in Jordan's history. It affirmed that 'freedom of expression is guaranteed for every Jordanian' and that the media should enjoy 'free distribution of news, information and commentaries' and it enjoined the authorities to 'facilitate the mission of the journalist and the researcher'. The 1993 law for the first time enshrined the right of individuals to own and publish newspapers and it required the state to reduce its ownership stake in publishing houses to no more than 30 per cent by 1997. The law permitted the government to suspend publications temporarily but required a court ruling for more drastic closures. This was a significant advance as previously the government had been able to close publications at will. At the same time, however, Article 40 listed nine loosely-defined prohibited topics: news touching on the king and royal family; unauthorised information about the armed forces and security agencies; articles disparaging religions; articles that harmed national unity, incited crime or sowed hatred, disunity or discord in society; reports on the proceedings of closed sessions of parliament; articles that undermined confidence in the national currency; articles which insulted heads of Arab, Islamic or friendly states; articles that offended the dignity of individuals or tarnished their reputations; and articles contrary to ethics and public decency. It was stipulated that foreign publications that violated any of these prohibitions should be denied entry to the country. The 1993 law also reaffirmed that publications required licences from the minister of information, and it reiterated the official definition of a journalist as a member of the Jordan Press Association (see p. 218).

Despite its heavy restrictions, the 1993 press law encouraged a flourishing of the Jordanian media. Privately owned journals, mainly weeklies, proliferated, offering very different perspectives from those of the longer-established state-owned or influenced dailies. 'For the first time, Jordanians had access to a multitude of views concerning issues fundamentally vital to their lives, thoughts and beliefs', observed media analyst Sa'eda Kilani. 'While government and pro-government newspapers were only publishing the official point of view with little and mostly censored information of opposing arguments, the private press would be quick the next day to release statements and views of the opposition and independent voices in full'.[19] This did not mean that the establishment did not fight back tooth and nail. In the three years from July 1993 until July 1996 the government filed no less than 63 legal actions against journals.

The post-1993 vigour of the press, and its sharp criticisms of the 1994 peace treaty with Israel in particular, proved too much for the authorities. In May 1997, while parliament was in recess, the government of Abdul Salam Majali issued a temporary press law that increased the number of banned topics and, in a clear swipe at the privately owned weeklies, raised their minimum capital requirement from $21,150 to a crippling $423,000. It revoked the provision of the 1993 law requiring the state to reduce its stakes in publishing companies to a maximum of 30 per cent. In the 1993 law, fines for violations did not exceed $1,410 but the May 1997 law set fines at between $21,150 and $35,250. The new law stipulated a three-month deadline for implementing the new minimum capital requirements. Many publications were unable to comply and the government suspended 13 of them. The stricken journals took legal action, claiming that the law was unconstitutional, as Article 94 of the Constitution stipulated that while parliament was in recess, laws could be issued only in respect of 'matters which require necessary measures which admit of no delay or which necessitate expenditures incapable of postponement'. On 26 January 1998 the Higher Court ruled in favour of the plaintiffs. Undaunted, the government in August 1998 submitted to parliament a new press law that was very similar to that of May 1997 and in some respects even more draconian. It was swiftly approved by parliament and ratified by Prince Hassan, at the time crown prince and regent, on 1 September. To the 1993 law's list of prohibited subjects, it added bans on articles containing false information or rumours, and articles instigating strikes, sit-ins or public gatherings. Also banned was reporting on court cases unless authorised by the courts. The new law set reduced but still heavy minimum capital requirements, of $705,000 for dailies and $141,000 for weeklies, and it reaffirmed the requirements for publications to be licensed and for journalists to be members of the JPA. The law sparked a storm of protest by the local media and international human rights and media freedom agencies. Amnesty International, for example, declared that it 'seriously limits freedom of expression and the liberty of the press in Jordan'.[20]

Hopes were high that King Abdullah's succession to the throne in February 1999 would inaugurate a new, more liberal era. The first months of his reign saw a major debate about the role of the press and the king repeatedly declared his commitment to greater media freedom. The hopes were soon dashed. A new Press and Publications Law was promulgated in September 1999 which, while removing some of the most restrictive aspects of the 1998 law, introduced a series of new constraints. The law abolished the list of prohibited subjects but the effect was all but nullified by a reaffirmation of an article of the 1998 law requiring the media to 'respect the truth and refrain from publishing anything that conflicts with the principles of freedom, national responsibility, human rights and values of the Arab and Islamic nation'. Also prohibited was the publication of 'anything that might incite violence or discord among citizens'. The new law reduced the minimum capital requirement for weeklies to $70,500. But it maintained the government's right to licence publications and the requirement for journalists to be JPA members and sanctioned the pre-trial detention of journalists. Contrary to the official rhetoric about economic liberalisation, the law explicitly forbade foreign ownership of Jordanian publications. It also reaffirmed a ban, first introduced in the 1997 law, on research centres accepting local or foreign funding without the approval of the information minister.

As if all this were not enough, the media is also severely constrained by other laws including the Penal Code, the Contempt of Court Law of 1959, the Jordan Press Association Law of 1983 and the Law on State Secrets and Classified Documents. The Penal Code, for example, defines defamation very widely. Article 191 stipulates that it is punishable by imprisonment of between three months and two years if aimed at parliament or its members in the course of their work or at an official body, a court of law, a public institution, the army or any public servant in the course of his duties. Articles 189 and 196 make 'innuendo' and 'affronts' offences distinct from defamation that are punishable by imprisonment or fines if directed against any of the persons and parties specified in Article 191.

Amendments to Penal Code provisions relating to the press were promulgated on 2 October 2001, while parliament was suspended, as part of a wider package of measures prompted by the 11 September attacks in the United States. Article 150(a) was amended to provide for imprisonment of between three and six months for those guilty of 'disseminating false information and rumours' and those who published anything 'harming national unity'; 'harming the prestige, integrity and reputation of the state'; 'inciting disturbances, sit-ins and unauthorised public meetings';

'causing harm to the dignity, reputation or personal freedom of individuals'; and 'destabilising society through the promotion of deviance and immorality'. Article 195 was amended to criminalise any publication that infringed on 'the dignity of the king and other members of the royal family', and to bring violations of these Penal Code amendments under the jurisdiction of the State Security Court, whose procedures offer only limited safeguards for defendants (see Chapter 13). The amendment to Article 195 (though not that to Article 150(a)) was annulled in April 2003, perhaps because it had occurred to the authorities that nothing undermined Jordan's 'prestige, integrity and reputation' more than the promulgation of such repressive legislation.

Informal pressures

In addition to the formal, legal constraints, Jordan's media is subject to a range of informal pressures. The General Intelligence Department (GID) monitors the media closely via a dense network of agents and informers within the journalistic community. 'They [the GID] have their people in the press who are infiltrators', said Abdullah Hasanat, then chief editor of the *Jordan Times*. 'They report every movement, every trend. They also control the Jordan Press Association. In fact, they are all over. The intelligence department interferes in everything: hiring journalists, dismissing them, even they interfere in the raises journalists get every year'.[21] As a result, the authorities quickly learn of any forthcoming 'negative' media items and can take steps to block publication. Usually, a friendly telephone call to an editor does the trick. With opposition publications, other methods are used. Many of the weeklies use the presses of the major state-influenced dailies. When the authorities wish to prevent something from reaching the public, they often do so via the printers. One instance involved the weekly *Al-Wahda*, which prints at the presses of *Ad-Dustour*. In September 2003 *Al-Wahda* planned an issue revealing that detainees had been tortured. 'An employee in the printing house informed the *mukhabarat* [intelligence service]', said the paper's editor, Muwafaq Muhardeen. 'It always happens like that. So the GID called the management of the printing house and told them not to print'.[22] *Al-Wahda* was told that there had been a 'technical problem' with the printing process. 'At first we believed them, and the following week we sent the same issue to be printed', continued Muhardeen. 'This time, the prosecutor general at the State Security Court telephoned the printing house demanding that the issue be blocked. They wouldn't even give us a written statement. They just called by telephone! They might as well have sent an SMS!' Other informal methods of pressuring the media include the withholding of advertising by state companies and agencies, and the withholding of official news.

Unlike in some neighbouring states, officially inspired physical assaults on journalists are rare. Where journalists have been attacked, it has been because of articles that upset individuals or families. Especially in rural areas, there is little acceptance of the journalist's right to report embarrassing news. 'Journalism thrives only in open societies', said *Al-Hadath*'s editor, Nidal Mansour. 'In closed societies journalists' rights have no roots. There is progress of sorts in Amman. In villages, people can attack you'.[23] The same point was made by Ibrahim Izzadine, president of the Higher Media Council (see p. 220). 'We still have a conservative society, and it's not only the government that can be annoyed if the media goes out of bounds. [Ordinary] people can be annoyed too'.[24]

The establishment looks after its own. In addition to the stick, there is the carrot. Journalists who toe the line can expect career advancement. Many senior editors have gone on to top appointments in government, the Royal Court and the civil service. Journalists 'can be awarded a programme on television...or can be given another job (whether in the private or public sectors) to improve their financial situation', wrote Sa'eda Kilani. 'The government sometimes intervenes to employ them as correspondents for Arab and foreign publications, satellite channels and magazines that pay a higher salary'.[25]

The formal and informal constraints mean that most journalists and journals habitually censor themselves. 'I'll usually opt for caution', said Jennifer Hamarneh, chief editor of the *Jordan Times*. 'You get an instinct: what's going to work, what's not going to work'.[26] I asked *Al-Majd*'s Fahd al-Rimawi if he practised self-censorship. He replied without hesitation: 'There's no doubt about that'.[27]

Jordan Press Association

The Jordan Press Association (JPA), originally established in 1953 but regulated by a 1983 law, is the official journalists' union and has about 600 members. Membership is compulsory for those wishing to be recognised legally as journalists but is open only to those with a university degree or who have undergone at least three years' training with a Jordanian publication. As a result, a number of journalists are not JPA members. While the JPA has on occasion moved to defend press freedoms, it has frequently collaborated with government efforts to tame the media. It is 'considered by most Jordanian journalists, both members and non-members, as a state body whose aim is to control journalists. [The JPA's] history shows little in the way of achievement for the profession as a whole, enhancing press freedom or defending its members' rights', commented Article 19.[28] It added: 'During the period since the enactment of the Press and Publications Law in 1993, the JPA has particularly attacked private opposition newspapers and has accused them of offending against general morality and traditions and of violating general ethics'.[29]

Tariq al-Mumani, the JPA's secretary-general who is also deputy chief editor at *Ar-Ra'i*, rejects the suggestion that the JPA functions as a press watchdog for the government. 'We have a real role protecting journalists', he insists. 'We issue statements against the arrest of journalists and against anything that hinders journalistic freedom'.[30] He noted that he had personally intervened in the *Al-Hilal* case, guaranteeing bail for its editor. 'I tried to guarantee bail for the three others, and I tried to persuade [the authorities] to hear the case in an ordinary court, not the Security Court, but they refused'. He added that in the previous eighteen months the JPA had succeeded in securing the transfer of some ten other cases from the State Security Court to the criminal and civil courts. Mumani stressed, however, that the JPA favoured mediation over confrontation, observing: 'We have to co-operate with the authorities'.

A different stance is taken by Nidal Mansour, owner and editor of the weekly *Al-Hadath* and director of the independent Centre for Defending Freedom of Journalists (CDFJ). In 1999–2000 Mansour was the JPA's assistant secretary-general. His work with the CDFJ prompted the JPA's disciplinary committee to launch an investigation against him in July 2000. Concluding that he had violated JPA regulations by not working full time as a journalist and by accepting foreign funding for the CDFJ, the JPA on 5 September 2000 stripped Mansour of his JPA membership and imposed a permanent ban on future membership, barring him from ever working legally as a journalist in Jordan. Subsequently, UNESCO selected Mansour as a member of its Press Freedom Advisory Group. He insists that the JPA 'has no real independence and no capability to fight against the government because its membership is from entities such as *Ar-Ra'i*, *Ad-Dustour* and Petra that are government-controlled'.[31] Mansour and four other journalists founded the CDFJ in 1999 'because of the need for an independent centre to defend the media'. As part of its media freedom activities, the CDFJ works to deepen journalists' knowledge of the law and the judicial system and in June 2002 established a Media Legal Aid Centre to provide free advice to journalists facing prosecution. It also runs programmes to improve journalistic standards and encourage use of the internet.

Higher Media Council

In October 2001 the king called for the abolition of the powerful information ministry, the key agency through which the regime promoted its views and countered alternatives, and its replacement with an independent Higher Media Council. The change, he asserted, would widen media freedoms. The project was fraught with difficulty. The Council was created in December 2001 as a body with executive powers, charged with drafting a new regulatory framework for the media including new laws and a journalistic code of ethics. Disputes swiftly arose over its precise mandate, however, and there were claims that the government at that stage was resisting any relinquishment of its responsibilities for the press. Before long, the Council was paralysed and in July 2002 its president, Kamel Abu Jaber, a former foreign minister, resigned. In December 2002 the Council was reconstituted as a non-executive agency to undertake research, training programmes for journalists and press officers and to mediate disputes between the press, on the one hand, and the public and government agencies, on the other. The information ministry meanwhile lived on, to be abolished only in late 2003.

The Council, whose eleven members were all appointed by royal decree, was 'a real press council, like any press council anywhere, in any democracy' and was 'totally independent', said its new president, Ibrahim Izzadine, a former information minister and press secretary to King Hussain and an ex-ambassador to both London and Washington.[32] Operating from newly-built premises perched on a hill on the airport road, adjacent to the foreign ministry, the Council by mid-2003 had consulted widely with interested parties, prepared a review of all Jordanian media-related legislation and drafted a future work programme, and was preparing to open a small training centre. It had managed all this despite having a staff of only 12, all part-timers. Izzadine shares the conventional establishment view of the media's role, using the word 'professional' in the same way that other officials use the word 'responsible'. 'We know that we have to have a free press', he explained. 'We have to have less control. [But] we have to have a more professional press. We have to combine freedom of the press with professionalism'. Coming perilously close to advocating self-censorship by journalists, he averred: 'If you are professional, you can write exactly what you want and you can be sure that you won't be taken to court. If you know exactly how to write your article…' Central to the Higher Media Council's outlook is a belief that sufficient common ground can be found as the basis for harmonious co-existence between the media, officialdom, civil society organisations and a still socially and religiously conservative public. Izzadine's key aim is to build 'some sort of consensus' about the media's role.

Many in the media are deeply sceptical. 'I'm not against the Higher Media Council', said Nidal Mansour. 'I was happy when it was established. But I have a question: what is this Council's *real* role? Under the law establishing it, it cannot do any real work. It can't take executive decisions because the government has that power. And it cannot make laws, because that is for parliament'.[33] All that was left were the areas of professional ethics and mediation, but in these areas the Council's powers were ill-defined and lacked legal force, he continued. 'In the UK, India or Germany, the law is very clear on the rights of those countries' press councils. Here, it's a gift, not a right'.

Al-Majd's Fahd al-Rimawi was more scathing. 'The Higher Media Council and the government have a very nice and elegant discussion about the media, but actual practices are totally against us', he said. 'We say very nice things, in order to win aid from Europe and the United States. We show them that we're a forward-looking and civilised country compared with others in the region. But in practice it's the opposite'.[34]

Notes

1   'Jordanian editor speaks to *Khaleej Times*', *Khaleej Times*, 14 May 2004.
2   Alia Shukri Hamzeh, 'Al Majd to resume publication today', *Jordan Times*, 27 September 2004.
3   Interview with author, Amman, 9 October 2003.

4   Ibid.

5   Amnesty International, *Jordan: Security Measures Violate Human Rights*, February 2002.

6   Interview with author, Amman, 9 October 2003.

7   Nicolas Pelham, 'Jordanian blasphemy verdict shakes the free press', *Christian Science Monitor*, 18 February 2003.

8   Alia Shukri Hamzeh, 'IAF clerics issue *fatwa* against *Al-Hilal* journalists', *Jordan Times*, 22 January 2003.

9   Reporters Sans Frontières, *Chief Editor of Weekly Detained over Cartoon*, 17 August 2002.

10   Reporters Sans Frontières, *Al-Jazeera Office in Amman Shut Down*, 8 August 2002.

11   Interview with author, Amman, 9 October 2003.

12   Interview with author, Amman, 24 February 2003.

13   www.kingabdullah.jo

14   Interview with author, Amman, 29 June 2004.

15   Interview with author, Amman, 20 July 2003.

16   Article 19, *Blaming the Press: Jordan's Democratization Process in Crisis* (London: Article 19, October 1997), p. 24.

17   Interview with author, Amman, 20 July 2003.

18   Interview with author, Amman, 23 February 2003.

19   Sa'eda Kilani, *Press Freedoms in Jordan* (Copenhagen: Euro-Mediterranean Human Rights Network, February 2002), p. 17.

20   Amnesty International, *Jordan: An Absence of Safeguards* (London: Amnesty International, 1 November 1998), p. 7.

21   Sa'eda Kilani, *Press Freedoms in Jordan*, p. 43.

22   Interview with author, Amman, 9 October 2003.

23   Interview with author, Amman, 22 July 2003.

24   Interview with author, Amman, 20 July 2003.

25   Sa'eda Kilani, *Press Freedoms in Jordan*, p. 43.

26   Interview with author, Amman, 23 February 2003.

27   Interview with author, Amman, 9 October 2003.

28   Article 19, *Blaming the Press*, p. 35.

29   Ibid., p. 91.

30   Interview with author, Amman, 24 July 2003.

31   Interview with author, Amman, 22 July 2003.

32   Interview with author, Amman, 20 July 2003.

33   Interview with author, Amman, 22 July 2003.

34   Interview with author, Amman, 9 October 2003.

CHAPTER 15

'Investing in a Mobile Resource':
Higher Education

AHLIYA UNIVERSITY COULDN'T be anything but a private institution. Small red-and-white Kit-Kat chocolate bar advertisements adorn the sturdy three-seater wooden benches with black metal arms outside its magnificent 5,000-seat Arena. Nearby, and at other strategic locations on the campus, are double-sided free-standing billboards, two metres high and a metre wide, proclaiming the wonders of fashion houses such as Massimo Dutti and Pull & Bear, both Spanish-based. The 172,000-square-metre campus, its buildings faced with honey limestone, is beautifully maintained. Aleppo pines and other conifers scent the air and offer shade, contrasting with the barren surrounding hills. Near the entrance is the 'Abdoun Circle', a coffee bar named after one of Amman's chicest neighbourhoods (see p. 21), where young men and women sip drinks, chat and joke. All are casually but stylishly dressed, many in jeans and T-shirts – even the few girls with head scarves. These students are unmistakeably well-heeled. Ahliya has faculties of engineering; law; administration and financial services; pharmacy and medical services; arts and fine arts; and information technology. All are strikingly well equipped. The administration faculty, for example, has a 50-unit computer laboratory. The Arena, an immense modern sports and cultural complex that cost over $28 million, is unique in Jordan. It boasts a 25-metre swimming pool, a six-lane bowling alley, squash courts, a billiards hall and a fitness centre, all arranged around a 5,000-seat sports and concert hall. Stars who have recently played here include Sting, Celine Dion and the immensely popular Lebanese singer Fairouz. When I visited in October 2003 negotiations were under way for a concert by Colombia's Shakira, whose father is of Lebanese origin. Instead of a point on the undulating limestone plateau north-west of Amman, about midway between the capital and Madaba, Jerash and Salt, this could easily be North America – except for the mosque.

Founded in 1990, Ahliya was one of Jordan's first private universities. Today it has 5,000 students, 186 teaching staff and 260 administrative and support staff. 'We are certified by the Ministry of Higher Education for 6,000 students, but we're highly selective', said Ahliya's president, Abdul Rahim Hamdan, a 61-year-old petroleum geologist from Amman who gained his first degree from Cairo in 1965 and his Ph. D. from Queen's University in Kingston, Ontario, in 1972.[1] 'We're highly selective, and not everyone can afford our fees'. Most of the students come from wealthy Jordanian families but over one third hail from other Arab countries. They include 500 Arab Israelis and 370 Palestinians from the West Bank. No less than 33 different nationalities are represented in Ahliya's student body. About two thirds of the students are girls. Cultural and political Islamism is far less pronounced at Ahliya than in the public universities, where the social and religious mix reflects the wider society more closely. 'We are a liberal society', said Hamdan, who took up his post in September 2002 and previously was dean of the Science Faculty and vice-president of the state-sector Hashimiya University. 'You may find 60–70 per cent of females without a scarf. If you go to the [public] University of Jordan, the opposite is true. Our university reflects the families and particular societies these students come from. Most come from liberal families – although whether they are Muslim or Christian they observe their religion'.

The biggest faculty is financial and administrative services, followed by pharmacy, with engineering and IT in joint third place. Engineering students take four-and-a-half to five years to complete their course while the other programmes are shorter, requiring between three and four years. The curricula differ from those in the public universities, with an emphasis on fields directly relevant to a modern economy. 'In business and accounting, for example, we give great attention to providing our students with the IT tools needed in their profession', explained Hamdan. 'That's why most of our graduates have no problems finding jobs with good establishments in the country, and in neighbouring Arab countries too'. For engineering, pharmacy and IT, the fees are $2,500–$2,800 per year. Degree courses in the other faculties cost $2,000–$2,300 per year. Teaching staff salaries are 25–50 per cent higher than in state-run universities. 'A lecturer here with an MA degree would average $1,050 per month, compared with about $630 in public universities', said Hamdan. For Ph. D. holders, salaries vary from faculty to faculty. 'Just yesterday I appointed an assistant professor [with a Ph. D.] in the IT faculty and I gave him $3,250 per month', he said, adding: 'That's more than any IT professor can get in public universities'. Ahliya receives no financial support from the government. Student fees account for most of its income while the Arena, whose facilities are used for profit-making cultural, social and artistic events, is another significant source of income. The university is owned by a company whose biggest shareholder is Dr Ahmad al-Hourani, a wealthy self-made businessman and former Central Bank official, originally from the West Bank, who is also Ahliya's chairman. Hamdan consults him closely on financial matters but stressed that Al-Hourani 'never, ever interferes in academic matters'.

Impressive progress

From the kingdom's earliest days, when skilled Transjordanians were scarce, governments have given high priority to education. Initially, the key motive was the need to develop cadres to administer the new state. Later, and especially since the 1970s oil boom in the Gulf, an educated population was seen as a major economic resource. Thousands of Jordanians, many of Palestinian origin, found lucrative employment in the oil states and their remittances to their families back home became a major pillar of the kingdom's economy. 'We value education greatly', explained Bassam Saket, head of the kingdom's Securities Commission. 'We had to invest in a mobile resource – manpower – that could both render services to the country and be transferred to the region, and that could compensate us for our limited natural resource base'.[2] Parallel to such hard-nosed commercial considerations lie more altruistic motives for Jordan's educational development efforts. For King Abdullah, education is much more than a means of boosting Jordan's invisible exports. Above all, it is a means of redressing societal imbalances. 'Poor people may not have had the opportunities because they didn't have the chance of education', he told me. 'I think education is the major balancing factor in society. If you give everybody a decent chance to make something of themselves, then the sky's the limit. That's why we're putting so much into education. Basically, we're giving the poor the same chance as the rich'.[3]

In 1921, when the Emirate of Transjordan was established, the country's entire educational establishment comprised 25 religious schools. By 1938–39, after some twenty years of British tutelage, there were still only 13,854 pupils in all Transjordan's schools (elementary and secondary, government and private). There were only four government secondary schools for boys, in Salt, Amman, Irbid and Karak, with only 243 pupils. Only Salt offered a complete four-year curriculum while the other three taught two-year programmes. There were no government secondary schools for girls. Two private schools, both linked to churches, had opened in 1937.[4] A very small number of students pursued secondary or higher education in Jerusalem or Beirut. 171,000 pupils, only 27 per cent of them girls, were attending school in 1952.

By any measure, Jordan's progress since has been impressive, especially when set against its limited financial resources and very rapid population growth. In 1952–79 the population was expanding by 4.8 per cent per year and although this has now slowed to 2.8 per cent annually, young people of school and university age continue to outnumber older Jordanians by far. In 2003 no less than 49 per cent of the population was aged between 5 and 24. A further 12 per cent was aged below five. About one third of the entire population is now engaged in education, either as students or teachers. In 1960 only 33 per cent of Jordanians aged 15 and over were functionally literate.[5] Today, the proportion is over 90 per cent – one of the highest literacy rates in the Arab world. Such progress comes at a price. The Ministry of Education's annual outlays have steadily increased. In 1991–2003 alone they nearly trebled, from $149 million to $400 million. In the same period the per capita figure expanded from $43 to $73.[6] A further $3.95 million was spent in 2003 by the Ministry of Higher Education and Scientific Research.[7] Schooling is compulsory and free from ages 6 to 15. On completing the ten-year compulsory basic stage, pupils can spend two further years of free education, either in secondary academic schools or in vocational schools. These latter are overseen by the Vocational Training Corporation, an agency of the Ministry of Labour. Despite the pressures, class sizes in Jordan's schools are manageable, averaging 28 pupils in 2002/3.[8]

As of the 2002/3 academic year, Jordan could boast 5,376 schools with 1,494,446 pupils – 49 per cent of them girls. Community colleges – vocational training establishments (see below) – accounted for a further 26,967 students, while 150,039 undergraduates were studying at the kingdom's 21 universities.[9] Fifty-six per cent of the kingdom's schools in 2002/3 were run by the Ministry of Education and other state agencies while 41 per cent were private. Of the pupils, 72 per cent were in state schools and 19 per cent in private schools. The UN Relief and Works Agency for Palestine refugees (UNRWA) operated 192 schools with 136,236 pupils.[10] The UNRWA schools use the national curriculum so that students can readily integrate with the higher education system.

The universities

Higher education, embracing community colleges and universities, is the responsibility of the Ministry of Higher Education and Scientific Research, established in 1985. Graduates of vocational schools who have passed their final exams may enter a community college, of which in 2003/4 there were 47 throughout the kingdom – 27 of them public (including six for the armed forces) and twenty private.[11] These offer two- or three-year advanced vocational and technical programmes in fields such as teacher-training, banking, commerce, engineering and electronics. One, for girls, offers secretarial, home economics and office management courses. Since 1997 all public community colleges have been overseen by Salt-based Balqa Applied University. At the end of their courses, community college students sit for an Intermediate Diploma, entitling them to apply for entry to university.

Graduates of secondary academic schools can apply to enter universities or community colleges, with entry dependent on their performance in the school-leaving exam, the General Secondary Education Certificate, or *Tawjihi*. The entry thresholds, which change each year to allow a balance between the numbers of applicants and places, are set by a Council of Higher Education chaired by the Minister of Higher Education and Scientific Research, vice-chaired by the Minister of Education and including the presidents of all public universities and of four private universities. In 2002/3 entry to community colleges required a score of at least 55 per cent in the *Tawjihi*. For courses in public universities, the *Tawjihi* score requirement varies according to the subject. In 2002/3 a score of 76 per cent was the threshold for pharmacy and engineering, provided that scores of at least 80 per cent were achieved in scientific subjects in the *Tawjihi*. For other disciplines the threshold was 55 per cent. The private universities, for which demand is intense, generally set higher admission standards. In 2002/3 their applicants for medicine and dentistry required a *Tawjihi* score of at least 85 per cent, and those for pharmacy and engineering needed 80 per cent. The usual requirement for other subjects was 65 per cent.

Public universities accounted for 70 per cent of the students pursuing undergraduate courses at Jordanian universities in 2002/3. The kingdom's first university, Jordan University, was established in Amman in 1962. It was followed by Yarmouk University in Irbid in 1976, Mu'tah University in Karak in 1985 and the University of Science and Technology, at Ramtha, near the Syrian border, in 1986. Two public university-level colleges and four other public universities were established in the 1990s: the Amman College for Applied Engineering Technology (1990) and the College of Islamic Preaching and Fundamentals of Religion (1991) – both now forming part of Balqa Applied University; Aal al-Bayt University in 1994; Hashimiya University in 1995; and Balqa Applied University and Al-Hussain Bin Talal University, both in 1997. Private universities and university-level colleges were authorised by a 1989 law and, by late 2004, 13 had been established. Public universities offer two year Master's degree programmes and the Yarmouk, Jordan, Mu'tah and Science and Technology Universities offer three- to five-year Ph. D. programmes. The only private university offering Master's and Ph. D. degrees is the Amman Arab University for Graduate Studies. In 2002/3, 7,727 students were pursuing post-graduate courses at public universities.[12]

Many Jordanians pursue higher degrees abroad, sometimes because their specialisations are not available locally but also because of the prestige that attaches to foreign, especially European and North American degrees. In 2002/3, 19,221 Jordanians were engaged in higher studies abroad. Of these, 36 per cent were in Egypt, Syria, the United Arab Emirates and Qatar; 29 per cent in Russia, Ukraine and Moldova; 10 per cent in the United States; and 6 per cent in Western Europe.[13] The numbers pursuing foreign studies have been declining in recent years, partly because of the collapse of the Jordanian dinar in the late 1980s, which dramatically increased the cost of study abroad, and partly because of the rapid expansion of higher educational programmes within the kingdom, offering students wider options locally. The high quality and relatively low cost of Jordanian higher education, combined with the kingdom's comparatively low cost of living have combined to attract substantial numbers of foreign students, some 13,000 of whom are enrolled at Jordanian universities, most from neighbouring Arab states.[14] Their outlays constitute a useful invisible export. An official study revealed, for example, that students from the UAE spend about $1,100 per month.[15]

Jordan's older, public universities are bigger by far than the private establishments. At one end of the scale, Jordan University had 23,768 undergraduate students in 2002/3 while, at the other, Hashimiya had 11,627. The biggest private institution, Applied Sciences University, had only 6,633 students in 2002/3, while most of the other private universities had only between 3,000 and 6,000 students.[16] In view of the prevalence of traditional, restrictive, attitudes to women, their high rate of participation in higher education is striking. In 2002/3 they accounted for half of all university undergraduates and they vastly outnumbered males in all public universities other than the Science and Technology University. Explanations for this vary. 'There are many other options for males [in Jordan], such as the army', offered Abdul Rahim Hamdan, president of Ahliya University,[17] where a 1:2 ratio of boys to girls in 2001/2 was reversed in the 2003/4 academic year. Dr Salman al-Badur, president of Aal al-Bayt University, opined: 'University admission depends on the *Tawjihi*, and the females, because they sit at home and study all the time, get better scores than the boys'.[18] In all but two of the private universities, the pattern was reversed,[19] perhaps suggesting that traditional attitudes die hard when hard cash is involved.

Tolerance

The development of specialised science and technology universities reflects a longstanding official desire for educational programmes to meet the needs of society and the economy. But ideological considerations have also played a part in shaping higher education programmes. Aal al-Bayt University, whose sprawling modern campus was developed from scratch on the semi-desert just outside the northern town of Mafraq, has a 'special mission', says its president, Dr Salman al-Badur: 'to teach students academic subjects; and to create Islamic moderation, Islamic tolerance'.[20] Aal al-Bayt was part of Jordan's answer to the rising regional tide of Islamic fundamentalism. 'When King Hussein dedicated this university, he stated this very clearly', said Dr Al-Badur. 'We are here to teach tolerance. We're not limited to one point of view – the Sunni, or the Shia, the Zaidi or the Alawi. We teach all Islamic traditions. Every student, even those studying subjects such as computer science, physics and chemistry, has to be acquainted with the problems facing the Islamic world, with the differences between Muslims themselves. Every student has to study comparative religion'. His words closely echo a university handbook which explains that Aal al-Bayt ('family of the house of the Prophet') was established 'to meet an urgent need for a new kind of university, one that combines the requirements of scientific methodology in teaching and research, on the one hand, and the requirements of belief and clarity of vision on the other, thus creating harmony between the rounded personality of the Muslim and his new environment'. The institution, it continues, 'is also intended to uphold the principles of freedom, justice, tolerance, respect for other people's beliefs and faiths and co-existence'.[21] Aal al-Bayt has some 7,000 students and 300 teaching staff. Most of the students are Jordanian but a significant number are foreign. 'We have students from Malaysia, Iran, Indonesia, Brunei, the US, Russia, Herzegovina, Ghana and Senegal', said Dr Al-Badur, a philosopher who has studied and taught at universities as diverse as Damascus, Tehran, Princeton and Harvard. As in all Jordan's public universities, academic standards are high and competition for places is fierce. The university's preoccupation with Islam does not mean that the students are all Muslims. Echoing the kingdom's religious structure, they include some Christians.

Fees at public universities vary but are only about 20 per cent of those for private universities. While the private institutions are prospering commercially, the public universities face severe funding pressures stemming from the kingdom's efforts to reduce its perennial budget deficits. 'All the public universities are suffering from government budget cuts', said Dr Al-Badur. 'It's a small cake. First it was divided between two establishments, Jordan University and Yarmouk University; and then between three; and then between eight'. One method devised to boost funds was a so-called 'parallel system' under which students who do not have the requisite *Tawjihi* grade can enrol in public universities if they pay fees comparable to those charged by private universities. 'It was first introduced in the University of Science and Technology in Irbid and has since been extended to all our universities', explained Al-Badur. Pressures are mounting, meanwhile, for *Tawjihi*-score entry thresholds to be lowered as a means of boosting student numbers and therefore fee income. The public universities are also introducing a range of new programmes to make them more competitive with the private establishments. The latter are feeling the heat. 'The most serious problem the private universities will face in the future is how to get enough students', said Ahliya University's Abdul Rahim Hamdan, noting that one proposal mooted in 2003 was for private universities to admit students who had attained only 50 per cent in the *Tawjihi* but who had left school at least two years prior to university entry.[22] 'I keep telling my colleagues that the only thing that will really enable us to face this challenge is to develop and improve our programmes and to be able to graduate students who can compete not only in the local market but also in the international market', he said.

Quotas

It is not only *Tawjihi* grades that determine university entry. Twenty per cent of all public university places are reserved for the offspring of the military, although only those who attain the necessary *Tawjihi* mark are accepted. Five per cent are earmarked for the children of Ministry of Education employees (many of them teachers). A variable annual quota of between 10 and 20 per cent of places are reserved for applicants from Jordan's least developed areas, mainly in the south. Further variable quotas are set annually for handicapped students, for applicants from refugee camps, for the children of officials working at the Royal Court and for officials attached to the prime minister's office. Human rights activists see this favourable treatment of selected groups as fundamentally unfair and a violation of the Constitution, Article 6 of which affirms: 'The Government shall ensure work and education within the limits of its possibilities, and it shall ensure a state of tranquillity and equal opportunities to all Jordanians'. Dr Fawzi Samhouri, former chairman of the now disbanded Jordanian Society for Citizens' Rights, said that discrimination in admissions to public universities was an issue on which his society had been working. 'A student from, for example, Tafila [in the south] can be admitted if he has only 65 per cent in the *Tawjihi*, whereas a person from Amman or Zarqa might have 88 per cent but cannot find a place', he said.[23] He estimates that at least half of all public university places are reserved for one group or another. The net result is that 'only about 10 per cent of all places are available to normal applicants from Amman, even though the city and its environs account for around half Jordan's population', Dr Samhouri said. Evidently it is not only in the electoral realm that the mainly Palestinian-origin capital suffers discrimination (see p. 178).

In itself, however, the actual selection process for university applicants is rigorously fair. There's none of the systematic cheating and *wasta* – the use of contacts and influence to gain favours (see p. 69) – that riddles the educational systems of Syria and other regional states, not to mention large swathes of Jordan's bureaucracy and economy. 'Not a single person is admitted to any public university who does not deserve it', insists Aal al-Bayt's Salman al-Badur: '*Wasta* doesn't exist'.[24] He concedes, however, that attempts to win favourable treatment do occur. 'Last term I received two calls, both from members of the new parliament, asking me to upgrade two students who had failed to achieve the marks required for a degree.' He ignored both pleas and both students failed. An important reason for the system's integrity is that university staff are secure in their posts and reasonably well paid, explained Al-Badur. 'Faculty members are settled. Their tenure is secure. There's no need for them to act as recommended by other people'. In consequence, the system of grading degrees was 'highly credible', he added. The methods of assessing university students in Jordan were similar to those used in Europe or North America. The latter, he joked, in one respect superficially resembled *wasta*. 'In England and the United States you have the recommendation system, which we also use', he explained. 'If I write a recommendation for you to be accepted in another university and I say that you are one of my top five students and you are excellent, it's a form of *wasta*, isn't it? The *wasta* in Jordan's·universities does not exceed this'.

Dr Abdul Rahim Hamdan, president of Ahliya University, agrees. 'I believe in organisational management. Anyone who wants to be appointed to our staff must go through all the proper channels. If he's the best, he will be appointed. If not, I say "sorry"'.[25] He conceded that in the past unsuitable individuals had been appointed to Ahliya's administrative staff through *wasta*. 'Most of those who received warnings and were fired were the ones who had been appointed on a non-competitive basis', he said. On accepting his post, he recalled, he had told the chairman, Ahmad al-Hourani, that the university could prosper only if the best people were appointed, and Al-Hourani had agreed without reservation. In public universities, said Hamdan, who had worked in them for many years, *wasta* could be a problem, but 'on the employee level, not when it comes to faculty appointments, where everyone must go through the proper channels'.

But Dr Samhouri is adamant. In his view, the reservation of 'between half and 70 per cent' of university places for favoured sections of the population is nothing but an application of wasta on a grand, formalised scale. 'They say there's no wasta!' he exclaimed with an ironic smile. 'Wasta accounts for 70 per cent of all university places, and they say there's no wasta!'[26]

Academic freedom

Generally, academic freedom is assured in Jordan, albeit within the legally defined limits on criticism of subjects such as the royal family. The authorities nevertheless keep a watchful eye on the universities, which in Jordan as elsewhere are centres of political activity. Sometimes they intervene, usually quietly and behind the scenes but occasionally heavy-handedly. 'The Government limited academic freedom', says the US State Department's *Country Reports on Human Rights Practices 2003 – Jordan*.[27] 'Some academics claimed that they received frequent threats of dismissal. During the year [2003], sources in the academic community claimed that there was an ongoing intelligence [i.e. General Intelligence Department – GID] presence in academic institutions'. The equivalent State Department report for 2001 noted that 'two university presidents were pressured to resign for their political views during the year [2000]. Some professors and students reported being asked by the GID to submit information regarding the political views expressed by colleagues in the classroom'.[28] All university appointments are now vetted by the GID, says Dr Mustafa Hamarneh, director of Jordan University's highly respected Centre for Strategic Studies (CSS). 'You have to go to the GID and obtain a Good Conduct Certificate – a clean bill of health'.[29] Pressures were not usually applied through formal channels. 'They do it over the telephone', he explained, adding that this was a 'regression' because such practices had been dropped during the brief period of liberalisation starting in 1989 when 'many exiles returned home and started teaching again and we even had the secretary-general of the Communist Party teaching in the economics faculty'.

One of the more draconian interventions came in mid-2002 when eight Islamic studies lecturers were summarily dismissed for refusing to amend their teaching curricula to describe Palestinian bombings in Israel as 'suicide bombings' rather than 'martyr operations'. Former students or teachers of shari'a law in Saudi Arabia, five were at the Jordan University, two at Mu'tah University and one at Yarmouk University. The UPI news agency said that officials at the universities had confirmed the professors' 'resignations' but had described them as 'an internal university issue'.[30] Government officials claimed that the dismissals had been 'purely administrative', said UPI, but the report cited Muslim Brotherhood sources as having been told by the lecturers that their universities had warned them 'either to resign or be dismissed on security orders'. A Muslim Brotherhood statement denounced the sackings as a measure designed to please the United States 'in its fight against terrorism'. A 'security official' contacted by UPI had been unaware of the sackings but commented: 'Some of these Islamic *shari'a* professors...tend to instigate their students towards subversion against the security of this country'. During 2002 four of the lecturers were reinstated.

An earlier case centred on Dr Hamarneh himself. In 1999 he was forced to resign as the result of what Human Rights Watch described as 'political pressure from Jordan's prime minister, Abdur-Ra'uf Rawabdah, and the chief of the General Intelligence Department, Samih al-Battikhi'.[31] The CSS is renowned for its public opinion and social surveys, whose results frequently upset the authorities. Often they have revealed unflattering levels of public confidence in governments. One, in 1997, disclosed that unemployment in Jordan stood at 27 per cent, compared with the official estimate of 17 per cent. 'The government never liked our polls, which have become a fixture of public life in Jordan, and they never liked our independence', said Hamarneh.[32] The pretext for his dismissal, however, was a *Newsweek* article, in which a quotation by him had been misrepresented in the Jordanian media as a slur on King Abdullah's dignity. On 14 July 1999 Hamarneh submitted his resignation to Dr Walid Ma'ani, the president of Jordan University, after having been informed that if he did not resign the CSS would be closed and its activities, including support for several Jordanians studying abroad, would be terminated. The ultimatum followed approaches from Rawabdah and Battikhi demanding Hamarneh's removal. Following the resignation, Dr Salah Bashir, a member of the university's Faculty of Law, was appointed in his place. In line with his contract with the university, Hamarneh initially continued working at the CSS as a researcher, but in late August Bashir dismissed him. 'It was ugly and nasty, and I almost went to jail', says Hamarneh.

His plight sparked international protests by academics and others. 'In London, Rosemary Hollis from Chatham House [the Royal Institute of

International Affairs] was a leader in this', he recalls. 'Laurie Brand from Los Angeles, who wrote several books about Jordan, was instrumental in getting the [US] Middle East Studies Association to send a petition to King Abdullah signed by 2,500 academics'. His case was taken up by Human Rights Watch, which wrote to Dr Ma'ani expressing grave concern that Hamarneh's 'exercise of his basic right to freedom of expression and his success in turning the Centre for Strategic Studies into an independent research and training facility – one of the very few in the Arab world – became the basis for his forced removal from office'.[33] Urging Hamarneh's immediate reinstatement, the letter reminded Ma'ani that 'university autonomy is a precondition of academic excellence'. The protests hit home. 'A few months later, I was back in my job', Hamarneh recalled. In Jordan, the authorities rarely hold long-term grudges and, having made their point, can treat critics magnanimously. Soon after his reinstatement at the CSS he was appointed to the board of the Jordan Radio and Television Corporation and in May 2004 became its chairman.

The dismissal of the eight lecturers in 2002 has not been the only sign of the authorities' concern over Islamism in the universities. Jordan has no national students' union. Instead, each university has its own elected student council which acts as a conduit between the student body and the university authorities. In March 2000 Jordan University amended the regulations governing student elections to grant its president the right to appoint half the university's 80-member student council, including the chairman. The move, 'viewed widely as an effort to curb the influence of Islamists' according to the US State Department,[34] sparked a series of demonstrations by students which police dispersed using 'physical force, water cannons and tear gas…injuring a number of students'.[35] The change brought the student council's structure into line with that of the Greater Amman city council, which in 2002 was extended to all Jordan's municipalities (see p. 180). To date, only Jordan University – the country's biggest – has had its student council's independence curbed in this way but there are fears that similar steps could be taken in other universities. Certainly the authorities are considering ways of boosting the non-Islamist vote in student elections as part of a wider attempt to curb Islamism (see Chapter 12).

Dr Fawzi Samhouri of the now disbanded Jordanian Society for Citizens' Rights insists that 'in the universities, the right of free expression is denied'.[36] While Islamists were the most affected, 'anyone who takes part in demonstrations, over Iraq or supporting the Palestinians, is considered an oppositionist'. Even those making entirely non-political demands can expect retribution. In 2001 a student at the private Applied Science University in Amman died of a heart attack. His colleagues staged protests, arguing that in view of the large sums they were charged for health insurance the university's clinic should have had sufficient equipment to have saved him. In response, the university suspended many of the protesters for several semesters.

Supply and demand

The emigration of workers to the oil states in the 1970s and 1980s caused serious local shortages of skilled labour and prompted concerted efforts to gear the education system more closely to the needs of the economy. One major result in the 1980s was a rapid expansion of vocational training and the establishment of the network of community colleges. The National Charter of 1991 urged that universities should 'enhance their role in developing Jordanian society and meeting its needs' (see p. 39). The Jordan First Document of 2002 likewise called for university research programmes to be linked with 'the needs of different national sectors'. Yet imbalances persist. A recent report on education by Amman-based Export & Finance Bank noted: 'A serious problem in the higher education system in Jordan is the mismatch between the education and training offered by higher educational institutions and labour market demand'.[37] Twenty-seven per cent of officially unemployed Jordanians in 2002 had completed secondary school or held Intermediate Diplomas from community colleges. Nineteen per cent were university graduates. Amongst unemployed women, the respective proportions were 44 per cent and 37 per cent.[38] Forty year-old Ismail ad-Dumour, the short, plump moustachioed co-owner of the Fida ('Sacrifice') Restaurant in Karak, 140 kilometres south of Amman, knows what it is to be well-educated but unemployed. After graduating from the local Mu'tah University with a BA in economics and politics, he spent eight years looking for a job. 'I couldn't find work, so I opened this restaurant, together with my brothers', he said, adding: 'People are very angry about the shortage of jobs'.[39] His predicament had not been unusual, although he noted that people 'don't blame the government because it's the situation outside Jordan that's the real cause'. When we met in mid-2003, the restaurant, a modest establishment in the shadow of Karak's magnificent Crusader castle, was deserted, another casualty of the tourism slump caused by the region's multiple crises (see Chapter 8). 'Yesterday only three vehicles came, a bus with six Germans and two cars with four French and two Belgians', sighed Ismail resignedly. On a nearby corner, hard by the Right Choice Supermarket, the 18-room Ram Hotel was shuttered, having closed a year before. The Shuhba Supermarket, also near the Ram, displays signs in Arabic, English, French and Hebrew – although the Israeli tourists are long gone.

A particular weakness of the education system, at least until recently, was a serious neglect of information technology. A joint UNDP/UNESCO report in 2001 found that 'professional computer-based tools and information resources are not much in use' and that 'computer-based educational delivery is almost non-existent'.[40] The authorities, and not least the king, are tackling the problems head-on. In his 19 June 2000 Designation Letter to Prime Minister Ali Abu Ragheb, King Abdullah stressed the need to enable 'both the teacher and the student to deal with modern technology and use it in the best way', and for educational programmes to 'meet the needs of society and aspirations for development and change'.[41] The universities are formulating new and more economically relevant courses, and at all levels of the system there is now a strong emphasis on equipping Jordanians to participate in the IT-driven global economy. English – the language of the internet and international business – is now taught from the first grade, and the education ministry is engaged in a major programme to introduce computer-based learning techniques at all public schools. September 2004 saw the inauguration of a University Learning and Research Network (ULRN), a broadband link between the kingdom's eight public universities. The ULRN is the initial component of a National Broadband Network that will ultimately interconnect all Jordan's schools and other educational institutions and also link them with 3,000 higher education establishments in Europe.

Supply is only one part of the equation, however. At least as big a problem is demand. Despite Jordan's high unemployment, serious labour shortages exist in certain sectors. The greatest demand, however, is for low-paid nurses and other health service workers and for unskilled manual labourers. Tens of thousands of Egyptians, Iraqis, Sri Lankans and Filipinos work in jobs that Jordanians shun as either too low paid or too undignified. It's a phenomenon that greatly exercises King Abdullah. 'We have an estimated 500,000 foreign workers in Jordan, most of whom are illegal, out of a [total] population of 5.5 million', he told me. 'They constitute about one third of the labour force. It's ridiculous. The idea is to replace the foreign workers with Jordanians'.[42] It is not self-evident, however, either that Jordanians will be any more attracted in the future than they are now to the types of work done by the foreigners, or that new businesses will arise in Jordan at a sufficient rate to absorb more than a limited proportion of the kingdom's graduates, regardless of their proficiency in IT or English. For the foreseeable future, many skilled Jordanians will continue to have to look abroad for work.

Notes

1 Interview with author, Amman, 8 October 2003.
2 Interview with author, Amman, 6 March 2003.
3 Interview with author, Amman, 29 June 2004.
4 Mary C. Wilson, *King Abdullah, Britain and the Making of Jordan* (Cambridge: Cambridge University Press, 1987), p. 249.
5 www.kinghussein.gov.jo.
6 Ibid, and Abeer Arafat, *Sector Report: Education* (Amman: Export & Finance Bank, undated), p.2.
7 *Hashemite Kingdom of Jordan Statistical Yearbook 2003* (Amman: Department of Statistics).
8 Ibid.
9 Ibid.
10 Ibid.
11 Telephone communication with Ministry of Higher Education and Scientific Research, 15 December 2004.
12 *Hashemite Kingdom of Jordan Statistical Yearbook 2003* (Amman: Department of Statistics).
13 Ibid.
14 Ibid.
15 Abeer Arafat, *Sector Report: Education*, p. 5.
16 *Hashemite Kingdom of Jordan Statistical Yearbook 2003* (Amman: Department of Statistics).
17 Interview with author, Amman, 8 October 2003.
18 Interview with author, Mafraq, 24 July 2003.
19 *Hashemite Kingdom of Jordan Statistical Yearbook 2003* (Amman: Department of Statistics).
20 Interview with author, Mafraq, 24 July 2003.
21 *Aal al-Bayt University* (Mafraq: Aal al-Bayt University, n.d.), p. 4.

22   Interview with author, Amman, 8 October 2003.
23   Interview with author, Amman, 5 October 2003.
24   Interview with author, Mafraq, 24 July 2003.
25   Interview with author, Amman, 8 October 2003.
26   Interview with author, Amman, 5 October 2003.
27   US State Department, *Country Reports on Human Rights Practices 2003 – Jordan* (Washington, DC: Bureau of Democracy, Human Rights and Labor, 25 February 2004).
28   US State Department, *Country Reports on Human Rights Practices 2001 – Jordan* (Washington, DC: Bureau of Democracy, Human Rights and Labor, 4 March 2002).
29   Interview with author, Amman, 24 February 2003.
30   Sana Abdallah, 'Jordan profs fired for suicide bomb views', *United Press International*, 5 June 2002.
31   Human Rights Watch, *Jordan University President Should Reinstate Ousted Director*, 8 October 1999.
32   Interview with author, Amman, 24 February 2003.
33   Human Rights Watch, *Jordan University President*, 8 October 1999.
34   US State Department, *Country Reports on Human Rights Practices 2000 – Jordan* (Washington, DC: Bureau of Democracy, Human Rights and Labor, 23 February 2001).
35   Ibid.
36   Interview with author, Amman, 5 October 2003.
37   Abeer Arafat, *Sector Report: Education*, p. 7.
38   *Hashemite Kingdom of Jordan Statistical Yearbook 2003* (Amman: Department of Statistics).
39   Interview with author, Karak, 19 July 2003.
40   Oula al-Farawati, 'Report cites minimal penetration of IT in higher education system', *Jordan Times*, 24 December 2001.
41   www.kingabdullah.jo
42   Interview with author, London, 5 October 2004.

CHAPTER 16

Visions and Realities: The Future

'Jordan is embarking on building a regional model through the implementation of a comprehensive reform agenda, with the aim of propelling growth and realising a sustainable improvement in the welfare of citizens', affirms the 'Vision for the Future' on King Abdullah's website. It continues:

> Jordan's vision is to develop a modern, tolerant and open society, and to establish itself as a successful model of reform and development conceived and implemented from within. With this in mind, Jordan is moving towards a society that respects diversity and regards it as a source of national strength and pride, where majority rule is coupled with minority rights, where the right to politically organize is guaranteed, and where personal and public freedoms are upheld.[1]

It's a message that lies at the heart of the official discourse, reiterated earnestly at every opportunity by the king and his ministers. There's no doubting their sincerity and, as a vision for the future, it's well and good. But it's far removed from the present reality, where democracy is fine, so long as it does not challenge the system's fundamentals; the rule of law prevails, but the laws protect and perpetuate the *status quo*; and media freedom is laudable, but only within 'responsible' limits. However attractive the vision may be to the Jordanian elite, their priority is to maintain their pre-eminence. Such change as they envisage will be strictly on their own terms. Much of Jordan's political life revolves around the attempt to minimise – or paper over – the awkward disparities between the liberal façade and the often harsh imperatives of power and privilege.

King Abdullah certainly rules with energy and enthusiasm but, fundamentally, his stance is little different from his father's. As Renate Dieterich has noted:

This concept of 'responsible freedom' and the inviolate 'higher national interest' did not vanish with the death of King Hussain but has been passed on to the new King Abdullah II who tells his subjects: 'It is not anybody's right or that of any side, whoever it may be, to monopolise the claim for truth or that of the higher national interest, or to exploit the climate of freedom, democracy or tolerance or to abuse the laws in this country, or its traditions and noble values, or to harm its image and bright reputation'.[2]

Jordanians have not been beguiled by the rhetoric. Perhaps the most striking feature of the relationship between rulers and ruled is the latter's cynicism. A public opinion survey conducted in autumn 2004 by Jordan University's Centre for Strategic Studies (CSS) revealed that some two thirds of Jordanians defined 'democracy' in terms of civil liberties and political rights and that only 49 per cent considered the system to be democratic.[3] Part of the explanation, said the CSS, was a 'perceived lack of belief among citizens that public freedoms are guaranteed to an extent that would allow citizens to exercise their rights of public expression without fearing government reprisal'. No less than 81 per cent of respondents felt that they could not publicly criticise the government without fear of reprisal against them or their families. This compared with 70 per cent in a similar poll in 1999, at the start of Abdullah's rule. Forty-seven per cent believed that the principle of equality of opportunity was not applied in Jordan, while only 10.5 per cent believed that 'justice and equality' were definitely applied.

Parliament and political parties are not spared. Ninety per cent of respondents expressed the view that none of the existing political parties represented their political, economic and social aspirations. Asked which of the parties they thought were qualified to form a government, 84 per cent replied 'none'. Forty-seven per cent felt that parliament did not effectively hold the government accountable and less than a third believed that parliament had successfully drafted laws dealing effectively with unemployment, poverty and corruption. Sixty-nine per cent believed that members of parliament were more interested in their own personal and family affairs than in serving the country as a whole. 'In all, parliament does not enjoy the trust of most citizens', commented the CSS. Against that background, it was perhaps unsurprising that 64 per cent of respondents said that parliament's suspension in 2001–03 had had no impact on them.

Façade democracy

'Jordan has not democratised successfully, but then there is strong evidence to suggest that democratisation was never truly the aim of the ruling regime', assert Milton-Edwards and Hinchcliffe. 'Rather, appropriate conditions were created to maintain a "façade or paper democracy", satisfying both local demands for greater participation and international and particularly American conditions at the beginning of [the 1990s], of liberalisation for aid-giving and other financial assistance'.[4] Jordan's establishment certainly wants to consolidate and perpetuate its privileges, and a commitment to 'democracy' doubtless does play well in London and Washington, the regime's key Western backers. Most certainly King Abdullah's vision does not include any development of democracy that would threaten the establishment with too rapid or dramatic change. Yet the elite's attachment to its privileges is not the only reason for the kingdom's democratic failings. Much deeper forces are at play. Jordanian society is simply not amenable to a wholesale transplant of Western-style democracy. The king may want a development of political parties of the centre, left and right, but these mean little for a society that is not divided on class lines to anything like the same extent as those of Europe or North America. What really matter to most Jordanians are family, tribe and religion: primordial ties that have little bearing on notions of 'left' and 'right'. As Mustafa Hamarneh, director of the CSS, has observed: 'There's no democratic trend in Jordan. There's an Arab nationalist trend and an Islamist trend. But an enlightened, modern, democratic current is nonexistent'.[5] It is a reality against which Jordan's democratic credentials and the king's vision for change must also be judged. That is neither to applaud the regime's parliamentary and electoral shenanigans nor to say that evolution will not occur and cannot be encouraged. With this in mind, the king's vision of a liberal democracy with programme-based parties of the left, right and centre, can be seen neither as an empty ploy to win plaudits abroad nor as an impossibly naïve dream, but simply as an ideal to be implemented as and when conditions allow.

The basic functions of democracy are to enable people to choose their rulers and to permit changes of government to be effected peaceably. Another key purpose is to guarantee personal freedoms, but democracy is not the only means by which this latter can be attained. George Joffé of Cambridge University's Centre of International Studies explains:

A fundamental interest of people in the Middle East is social justice – the sense of individual security and fair treatment by the state. Democracy may be one way of achieving this, but they do not feel that it is necessarily the only one. They certainly want human rights and responsible, accountable, government. They certainly want to be protected by law from the depredations of unaccountable power. But the specific forms by which this should be done are still open to discussion. If it is to involve patronage–clientage or monarchical *dirigisme*, consultation rather than explicit democracy, so be it: provided that it delivers the all-important sense of personal inviolability within a generally-accepted cultural and legal framework'.[6]

Jordan may be essentially undemocratic and its elite largely unaccountable, but it is no Syria or Saudi Arabia. While the freedoms of 1989–93 have since been eroded, the margins of debate and criticism remain wide, especially when measured by regional standards. Eighty-one per cent of respondents in the 2004 CSS opinion survey may have felt that criticising the regime would invite retaliation, as did the taxi driver Abu Muhammad (see Chapter 8). But that does not mean that they would in fact automatically suffer retaliation. Certainly the press is constrained. Certainly a watchful eye is kept on dissidents and sometimes they are detained. But usually they are held only briefly, maltreatment is rare and the legal system offers a degree of real protection. Tellingly, the CSS poll disclosed that only 3 per cent of Jordanians feel that 'enhancing democracy and freedom of expression' is the biggest problem facing the country. Perhaps more fundamentally than from formal structures and mechanisms, the relatively high degree of freedom stems from the regime's benign political culture. Except when feeling cornered, Jordan's kings have preferred to rule by consent rather than fear. 'Jordan can be vicious sometimes, but it's not vicious altogether', observed Hamarneh. Tribalism has played a part. Forming the regime's key support base and providing much of the manpower for the armed forces and state bureaucracy, the tribes constitute a powerful check on overweening authority and provide their members with crucial informal channels through which to seek redress. The elimination of *wasta* (see Chapter 3) in order to forge a fairer society may be an important official objective. But *wasta* (like its Western equivalent, the old boys' network) is used not only for personal gain but also for personal protection. And, in truth, *wasta* will remain so long as there are tribes. The difficulty about benign autocratic rule, however, is that it cannot be taken for granted. If, one day, a brutal and ruthless monarch were to succeed to the Jordanian throne, there would be little to constrain him.

Neither of the two main opposition trends meanwhile poses any threat to the establishment, whether within parliament or without. Arab nationalism is largely a spent force. The Islamic fundamentalist Ikhwan and their political wing, the Islamic Action Front (IAF), remain vibrant although the regime's manipulation of general elections makes it hard to gauge their true level of public support. Even bearing in mind the impact of the authorities' electoral engineering, however, it appears that their popularity may well have peaked. In the 2004 CSS poll only 7 per cent of respondents identified the IAF as representing their aspirations, with no other party coming anywhere close. But the IAF's proportion had fallen from 15 per cent in an equivalent poll a year earlier.

Unlike in other regional states, the regime's legitimacy is not at issue. The king remains the unchallenged focus of power, ruling through a complex network of relationships that extends way beyond parliament and largely by-passes it altogether. If King Abdullah wobbled at first in his management of the political elite (see Chapter 3), he has now more than found his feet. His confidence was underlined by the abrupt manner in which he relieved his half-brother, Hamzah, of his title of Crown Prince in November 2004. The succession too is not a burning issue. For one thing, Abdullah is young and healthy and expected to rule for many years yet. For another, Jordanians – including the royal family – acknowledge that it is the king's constitutional prerogative to name his successor and will not challenge his decision. At the time of writing, Abdullah was keeping his options open by declining to name a crown prince. Jordanians will be unsurprised, however, if he eventually names his son, Hussain, in accord with the traditional descent of Hashemite monarchs through the eldest male heir.

In short, for all the talk of developing democracy and widening freedoms, little real change seems in prospect. For the foreseeable future, the regime will continue to call the shots, widening or curtailing democratic freedoms according to its assessment of the risks.

Economic reform

King Abdullah is less autocratic than his father, seeking consensus wherever possible, although their fundamental approaches to democracy and freedoms have much in common. Not so their positions on the economy. While Jordan started liberalising its economy as the price of IMF support in the wake of the financial collapse of the late 1980s, Hussain was a reluctant reformer. Abdullah is a true believer. Since acceding to the throne in 1999, he has driven a frenetic liberalisation programme involving an easing of regulatory controls, the cutting of subsidies on basic commodities, sales tax increases and an accelerated privatisation of state enterprises. Jordan has joined the World Trade Organisation, signed free trade agreements with the US and the European Free Trade Association (EFTA) and an Association Agreement with the EU. A national Socio-Economic Transformation Plan (SETP) for 2002–04 has been succeeded by a Social and Economic Development Plan for 2004–06. The strategic objectives have been to reduce the public debt and boost hard currency reserves. The tactics have been to boost exports, thereby reducing current account deficits, and to rein in public spending in order to contain budget deficits. With a liberalised regulatory framework, a sound current account and solid public finances, it was asserted, investment would rise as part of a self-sustaining upward economic spiral.

The local and regional security backdrop has not been helpful. The Arab world has been plagued by terrorism, from which Jordan itself has not been spared. To the west, the Palestinian *intifada* has raged. To the east, the US-led invasion and occupation of Iraq have spawned a bloody war of resistance. Consider the front page of the *Jordan Times* on 22 April 2004. The lead story, from Iraq, was: 'Suicide bombers kill 68'. Below, from Palestine, was 'Raid on northern Gaza claims 13 lives', and below that, from Saudi Arabia, '10 die in Riyadh blast'. By dampening business confidence, instability has seriously dented the kingdom's plans. The achievements to date have been mixed. Although gross domestic product (GDP) has grown steadily if modestly, still rapid population growth means that expressed per capita it has hardly changed. The current account has shown some significant surpluses but these have been mainly the result of higher infusions of foreign aid (of which the US alone pledged $1.6 billion in 2003)[7] and a healthy influx of remittances from Jordanians working abroad. The public debt has declined, but slowly, and still totalled $10 billion in 2003.

The macro-economic picture, however, says nothing about the distribution of wealth within the country. Without doubt, the business community and the better-off have been the main beneficiaries of the liberalisation programme. The theory is that the new wealth at the top will eventually 'trickle down' to the mass of the population. As yet, there's scant sign of it happening. Around one third of the population live below the official poverty line and unemployment stands at around 25 per cent. The CSS 2004 public opinion survey found that 74 per cent of Jordanians consider that the national economy does not benefit the mass of the population – the same proportion that held this view in similar polls in 2001 and 2003. Forty-two per cent reported that their economic situation had worsened in the previous twelve months, against 43 per cent who said that there had been no change and only 13 per cent who reported an improvement. Fifty-two per cent of respondents said that 'poverty and unemployment' were the biggest problem facing the country. In second place came 'financial and administrative corruption', mentioned by 27 per cent as Jordan's biggest challenge. Poverty's destabilising potential was dramatically underlined by the Ma'an crisis in 2002, of which it was an underlying cause, and by the riots that shook the south in 1989 and 1996 following bread price rises.

The authorities readily acknowledge the persistence of poverty and unemployment but insist that matters will improve with time. 'The talk that you'll hear from everybody is that society still has not felt the impact [of the reforms], and I'm very aware that poor people will say, "we're still poor"', said King Abdullah. 'And only when the lower middle class and the lower class start to say, "OK, my lot is getting better" can we start to rest on our laurels, and I think we've still got a long way to go on that'.[8] Despite the mixed results to date, his faith in his economic strategy remains unshaken. 'We have to stick to our guns', said the king. Further privatisations, of the National Electric Power Company, the Jordan Phosphate Mines Company and the Jordan Telecommunications Company, are planned. All subsidies on oil products will be phased out in 2005–07.[9] The 2004-6 Social and Economic Development Plan anticipates an annual GDP growth rate of 6 per cent by 2006, with similar rates thereafter. The public debt/GDP ratio is projected to fall to 78 per cent by 2006, compared with 101 per cent in 2003 and 89.5 per cent at end-September 2004.[10] Whether these targets can be met remains uncertain. For all the efforts expended on reform, Jordan remains essentially what it has always been: a small, resource-poor country in a troubled part of the world, where the non-productive service sector accounts for over two thirds of the economy and whose financial wellbeing depends critically on foreign aid and the funds sent home to their families by the tens of thousands of its citizens working abroad. Most likely is that the reforms will bear some fruit, albeit at the cost of continued hardship for the poor, but that the real determinants of economic performance will continue to be workers' remittances and aid – both of which are intimately linked to the kingdom's foreign relations.

Iraq

The crisis over Iraq, starting in late 2002 and persisting until now, has been King Abdullah's biggest foreign policy challenge by far, requiring him to balance his strategic alliances with Washington and London with the markedly pro-Saddam Hussein (and, perhaps more to the point, anti-US) sentiment of the majority of Jordanians, particularly those of Palestinian origin. Adroitly, and in contrast to his father during the 1990–91 Kuwait crisis, he has managed to have it both ways. In the prelude, he repeatedly warned of the dangers and difficulties and declined any direct role. At the same time, however, he allowed the US to station anti-missile batteries in Jordan to counter possible Iraqi strikes against Israel. But, more discreetly, he also allowed US and British Special Forces to conduct operations from remote bases in Jordan's eastern desert. His immediate reward was a sharp hike in US economic and military aid that explained much of Jordan's improved economic performance in 2003.

Following the end of the main hostilities and especially after the establishment of Iraq's interim government in June 2004, Jordan worked determinedly to forge links with the new Baghdad, not least with an eye to the rich potential economic rewards. In late 2003 Amman started training 26 Iraqi air traffic controllers. More significantly, at the same time it started a $1 billion, two-year programme to train 32,000 Iraqi police cadets. Jordan is also training personnel for the new Iraqi armed forces.

Trade with Iraq has boomed, and Amman has been the venue for several conferences and seminars on Iraqi reconstruction, with local enterprises selling themselves as middlemen for international companies. An example was Iraq Procurement 2004, a three-day conference in November 2004 which, said the *Jordan Times*, would seek 'to connect Iraqi businesses with global companies looking for prospects in the oil-rich but war-ridden country'.[11] Another such event, the Second International Trade Exhibition for the Rebuilding of Iraq, took place in

April 2005. Hailing Amman as 'Jordan's secure gateway to business with Baghdad and the rest of Iraq', the exhibition's publicity material noted that 'Jordan's geographical proximity to, and history of trade with, Iraq makes Amman the natural and preferred venue for international companies eager to meet and do business with Iraqi entrepreneurs'.[12] In April 2004 Jordan became the first Arab state to offer to send peacekeeping troops to Iraq, and Iraq's interim prime minister, Iyad Allawi, later became a frequent visitor to Amman. Plans for a far-reaching expansion of ties were laid at the first meeting in Amman in November 2004 of a bilateral Joint Higher Committee, chaired by Allawi and his Jordanian counterpart, Faisal Fayez. Joint projects were approved to rehabilitate customs and immigration posts on each side of the border; to create a free trade zone at the border; to build a new, 642 kilometre highway to the frontier from Jordan's Red Sea port of Aqaba; to modernise the port to enable it to handle larger volumes of Iraq-bound cargo; to build a railway linking the two countries; and to lay a pipeline to convey 350,000 barrels per day of Iraqi crude oil to Jordan's refinery at Zarqa, near Amman. Within days it was reported that the two countries had appealed to 'the international donor community' for $1.08 billion to fund the projected schemes.[13] Allawi and Fayez also agreed to form joint commissions to promote collaboration in the fields of finance, technology, trade, transport, oil and energy, labour, training and investment promotion, and in military and security matters. It was eerily reminiscent of the 1980s, when Jordan was Iraq's closest ally in its war with Iran. Then, exactly similar projects were agreed and some were implemented, and Iraq had been Jordan's biggest export market by far. By late 2004, King Abdullah plainly viewed Iraq as a key to Jordan's future economic security, no doubt calculating that any misgivings the Jordanian public might have about the kingdom so brazenly supporting the US project in Iraq would take second place to improved living standards. Amman's Iraqi prospects were seriously dented, however, by the emergence of the Shias as a commanding political force in Baghdad as a result of the Iraqi elections in January 2005. Iraq's Shias have little love for Jordan, recalling that King Hussain was one of their oppressor, Saddam Hussain's staunchest allies. In December 2004 King Abdullah had caused them deep offence by alleging extensive Iranian interference in Iraq and warning that if a Shia-dominated, pro-Iranian government took power in Baghdad the result could be a 'Shia crescent' stretching from Iran through Iraq, Syria and Lebanon that could destabilise the region.[14] In March 2005 a brief but fierce diplomatic row erupted between Baghdad and Amman after Iraq accused Jordan of taking insufficient steps to prevent the infiltration of Islamist militants across its border into Iraq.

On Palestine, which like Iraq is simultaneously a domestic and foreign issue for the kingdom, Jordan can be expected to continue playing a supportive role in Western attempts to secure a peace settlement. In the immediate future, a particular focus for Amman will be continued efforts to revive the so-called Road Map plan, in which King Abdullah has invested much personal prestige (see Chapter 3). Pending progress, however, the kingdom will continue its routine expressions of support and sympathy for the Palestinians under Israeli occupation. Given the Palestine issue's extreme domestic sensitivity, relations with Israel can be expected to remain little more than correct until a settlement has been achieved.

Elsewhere in the region, Jordan will endeavour to maintain good ties with its powerful northern and southern neighbours, Syria, Saudi Arabia and Egypt, carefully modulating its rhetoric as required by its established 'all things to all men' approach to foreign policy. It will continue to give particular attention to the Gulf states, where many Jordanians live and work and which have been important, if sometimes capricious, sources of budgetary and other aid. Beyond the region, Jordan will maintain its intimate strategic relationships with the US and UK and its support for President Bush's 'war on terrorism'. At the same time it will continue working to bolster ties with Europe – another important source of funds – and Russia, still a major power despite its straitened circumstances.

Crossfire

Eighty-three years after the first King Abdullah arrived at the dusty little railway station in Ma'an to claim a largely barren and unpopulated territory that no-one else wanted, Jordan has much reason for pride. At the start, after all, there was not even an embryonic sense of national identity. The south was part of the doomed kingdom of Hejaz. The rest, though formally part of Britain's Palestine mandate, had in practice been ignored and unoccupied by the British and lacked any central administration. The south and east were the domain of nomadic *bedu* tribes. Only the north-western corner was capable of sustaining settled agriculture. There were no cities and only a handful of towns. Amman was just a large village. Under British patronage and control, Abdullah forged this backwater into a functioning state and, highly controversially, expanded its frontiers westwards by seizing the West Bank in the 1948 Palestine war, endowing his kingdom with a clear Palestinian majority, over half of them refugees. Abdullah's legacy was the creation of Jordan. That of his grandson, Hussain, was its survival and consolidation, sometimes against heavy odds. In the first two decades of his rule Jordan was in ferment, swept by the political tides of Arab nationalism and subject to sustained subversion by radical Egypt and Syria. In 1967 the West Bank was lost, sparking a new influx of refugees, and in 1970–71 the kingdom was engulfed by civil war. In the 1980s Islamic fundamentalism emerged as a new threat to the Hashemite order, to be followed by economic crisis and attendant rioting. Then came the Kuwait crisis, when the kingdom was ostracised by its key backer, the United States, and had to absorb a third wave of refugees, this time from Kuwait and other Gulf states. In 1994 a peace treaty was signed with Israel, inflaming anew the tensions between East Bankers and Palestinian Jordanians. The new king, Abdullah, has started well. Above all, he has weathered the storm of the Iraq crisis sparked by the US-led invasion of 2003.

Despite its inauspicious start and troubled history, the kingdom has developed into one of the region's more prosperous and liberal states, albeit one with a strong streak of authoritarianism. 'Jordan stands out as a success story in terms of the quality of life of its citizens', said the CSS's Mustafa Hamarneh. 'Basically, that is the result of the success of Hashemite policies and the failure of all others'.[15] Its kings had successfully 'navigated a small ship in very rough waters'. Libya, he continued, had 'nothing to show for all its billions in oil money. Iraq is a disaster. Who would want to live in Saudi Arabia, under Wahhabism? Look how Algeria went, and Syria next door. Jordan had nothing, and yet we enjoy a lifestyle that's much better than anyone else's in the region'. Luck had played a part. 'It just happened that America won the Cold War', he observed. 'Had the Soviet Union won, it would have been a different story altogether. The Hashemites would probably be somewhere in the south of France, living in apartments paid for by European monarchies'

Although it has had an authentic national life of its own, Jordan has never been fully the master of its fate. Forming the pivot between Israel and Palestine to the west, Iraq to the east, Saudi Arabia and Egypt to the south and Syria to the north, dependent on foreign aid and foreign markets, and with first Britain and then the US as the ultimate guarantor of its regime, the kingdom has always been largely 'an object of the politics of others'.[16] The coming decades cannot be much different for, by Jordan's very nature, its destiny has always been to live in the crossfire.

Notes

1 www.kingabdullah.jo
2 Renate Dieterich, 'The weakness of the ruled is the strength of the ruler: the role of the opposition in contemporary Jordan', in George Joffé (ed.), *Jordan in Transition 1990–2000* (London: Hurst & Company, 2002), p. 134.
3 *Democracy in Jordan*, Public Opinion Poll Unit, Centre for Strategic Studies, University of Jordan, October 2004.
4 Beverley Milton-Edwards and Peter Hinchcliffe, *Jordan: A Hashemite Legacy* (London: Routledge, 2001), p. 63.
5 Interview with author, Amman, 24 February 2003.
6 Email communication with author, 27 August 2004.
7 www.mfa.gov.jo.
8 Interview with author, Amman, 29 June 2004.
9 *Middle East Economic Digest*, Vol. 48, No. 27, 2–8 July, p. 8.
10 Rami Abdelrahman, '"Third generation of reforms" will mark next stage of Socio-Economic Transformation Plan', *Jordan Times*, 9 April 2004; and *Jordan Times*, 2 November 2004.
11 Ibid., 22 November 2004.
12 www.rebuild-iraq-expo.com
13 *Jordan Times*, 12 October 2004.
14 *Washington Post*, 8 December 2004.
15 Interview with author, Amman, 24 February 2003.
16 Philip Robins, *A History of Jordan* (Cambridge: Cambridge University Press, 2004), p. 77.

Select Bibliography

Abu-Odeh, Adnan, *Jordanians, Palestinians and the Hashemite Kingdom in the Middle East Peace Process* (Washington, DC: United States Institute of Peace Press, 1999).

Article 19, *Blaming the Press: Jordan's Democratization Process in Crisis* (London: Article 19, October 1997).

Asher, Michael, *Lawrence: The Uncrowned King of Arabia* (Harmondsworth: Penguin Books, 1999).

Brand, Laurie A., *Jordan's Inter-Arab Relations: The Political Economy of Alliance Making* (New York: Columbia University Press, 1994).

Bruce, Anthony, *The Last Crusade. The Palestine Campaign in the First World War* (London: John Murray, 2002).

Dallas, Roland, *King Hussein: A Life on the Edge* (London: Profile Books, 1999).

Dalrymple, William, *From the Holy Mountain* (London: Flamingo, 1998).

Department of Statistics [Jordan], *Household Expenditure and Income Survey 1997* (Amman: The Hashemite Kingdom of Jordan Department of Statistics, March 1999).

Department of Statistics [Jordan] and ORC Macro, *Jordan Population and Family Health Survey 2002* (Calverton, Maryland: ORC Macro, 2003).

International Crisis Group (ICG), *The Challenge of Political Reform: Jordanian Democratisation and Regional Instability* (Amman and Brussels: ICG, 8 October 2003).

International Crisis Group (ICG), *Red Alert in Jordan: Recurrent Unrest in Maan* (Amman and Brussels: ICG, 19 February 2003).

Jeffreys, Andrew, (ed.), *Emerging Jordan 2003* (London: Oxford Business Group, 2002).

Joffé, George, (ed.), *Jordan in Transition 1990–2000* (London: Hurst & Company, 2002).

Kilani, Sa'eda, *Press Freedoms in Jordan* (Copenhagen: Euro-Mediterranean Human

Rights Network, February 2002).

Kilani, Sa'eda, and Sakijha, Basem, *Wasta: The Declared Secret* (Amman: Arab Archives Institute, March 2002).

King Abdullah of Jordan, *My Memoirs Completed: "Al Takmilah"* (London and New York: Longman, 1978).

Lawrence, T.E., *Seven Pillars of Wisdom: A Triumph* (London: Penguin, 2000).

Layne, Linda, *Home and Homeland: Dialogics of Tribal and National Identities in Jordan* (Princeton, NJ: Princeton University Press, 1994).

Milton-Edwards, Beverley, and Hinchcliffe, Peter, *Jordan: A Hashemite Legacy* (London: Routledge, 2001).

Ministry of Planning and International Co-operation; UNDP, *Jordan Human Development Report 2004: Building Sustainable Livelihoods* (Amman: MoPIC and UNDP, 2004).

Queen Noor, *Leap of Faith: Memoirs of an Unexpected Life* (London: Phoenix, 2003).

Robins, Philip, *A History of Jordan* (Cambridge: Cambridge University Press, 2004).

Rogan, Eugene L., and Tell, Tariq, (eds.), *Village, Steppe and State. The Social Origins of Modern Jordan* (London and New York: British Academic Press, 1994).

Sakijha, Basem and Kilani, Sa'eda, *National Integrity Systems: Country Study Report: Jordan – 2001*, (Berlin: Transparency International, 2001).

Salibi, Kamal, *The Modern History of Jordan* (London: I B Tauris, 1998).

Shlaim, Avi, *Collusion across the Jordan: King Abdullah, the Zionist Movement, and the Partition of Palestine* (Oxford: Clarendon Press, 1988).

Tourret, R., *Hedjaz Railway* (Abingdon: Tourret Publishing, 1989).

US Library of Congress, Federal Research Division, *Jordan: A Country Study* (Washington, DC: Library of Congress, 1989).

US State Department, *Country Reports on Human Rights Practices 2003 – Jordan* (Washington DC: Bureau of Democracy, Human Rights and Labor, 25 February 2004).

Wilson, Mary C., *King Abdullah, Britain and the Making of Jordan* (Cambridge: Cambridge University Press, 1987).

Index